MEDIA, CULTURE AND SOCIETY

'Introductory texts are notoriously difficult to write; they have to be accessible, engaging, well organised and well written. Hodkinson has succeeded in writing a book which makes a distinctive and engaging contribution to the literature; it is a work which combines scholarship and imagination. The book is carefully organised and sets an agenda which will be useful to students in a wide variety of contexts. It manages to combine traditional approaches to understanding the media with new and emergent issues and areas. Contemporary examples and illustrations are used throughout to ensure that general analysis is always embedded in particular case studies and each section is rounded off with a summary conclusion which allows students to reflect on their reading. The book is fully supported by key references and succeeds in providing an introduction to which students will return throughout their studies.'

Tim O'Sullivan, Professor of Media, Film and Journalism,
De Montfort University

MEDIA, CULTURE AND SOCIETY

an introduction

Paul Hodkinson

Los Angeles | London | New Delhi
Singapore | Washington DC

© Paul Hodkinson 2011

First published 2011
Reprinted 2012, 2013

Apart from any fair dealing for the purposes of research or
private study, or criticism or review, as permitted under the
Copyright, Designs and Patents Act, 1988, this publication
may be reproduced, stored or transmitted in any form, or by
any means, only with the prior permission in writing of the
publishers, or in the case of reprographic reproduction, in
accordance with the terms of licences issued by the Copyright
Licensing Agency. Enquiries concerning reproduction outside
those terms should be sent to the publishers.

SAGE Publications Ltd
1 Oliver's Yard
55 City Road
London EC1Y 1SP

SAGE Publications Inc.
2455 Teller Road
Thousand Oaks, California 91320

SAGE Publications India Pvt Ltd
B 1/I 1 Mohan Cooperative Industrial Area
Mathura Road, Post Bag 7
New Delhi 110 044

SAGE Publications Asia-Pacific Pte Ltd
3 Church Street
#10-04 Samsung Hub
Singapore 049483

Library of Congress Control Number 2009941862

British Library Cataloguing in Publication data

A catalogue record for this book is available from the British
Library

ISBN 978-1-4129-2052-0
ISBN 978-1-4129-2053-7 (pbk)

Typeset by C&M Digitals (P) Ltd, Chennai, India
Printed in Great Britain by MPG Printgroup, UK
Printed on paper from sustainable resources

MIX
Paper from
responsible sources
FSC® C018575

Contents

List of illustrations

Acknowledgements

My sincere thanks go to the Department of Sociology at the University of Surrey for providing me with a wonderful place to work and, specifically, for enabling me to have the time to write this book.

I would also like to specifically thank Cornel Sandvoss, Victoria Alexander and Vivienne Boon for their invaluable comments on draft chapters.

Acknowledgement is also due to Graham McBeath, from whom I learned so much at the University of Northampton, and to all those who inspired my interest in the study of media, culture and society when I was a student in the Department of Cultural Studies at the University of Birmingham.

Thanks also to the team at SAGE Publications for all the help and support provided throughout the process of producing this book.

Thanks, too, to all my students, for whom a good deal of what is written here will (hopefully!) be familiar and without whom my enthusiasm and understanding would be so much less.

Finally, my deepest thanks to Holly Cummins, for her tireless, meticulous and always entertaining proofreading – and for everything else, too.

1

Introduction

Focal points

- Introduction to the notions of media, culture and society.
- The relationship between media representations and society.
- Linear models of the communication process.
- A suggested model of the elements of media in socio-cultural context.
- Summary of the chapters to follow.

Introduction

Perhaps more than ever before, *media* and communication are at the centre of our everyday lives. At work, at home, in public spaces or while travelling from one location to another, we are rarely far away from mediated sounds, images or words, whether in the form of television, radio, newspapers, magazines, mobile phones, personal music players, games machines or the Internet. Sometimes on our own and sometimes in the company of others, media entertain us, enable connections with friends and communities, provide interpretations of the world around us and offer resources for the forging of identities and imaginations. Their importance to everyday lives and routines suggests that media also must have the most significant implications for the nature and character of the broader *culture* and *society* that surround us. We live, it may be argued, in a media culture, a media society. This book provides an introduction to the relationships between media and the broader social and cultural world in which they operate.

Media, culture, society

It should always be remembered that *media* is the plural of the term *medium*, which refers, essentially, to the means by which *content* is communicated between an origin and a destination.

It could be argued that the human body acts as the first and most fundamental medium in this respect, transferring thoughts, ideas and emotions into speech or gestures audible or visible to others. Yet our concern here is with the use of artificial forms of media that enhance and extend our communicative capacity beyond the capabilities of our own bodies, transforming the range of expression open to us and mediating what we say over longer distances or to greater numbers of people, for example.

At one extreme, such media may enable each of us to interact with friends without the need to be in the same room, the same city or even the same country, while at the other, they may enable a relatively small number of professional media producers to transmit large volumes of content simultaneously to audiences of millions. Such producers, along with the technologies they utilize and the content they distribute, are often collectively referred to as 'the media' and this certainly has become an acceptable use of the term. It remains important, however, to understand media as plural and diverse. Although large-scale *mass media* will figure heavily in our discussions, we'll focus on a broad range of different types and scales of communication involving a plethora of organizations, communities and individuals.

Two connected senses of the word *culture* are of importance to our discussions in this book, both of which are identified in the influential writings of Raymond Williams (1988; 1989) on the subject.

First, culture is sometimes used in a specific sense to refer to the worlds of creative expression or, as Williams puts it, 'the works and practices of intellectual and especially artistic activity' (1988: 90). Traditionally, this sense of the term was reserved for elite or 'high' forms of literature, music, art and theatre, but increasingly its use also encapsulates the larger realm of so-called *popular culture*, including pop music and popular fiction or drama, for example. As Williams puts it, 'culture is ordinary' (1989: 3). At certain points, we'll use the term culture in this more restricted sense, including as a means to refer to mediated forms and practices of expression.

Importantly, however, such creative forms and activities form just part of a crucial second sense of the word culture, as a means of referring to the whole way of life of a society or group, including values, meanings, identities, traditions, norms of behaviour and ways of understanding the world.

As Williams argues, although they are different, these two senses of culture are closely related. After all, the practices of creative, artistic and intellectual expression in a given society encapsulate anything from the production and consumption of famous art, literature, music or television programmes to grass roots dancing, music-making, dress and acts of worship, all of which form an integral part of the overall ways of life of that society. The word culture, then, often refers simultaneously to creative practices and broader ways of life, whether in reference to the distinctive identities, rituals, practices and forms of expression associated with a particular group (as in 'punk culture') or a certain activity (as in 'television culture') or as a more general way to invoke the range of cultural features and practices across a broader range of people.

Society, meanwhile, is a closely related but somewhat broader term that refers to the whole social world in which we exist, or, 'the body of institutions and relationships within which a relatively large group of people live' (Williams, 1988: 291). Society particularly invokes an emphasis on social relations, including the detail of everyday interactions and the operation of broader social groupings and categories of social differentiation, such as those based on class, ethnicity and gender.

Patterns of wealth, power and inequality are a further core element of societies, as are social institutions, including the apparatus of government and law, education systems, religious organizations, commercial enterprises and smaller-scale organizational units, such as the family. Together with established hierarchies of wealth, power and control, such institutions form a complex set of *structures* through which social relations are lived out.

Among those who study societies, a key question concerns the relationship between these established structures and human *agency,* which means people's ability to be self-determining. Are we shaped by the gender, social class or ethnic category into which we were born – or, indeed, the family structure, education system or religious institutions that play a role in our lives? Or do we have the power to determine our own futures? The importance of media at so many levels of contemporary social life renders it a crucial consideration in such questions of structure and agency.

Crucially, it is difficult to envisage a study of such questions about the make-up of society, the arrangement of social relations or the balance of structure and agency that omits the cultural ways of life and expression, which, after all, lie at the heart of all societies. It is equally difficult to imagine how one might examine questions about cultural rituals, understandings, identities or creative practices without reference to the society in which they take place.

The emphasis associated with the term 'culture' and with the term 'society' differs in some respects, then, but there are extensive overlaps and ambiguities – something that particularly applies to the connection between society and the broader sense of culture as way of life. I would urge readers to feel comfortable with this fuzziness. The particular emphasis of one term or the other will be invoked at different stages of the discussions ahead, but our ultimate concern is with the relationship communications media have with the range of phenomena covered by the two terms. We will explore the possibility, then, that media have, in one way or another, become integral to what we might term the broader social and cultural environment – something that includes the distribution of wealth, power and influence, the operation of social structures and institutions, class, gender and ethnic relations, patterns of identity and *community*, ideas and understandings, practices of intellectual, artistic and creative expression and broader ways of life.

Starting points: shaping, mirroring and representing

Needless to say, the development of a detailed understanding of the role of media in relation to these various features of the broader social and cultural environment in which we live is a far from simple task. So let's take things one step at a time and consider, by way of a starting point, two simple and contrasting approaches to the relationship between mass media content and society. For the purpose of the discussion, let's assume that 'society' here can be taken to include, among other things, culture in its broad sense as a reference to overall ways of life.

Some approaches regard media as constructors or *shapers*, arguing that the content they distribute has the power to influence people and affect the future of society (Figure 1.1).

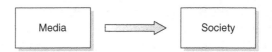

FIGURE 1.1   Media as shaper

There are all sorts of arguments that fit with this approach. Some suggest, for example, that media depictions of sex and violence are liable to influence viewers to the extent that people's *real* lives may become more dominated by promiscuity or danger, while others warn that stereotypical portrayals of ethnic or sexual minority groups might increase the marginalization of such groups within society. Arguments that political or moral *bias* in the media may lead to a predominance of certain opinions among audiences also come into this category, as do assertions that the general quality of media content in a given society may affect how informed, engaged or creative its *population* is. Such perspectives all focus on the ways in which media may be affecting or influencing us.

Others focus not on how media content shapes us but on the way it reflects or *mirrors* society (Figure 1.2). The predominant role of media, according to

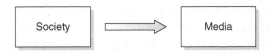

FIGURE 1.2 Media as mirror

this view, is to reflect back to us events, behaviours, identities, social relations or values that already are important. Media, then, are deemed more significant for the way they follow rather than the way they lead.

From this perspective, if media are dominated by sex and violence, that is because we already live in a society in which these are important, and if particular opinions or values are given prominence in media content, this reflects their existing currency. Thus, when accused of manipulating public opinion through bias, news media professionals often defend themselves by reciting the cliché 'don't shoot the messenger'. The implication is that news is neutrally reflecting the world and that, if we don't like it, we should seek to improve the world rather than blame media.

As Victoria Alexander (2003) shows, the belief that media reflect society has prompted some analysts to try and learn about changing structures, cultural norms or politics within real society by studying media content. Such analysis can be instructive up to a point. For example, during the 1980s, the baddies in Hollywood action or war films (*Rocky, Top Gun, From Russia with Love*) often were from the former Soviet Union, reflecting real-world Cold War tensions at the time between that country and the USA. By the 1990s, the Cold War was largely over and a switch of US foreign policy towards the Middle East was apparently mirrored by a greater emphasis on Arab or African Hollywood enemies (*Patriot Games, Black Hawk Down, The Siege*).

In their extreme form, however, suggestions that media content *either* shapes or mirrors society are both simplistic. An improvement would be to understand the relationship as being a circular one, involving elements of both processes. The media-as-mirror approach is useful in reminding us that, rather than being invented out of thin air, media content often relates closely to real events and prevailing social trends and cultural values. Media content does not reflect these perfectly or neutrally, however. Media producers are highly selective with respect to what they include and they present the elements they do include in very particular ways. They do not, then, offer us a *mirror* but a selective, manufactured set of *representations* (or re-presentations) of the world. As Stuart Hall (1982: 64) explains: 'representation is a very different notion from reflection. It implies the active work of selecting and presenting, of structuring and shaping.'

The content of television soap operas, for example, relates closely to scenarios and dilemmas that are already of significance within broader society. Such programmes do not simply mirror society, however, because only certain characters, issues and incidents are included and these are represented to audiences in particular, dramatically appealing ways. Likewise, there may indeed be a relationship between the race or nationality of Hollywood villains and real US foreign policy, as discussed above, but, rather than comprising a neutral reflection of the world, this demonstrates a selective emphasis on particular US-orientated perspectives.

Because media representations are selective and manufactured, this makes them distinct from the world they sometimes claim to reflect. It is this that creates the possibility that media may also have the potential to influence us. The repeated emphasis on certain opinions, themes, events or practices across media and the consistent exclusion of others may have a bearing on future attitudes, identities, behaviour and social patterns. Rather than deciding between the shaping and mirroring approaches, then, a more useful starting point is to conceive of an ongoing process whereby selective media representations constantly feed into and are themselves fed by the make-up and character of society (Figure 1.3).

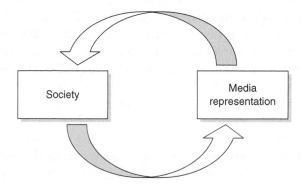

FIGURE 1.3   Circular model of representation and influence

The communication process

The circular representations model outlined above provides a helpful starting point for an understanding of the socio-cultural significance of media, and it can be usefully applied to many of the specific topics covered throughout this book. Nevertheless, as well as rather oversimplifying the complex range of phenomena included within our earlier discussion of culture and society, this model remains too general to facilitate a detailed analysis of the way media work. In order to take us a step further in the latter respect, we need to break the process of media communication into its different components and consider the significance of each one. This involves thinking not just about the content of media, as we did in the discussion above, but also about where such content comes from, how it is transmitted and what happens when people engage with it.

Transmitters, receivers and noise

One of the first attempts to develop a systematic understanding of the relationship between different components in the communication process was developed by Claude Shannon and Warren Weaver 1949, (Figure 1.4). The model was developed for the Bell telephone company, which wanted to improve the efficiency of communication using *technology*. It was not intended to represent broader processes of mass communication, but it became highly influential in this respect.

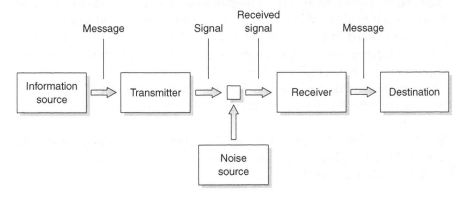

FIGURE 1.4   Shannon and Weaver's model of communication

The model comprises a one-directional process whereby a message goes through a number of stages. It is created by an information source (such as somebody's voice), encoded into an electronic signal by a transmitter (such as his or her telephone), decoded back into its original form by a receiver (such as another person's telephone) and received by a recipient at its destination.

The model also incorporates *noise*, which refers to interference that might distort the message en route so that what is received is different from what was sent. Shannon and Weaver's primary concern here is with *technical problems* relating to faults or technological limitations – a crackly or crossed line can make it hard to understand what people are saying and, even if the medium is working perfectly, we don't hear people on the telephone in quite the same way that we would if we were in the same room. However, they also consider the notion of *semantic problems*, which refers to the possibility that the recipient might misunderstand the message itself as a result of ambiguities in its content, and *effectiveness problems* relating to the failure of the message to have the desired impact on the recipient.

Shannon and Weaver's interest in semantic and effectiveness problems is largely focused on the ways in which such complications might be avoided by improving the technical efficiency with which messages are encoded and decoded (Fiske, 1990). Nevertheless, their focus on such matters opened the doorway to important issues about the human interpretation or 'decoding' of media content by audiences and the ways in which media might influence people.

'Who says what...?' and other questions

Emphasis on communication as a human as well as a technical process was taken a stage further by Harold Lasswell (1948), who produced a model orientated towards the development of a broader understanding of the role of mass media in society. The model is phrased as a question: 'Who says what in which channel to whom with what effect?'

Memorable and deceptively concise, this question sets out an agenda for the understanding of media by breaking up the communication process into its key components and formulating an interpretation of the relationships between them. If we separate out the components of the question and present them as a diagrammatic model, we can see clear similarities with the transmission model (Figure 1.5).

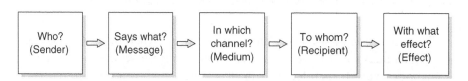

FIGURE 1.5   Diagrammatic representation of Lasswell's model

Whereas Shannon and Weaver had focused on the efficiency of the *technical* apparatus of communication, Lasswell's approach suggests that each of the components he identifies have equally important implications for the outcome of the communication process. I might conduct a detailed analysis of the content of a television programme, then, but unless I also investigate the status and motivations of those who created and distributed it, the capacities and limitations of television itself as a medium for transmitting it and the make-up and orientation of the audience, then my understanding will be partial and limited. Lasswell's model could also be applied to all manner of other forms of communication, from telephone calls to social networking site conversations and from magazine reading to university lectures.

Linear and one-dimensional

Although valuable in breaking the communication process down into components and considering the relationships between them, Shannon and Weaver's and Lasswell's models have been criticized for oversimplifying things. According to Daniel Chandler (1994a), Shannon and Weaver's model relies on a 'postal metaphor' of communication. That is, it treats communication as something centred on the effective (or ineffective) transport and delivery of a pre-existing message, complete with any meanings it contains, to a destination. Its overriding concern with the efficiency of the *delivery* system may make sense as a means for Bell to enhance its technical services, but provides a highly limited understanding of the broader operation of media in society.

As Chandler points out, Shannon and Weaver's model encourages us to view communication as an essentially one-way, linear process in which the sender of the message is active and the role of the receiver is limited to passively receiving and absorbing it. It implies what some have termed a *hypodermic syringe* approach to media, whereby messages are automatically injected into the minds of recipients, whether in their living room, at the cinema or in a lecture theatre.

What is not allowed for is the possibility that 'recipients' might do more than just receive, that they might engage with content actively, drawing on their existing identity and surroundings to produce their own interpretations of what senders present to them. The construction of meaning, then, might be seen as a joint project between senders and receivers.

Neither does the model refer to the possibility that receivers might directly influence the messages sent to them by virtue of their provision of different sorts of feedback to senders (Fiske, 1990). In the case of *interpersonal* communication, constant adjustment to the cues and responses of the other person is a critical part of effective communication. Likewise, mass media are intensely sensitive to audience responses, whether in the form of ratings, market research or direct communication.

Developed specifically as a means of understanding the role of communication in society, Lasswell's model has a little more going for it in this respect than Shannon and Weaver's approach. In specifically inviting us to ask questions about the status of senders and receivers, as well as about content and medium, the model goes further towards the development of a detailed understanding of media processes – something for which it is not always given appropriate credit. Yet the wording and ordering of the model tends to reproduce the linear approach of the Shannon and Weaver model. Although it encourages us to consider the *status* of the recipient, it is clear that the primary role of the latter is deemed a passive one: to be *affected* in one way or another by what is said to them. Later communications models that drew on the work of Lasswell and of Shannon and Weaver responded to this deficiency by building in feedback loops from recipients back to senders (Westley and Maclean, 1957) and/or the potential for audiences to interpret media in different ways (Gerbner, 1956), among other things. However, many of these adaptations tended still to present communication as a largely one-way process.

Perhaps the most important element of the communication process that is not accounted for in Shannon and Weaver's model is the broader social and cultural environment within which media communication takes place. The model encourages us to think about communication as a process centred on isolated individuals (Chandler, 1994a). Lasswell's approach represents an improvement in this respect because, through encouraging us to think in detail about the identity of the sender and receiver of the message, it allows for some consideration of the context of each. Yet, the lack of any explicit emphasis on the role of broader culture and society in the model seems to underestimate their importance.

Elements of media in socio-cultural context

In this book, we'll draw on the first four parts of Lasswell's question – 'Who says what in which channel to whom?' – as valuable contributions towards the identification of the key elements of the media and communications process. Consistent with the approach of many other contemporary scholars, however, the model I would advocate (Figure 1.6) focuses on 'media industry' and 'media users' rather than 'senders' and 'recipients'. By using these categories, we can specifically emphasize the power and significance of media organizations for the communications process while, at the same time, avoiding the automatic portrayal of those who engage with media as passive individuals whose only role is to absorb or be affected. The avoidance of a one-way, linear understanding of communication also can be achieved by the representation of a series of multidirectional flows between the different components of the model. And crucially, our understanding of

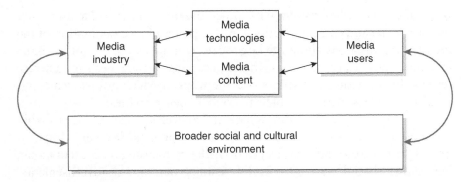

FIGURE 1.6   Simplified model of the elements of media in socio-cultural contexts

media processes has to incorporate the extensive and constant flows of influence both to and from a complex broader social and cultural environment, which consists of an established but developing overall world of social relations, ways of life and modes of expression. This broader environment, or world, forms an everchanging context within which industry and *users* – alongside the technologies and content they use, create and distribute – operate. It should therefore be regarded as integral to the operation of all four of the elements of the media process.

The four elements of media that are represented in the context of broader culture and society in the model above form the basis for the chapters in Part 1 of this book, Elements of media, but I'll briefly introduce them here.

Equating with the 'in which channel?' part of Lasswell's model, *media technologies* refers to the hardware by means of which media content is created, distributed and used. Crucially, rather than being neutral, technologies such as television, newspapers, mobile phones and Internet services each offer their own particular sets of possibilities and limitations. For example, books require all of my individual attention and have the capacity to provide extensive depth and detail via the written word, whereas television has greater potential to be enjoyed alongside other activities or with other people and, in comparison to books, it tends to facilitate a greater emphasis on what things look and sound like on the surface. Rather than simply shaping us, however, technologies are developed and used in ways that relate closely to the social and cultural context of industry and users.

Media industry can be seen as a more specific and contextualized formulation of the 'Who?' at the beginning of Lasswell's model. Media and related organizations are not the only creators of content but they also dominate its production and distribution and control the development and availability of technologies. An understanding of media processes, then, requires an appreciation of the motivations of these organizations, the ways in which they work and their relationships with other organizations, media users and broader social and cultural relations. At the centre of an examination of the industry are questions about the large-scale, commercial nature of the most influential media organizations, the implications of their need to generate revenue by attracting advertisers and the ways in which governments and regulators have sometimes sought to control their activities.

Media content comprises the 'What?' in Lasswell's model and is probably the most talked about element of the media process. We can't hope to understand the role and significance of media by focusing on content alone, but neither should we ignore it. Television programmes, advertisements, news articles, music videos, social networking site profiles and a plethora of other forms of media content all represent the world in partial and particular ways and this places limits on the range of likely interpretations or uses of them. This implies that content may have the capacity to influence the thoughts and lives of users and the broader ways of life and social relations of which they are a part. Careful analysis of what is included and excluded and the complex ways in which particular meanings are constructed remains a key element of the study of media, culture and society.

The notion of *media users* is a little broader than the 'To whom?' in Lasswell's model in that, rather than restricting their role to that of receivers who are affected by media messages, it recognizes that, although they still may be open to influence, those who engage with media play an active role in the communication processes. It is crucial, then, to learn about the circumstances in which users engage with media and the ways in which they contribute to the generation of meaning by bringing their existing identities, opinions and social position to their encounters with content and technologies. Users should also be understood as small-scale creators of content, whether through the provision of feedback to industrial media organizations, participation in phone-ins, talk shows or letters pages or the production and distribution of more substantive forms of amateur content.

The broader social and cultural environment is represented here as feeding, via users and industry, into each of the different elements of the ongoing media process, while at the same time developing and changing as a result of that process. It is impossible to understand the operation and significance of any one of the elements of media without placing it within this sociocultural context. Because of this, rather than having a separate chapter on the theme, different elements of culture and society are discussed throughout the chapters on technologies, industry, content and users that make up Part 1 of the book. The relationship between media processes and the various elements of broader culture and society also dominates Parts 2 and 3 of the book, which address a range of substantive issues and debates under the themes of media, power and control and media, identity and culture.

Media, power and control

Part 2 of this book focuses on a series of themes connected with the relationship between media and questions of power, influence, *regulation* and control. We start, in Chapter 6, by examining highly influential Marxist approaches, which regard media as a form of *ideology* or, more specifically, a means by which powerful groups manipulate people by reinforcing understandings of the world that serve to legitimate an unequal and exploitative capitalist system.

Concerns about ideology also figure, among other perspectives, in Chapter 7, which addresses the specific role of news media as a way of distributing particular representations of the contemporary world to media users.

In Chapter 8, our focus shifts to broader questions about what media are for and, specifically, whether their role in society might be improved if governments were to intervene in the way that they are run. Should we attempt to control media by having subsidized public service broadcasters or restrictions on content or would we be better served by an unfettered commercial media system?

Finally, Chapter 9 addresses the relationship between media, national identity and democracy, focusing in particular on the possibility that the increasing commercialization, *globalization* and diversification of media may be contributing to declines in cultural cohesion and socio-political engagement.

Media, identity and culture

Part 3 is the final section of the book and moves us towards a set of questions about the relationship between media and patterns of identity, culture and community.

Chapters 10 and 11 deal with two of the most discussed subjects within the study of media: race and gender.

In Chapter 10, we will consider debates about the exclusion and stereotypical representation of subordinated ethnic groupings within mainstream media before examining the implications of the increasing use by such ethnic minorities of specialist and sometimes transnational forms of media.

Chapter 11 centres partly on questions about the representation of femininities and masculinities, while also examining debates about how to make sense of audience interpretations of gender in media.

In Chapter 12 our focus will shift to the implications of media processes for patterns of collective identity in society. In contrast to theories that suggest media tend to *erode* collective forms of identity, the chapter examines a range of ways in which different forms of media – from local newspapers to online discussion groups and social networking sites – appear to *facilitate* communities, including youth *subcultures*, *fan* groups and sexual minorities.

The final chapter of the book, Chapter 13, addresses the possibility that, as a result of the rapid and ongoing expansion of media, everyday culture has become so saturated by communication, images and representations that we no longer know what, if anything, any of it means. Truth, reality and stability are all deemed to be under threat in a world dominated by *fluidity*, uncertainty and the loss of meaning.

Making connections

These thematic sections of the book offer a useful means of organizing and making sense of so large a range of material, but readers, hopefully, will identify a range of connections between the issues covered in each section. They may note, for example, that questions of national community clearly relate to identity as well as power, while discussions of gender and race connect to issues of domination and subordination as well as those of cultural differentiation. Also, as one would expect, the issues covered in the chapters of Part 1 – on technologies, *industry*, content and users – resurface at various points during the discussions of substantive topics that follow. Equally, a number of particular issues make themselves known at a number of different points in the book. Questions about commercialization and the quality and depth of media content, for example, appear in all three parts of the book, as do considerations of the relationship between media and advertisers and questions about the increasing specialization of media. Such interconnections are important and readers are encouraged to draw their own links between the various topics covered in the chapters that follow. It is only by making such connections that we can gradually develop a more rounded understanding of the themes and approaches that dominate the study of media, culture and society.

QUESTIONS AND EXERCISES

I Select a piece of media content of your choice and answer the following questions.

   a) In what ways does the content draw on elements of existing social relations or ways of life?

---

b) In what ways is it selective in doing so?

c) In what ways might these selective representations influence the future of society?

2 Taking the models presented in the chapter as a starting point, design your own diagrammatic model of the process of media communication and its relationship with the broader social and cultural environment. Think carefully about how you will represent the key elements of the communication process and the nature of the relationships between them.

PART ONE

ELEMENTS OF MEDIA

2

Media Technologies

Focal points

- Theories that suggest communications technologies influence the social and cultural world.
- Arguments about the socio-cultural impacts of print and electronic media.
- Criticisms of technological determinism.
- The need to study technologies in relation to the context of producers and users.
- The growth and significance of digital media and the Internet.

Introduction

When asked to think about media, the first thing to enter many people's minds would probably be an example of media content, whether a film, an advertisement, a website, a music video or a piece of news footage. Similarly, analysis of the social or cultural significance of media often focuses on questions of media content. Is newspaper coverage of current affairs biased? What do depictions of gender in advertisements tell us about attitudes to masculinity and femininity? What explains the emphasis on celebrity across so many genres of media? These and other questions about content are of great importance. This chapter, however, is not about content but the technologies or hardware through which content is transmitted. It is, in other words, about the significance of media themselves, remembering that media is the plural of medium.

For some commentators, known as *medium theorists*, the properties of communications technologies can have profound social and cultural impacts and the understanding of these impacts should be pivotal to any quest to make sense of media. From the development of newspapers to the growth of the Internet, the onset of new technologies with distinct capabilities has often been accompanied by intense debate about their likely impacts on power, politics, culture and everyday life. In recent times, debates have raged about the impact of games consoles, digital music players, mobile phones and social networking sites, while in the past equally intense discussions took place with respect to newspapers, radio, records, cinema and, of course, television.

This chapter begins by focusing on some of the contrasting conclusions drawn by prominent medium theorists about the development and impacts of print and electronic media technologies. As well as discussing case studies, we will examine criticisms of medium theories more generally, including the claim that such approaches tend to overestimate the extent to which technologies have inevitable or predictable socio-cultural effects. We will go on to discuss arguments about the significance of recent technologies, such as digital television and the Internet.

Contrasting medium theories

McLuhan: the medium is the message

> in operational and practical fact, the medium is the message. This is merely to say that the personal and social consequences of any medium – that is, of any extension of ourselves – result from the new scale that is introduced into our affairs by each extension of ourselves, or by any new technology.
>
> McLuhan, 2001: 2

The first of our case studies involves the most famous medium theorist, Marshall McLuhan, who famously argued in the 1960s that the study of media content was of little significance compared to the analysis of communications technologies. This is expressed through the often cited slogan 'the medium is the message'.

Essentially, McLuhan's argument is that the medium is more important than the message – that it is the capacities of media hardware, rather than the details of particular examples of content, that have real social significance. Debating the specifics of the content of newspaper articles, advertisements or radio broadcasts is regarded as an unnecessary distraction – something liable to result in a failure to see the forest for the trees. Thus, to study the social significance of television by focusing on the content of particular programmes is no more useful, from McLuhan's point of view, than trying to learn about the cultural impact of the telephone by referencing the precise subject matter of a particular conversation between two friends in Toronto or attempting to ascertain the impact of the iPod by conducting a close analysis of the music listened to by a particular individual on a Monday morning.

What is important, he argues, is not the detail of the content, but the broader fact that particular modes of communication are made possible. For McLuhan, each media technology enables a different extension of our communicative senses – in both space and time – beyond what was previously possible. Arguing that media should be regarded as 'the extensions of man', he writes that, 'after more than a century of electric technology we have extended our central nervous system itself into a global embrace, abolishing both space and time' (2001: 3).

In different ways, then, media technologies expand our physical sphere of communications – we can see, hear, talk or write across greater distances and at greater speed than before. It is this that leads to McLuhan's most famous pronouncement – that, as a result of the ease with which we can communicate across the world through electronic media, we increasingly inhabit a *global village*.

Crucially, each medium extends our senses in different ways, encouraging certain patterns of communication and preventing others. The central distinction made by McLuhan between different forms of media involves two categories: *hot* and *cool*. Hot media are high-definition and data-intensive with a large amount of information, conveyed – usually to a single one of the human senses. Including books, newspapers and radio, hot media occupy all or most of the attention of an individual and leave few gaps to be completed by the audience. In contrast, *cool media* are low in information intensity and high in audience participation – rather like a seminar as compared to a lecture.

For McLuhan, the cool medium par excellence of his time was television, whose ability to combine sound with low definition moving pictures is deemed to have enabled both senses to be engaged, but each less intensively than in the case of printed literature or radio. As a consequence, television did not spell out every detail, it is argued, leaving audiences more able to fill in the gaps themselves.

In order to appreciate McLuhan's point, we might imagine how he might have interpreted the difference between sports commentaries on the radio and those on the television. On the radio, numerous details have to be spelt out by the commentators, requiring intense concentration from listeners and strongly shaping their interpretation of events. In contrast, television commentators do not need to provide the same level of detail because their words are accompanied by moving pictures, which viewers are able to partially interpret for themselves.

The most important comparison for McLuhan was between print media, which he regarded as universally hot, and electronic media, which he believed were becoming increasingly cool. Outlining the social significance of the historical development of the printing press, McLuhan (1962) argues that the ability to mass produce books and, later, newspapers precipitated an end to the age of oral, informal, face-to-face communication and its replacement by a society so dominated by standardized print media that the human senses became fragmented because everything was reduced to and dictated by the format of the written word. The effect of this was to standardize dialect, language and culture, to dictate particular ordered ways of viewing the world and to homogenize societies into hierarchically organized nation states.

Inherently, McLuhan suggests, print media were amenable to such hierarchical arrangements. Isolated, individualized and silent, the reader is dictated to by the one-directional, linear organization and the intense detail of the information in the text, receiving a precise and literal set of messages from a small number of sources and unable to participate or interact with the material. For McLuhan, such technological biases rendered print media responsible for the development of an early capitalist society dominated by rigid cultural hierarchies, standardization and individual isolation.

In contrast, the ongoing development of electronic media is deemed to have culminated in television – a cool technology, which he believed would liberate audiences from the restrictions of the print age and herald a return to organic, participatory communicative practices. 'Mechanical, one-way expansion from centres to margins,' he argues, is 'no longer relevant to our electric world' (2001: 39).

While print culture served to homogenize language, television's emphasis on cool speech and pictures is deemed to have precipitated a shift away from such centralized officialdom and towards an emphasis on local dialects and everyday talk. More generally, television is regarded as spontaneous, intimate, informal and incomplete, inviting creative audience participation. Ultimately, the capacities of this cool, informal medium are deemed pivotal to the increasing development of a *global village*, envisaged in the most organic, decentralized and democratic of terms. Gone would be the individual isolation and one-way standardized, linear national communication that characterized print culture, to be replaced by a proliferation of multi-directional, decentralized electronic communication across the globe.

Kill your television

McLuhan's optimism about the social impact of electronic media is not shared by all commentators. Neil Postman (1987) looks back fondly on the age of print media and describes a range of social ills brought about by developments in electronic and visual communications. From this point of view, early newspapers offered a detailed, localized and relevant source of communication, filled with rich, coherent information of direct significance to the lives of readers. Far from being a disadvantage, as McLuhan had seen it, the level of concentration required from readers is deemed by Postman as having encouraged a rational, serious engagement with local issues and been important to the development of informed, reasoned forms of critical discussion and political engagement. For Postman, such engagement has gradually been undermined by a series of technological developments, beginning with the telegraph and ending with television.

Developed by Samuel Morse in the early 1800s, the telegraph enabled the transmission of coded electric signals across significant geographical distances (Figure 2.1). Among other things, this possibility had a profound impact on newspapers, which became able to report stories from distant places without the inconvenience and time delays associated with physical travel. In Postman's view, however, 'the dazzle of distance and speed' (1987: 67) prompted greater and greater emphasis on the superficial reporting of any number of unconnected enticing stories from elsewhere. Telegraphy is deemed to have been suited only to 'the flashing of messages, each to be quickly replaced by a more up-to-date message' (1987: 71) and this principle, according to Postman, rapidly imprinted itself on newspaper content, too.

FIGURE 2.1   Telegraph wires
© Robert Hillman

Instead of offering coherence, depth and relevance, each edition offered an arbitrary mixture of temporary sources of fascination from afar.

The ability to reproduce photographs as part of newspapers – first developed in the late 1800s – is deemed by Postman to have represented a further step in the direction of superficiality. Whereas printed text is capable of providing depth and context, and thereby encouraging rational engagement and critical thinking, photographs, it is argued, reduce the complexity of issues to particular observable fragments and encourage emotional, voyeuristic captivation. Worse still, this inherent superficiality is hidden by a veneer of realness and proximity as photographs entice us into the mistaken feeling that we have fully understood the situation being depicted.

Meanwhile, the desire for image-based journalism is deemed to have affected news priorities, the inclusion of issues increasingly being based not on importance but on visual appeal. For Postman, this made the photograph the ideal counterpart for the emphasis created by telegraphy on exciting short-lived stories from afar.

Together, the two developments are blamed for a reorientation of mass media towards empty spectacle. Such was the flow of pointless information, according to Postman that newspapers eventually had to include quizzes and crosswords to find some use for it all: 'Where people once sought information to manage the real contexts of their lives, now they had to invent contexts in which otherwise useless information might be put to some apparent use' (1987: 77).

Postman's strongest comments, however, are reserved for the transformation of society and culture in the twentieth century as a result of television. In contrast to McLuhan's optimism, Postman regards the small screen as having extended to near infinite proportions all the worst tendencies conceived by the alliance of telegraphy and photography, 'raising the interplay of image and instancy to an exquisite and dangerous perfection' (1987: 79) and bringing them to the centre of our domestic lives.

Television's emphasis on moving pictures, he argues, has extended the emotionally enticing qualities of the photograph, has combined them with sound, and, in doing so, has intensified the domination of communications by voyeurism and spectacle. That is because, even more so than photography, the ability to view moving pictures allows us to imagine we have seen all there is to know when, in reality, we have witnessed only superficial fragments. In place of the depth and coherence once provided by text-based media, the technological properties of television made it inevitable that it would, 'suppress the content of ideas in order to accommodate the requirements of visual interest' (1987: 92).

If television exaggerates the visual biases of photography, then its relentless emphasis on tempo and immediacy may be traced back, according to Postman, to the telegraph. It is no coincidence, argues Postman, that US television news reports are each over within a minute, that individual programmes rarely last more than 30 minutes and that rarely is there any sort of link or coherence between one segment of content and another. For Postman the 'now this!' tendency, whereby content rapidly shifts the attention of the viewer between an array of unrelated subject matter, has resulted from the inherent bias of television as a medium – its 'predisposition toward being used in some ways and not others' (1987: 84). And the impact of this predisposition towards superficial, fast-moving entertainment is that audiences are induced into any number of instant emotional responses to the spectacles placed in front of them, but are unlikely to understand or even remember them:

> There is no murder so brutal, no earthquake so devastating, no political blunder so costly – for that matter, no ball score so tantalising or no weather report so threatening – that it cannot be erased from our minds by a newscaster saying 'now this!' The newscaster means that you have thought long enough on the previous matter (approximately forty-five seconds), that you must not be morbidly preoccupied with it (let us say, for ninety seconds), and that you must now give your attention to another fragment of news or a commercial (Postman, 1987: 99-100).

The depth of Postman's concern also relates the ubiquity of television – its dominance of lives and imaginations across boundaries of class, age, gender and ethnicity. As a consequence, television's emphasis on short-term enter-tainment and superficiality is deemed to have had a profound impact on culture and society off the screen: 'Television is our culture's principal mode of knowing about itself. Therefore ... how television stages the world becomes the model for how the world is properly to be staged' (1987: 92–3).

Postman's attack on the social impacts of television shares some features with an earlier polemic entitled *Four Arguments for the Elimination of Television*, in which Jerry Mander asserts that the technological biases of television make attempts by governments or others to reform or regulate it futile: 'Far from being "neutral", television itself predetermines who shall use it, how they shall use it, what effects it will have on individual lives and ... what sort of political forms will inevitably emerge' (1978: 45). Like Postman, Mander argues that such biases create an emphasis on short, snappy content and a focus on style, presentation and entertainment.

While presenting us with all this superficiality, argues Mander, television consumption makes us believe that we understand the world: 'because of television we believe we know more, but we know less' (1978: 349). In con-trast to McLuhan's insistence that television would undo the centralized, top-down culture created by print, Mander also asserts that television is itself inherently a hierarchical, one-directional mode of communication that empowers an elite minority while distracting and disorientating a passive mass audience.

Technological determinism

There should be no doubt as to the importance of either McLuhan's highly influential optimistic approach to electronic technologies or the pessimistic approach taken by the likes of Postman and Mander. Alongside a range of other medium theorists, including Harold Innes (1951), Walter Ong (1977) and Joshua Meyrowitz (1985), they offer a crucial reminder that those seeking to understand the relationship between media, culture and society must consider the significance of different forms of media hardware. More specifically, they remind us that questions of power, space and time, as well as patterns of interaction and understanding, can be intimately connected with the dominant means of communication within different societies and eras.

Nevertheless, there are also significant problems with medium theory, whether it is optimistic, pessimistic or neither. Difficulties vary somewhat from theorist to theorist, but, as a whole, the approach has tended to overplay and simplify the role of technologies, regarding them as the primary cause of social change and giving insufficient consideration to the broader context in which they are developed and used. Let's examine this in some more detail in relation to our case studies of McLuhan, Postman and Mander.

Hot, cool or both?

It should already be clear – not least from the disagreement of Postman and Mander – that McLuhan's specific interpretations of the qualities and impacts of media technologies are open to question. Notably, his distinction between high-intensity, low-participation (hot) technologies and low-intensity, high-participation (cool) technologies is confusing, especially when one considers his own categorization of different examples.

In some respects, McLuhan's categorization of print media as hot makes sense – books and newspapers do indeed place emphasis on linear textual detail and tend to require intensive engagement from an isolated individual reader. Yet, these media surely also have potentially cool characteristics. Is it not the case that reading can generate participation, imagination and critical thought, for example, not least through the construction of our own visual representations of what is being described by the text? Some degree of co-construction of meaning is surely taking place here – arguably more so than in the case of many encounters with television content, where pictures, sounds and sometimes text are each shaped by media producers.

Another dichotomy presented by McLuhan – between cinema, which he regards as hot and television as cool – is even more questionable. McLuhan argues that the cinema viewer is in a darkened, silent room in front of a single linear text and that this has a hierarchical and individualizing effect that is similar to the consumption of print media. In contrast, television viewing is argued to be more social and less prescriptive. A further factor here is that, during the 1960s, the cinema screen produced a far higher-quality and more intense image than the fuzzy, black and white images broadcast on early television screens.

Now, we may agree that, of the two viewer experiences, the cinematic one probably was – and is – of a higher order of intensity and individualization than the televisual. It is curious, however, for this difference of degree to be regarded as the basis for categorizing two such apparently similar forms of communication at opposite ends of the hot–cool spectrum. After all, both combine moving pictures and sound, both tend to have a largely linear for-mat and both tend to occupy a significant proportion of the attention of viewers. Further, McLuhan's emphasis on differences in technical quality has become increasingly redundant as a result of predictable improvements in the size and quality of television screens, culminating in the development of huge LCD and plasma screens, high-definition pictures and surround sound sys-tems, all of which seek to imitate the experience of the cinema. Confusingly, McLuhan acknowledges such a possibility, but side-steps it by claiming that if it were of a higher quality, television would no longer be television:

> If anybody were to ask whether all this were to change if technology stepped up the character of the TV image to movie data level, one could only counter by enquiring 'Could we alter a cartoon by adding details of perspective, light and shade?' The answer is 'Yes,' only it would then no longer be a cartoon. Nor would 'improved' TV be television (2001: 341).

Leaving aside this curious point, McLuhan's recognition that higher-quality television would not fit well with his cool designation raises substantial ques-tions as to the basis for his broader optimism about the 'cool' electronic future.

What these confusions draw attention to is that the very exercise of cat-egorizing technologies as inherently 'hot' or 'cool' is hazardous, as is the broader assumption that the inherent properties of technologies predeter-mine their use and social impact in predictable ways. When I ask my students to categorize different media technologies as hot and cool, their most frequent response is, quite rightly, to point out that levels of intensity and audience participation are dependent on content as much as they are on medium, to say nothing of the circumstances of media users. If one listens to a complicated play on the radio, then this may require intense concentration, but, if the same medium is used for the transmission of popular music, the intensity required may be considerably lower, making it possible to combine the activity of listening with working or socializing. The technical capacities of radio are important here, but the kind of communication engendered is equally dependent on the content and on the context of use.

Contrary to McLuhan, then, we need to examine the message *as well as* the medium, and we need to examine the context of media users, too.

Generalization and reification

The negative commentaries of Postman and Mander also suffer from an assumption that technologies have automatic social effects, regardless of content or context.

Both insist the deficiencies in television content that they refer to are an inevitable result of the technical biases of television. For Mander, there is no possibility of reforming or regulating television in order to make it more compatible with a culturally rich, democratic society and, by implication, no possibility of producing television content that has any value in this respect. Yet both Postman and Mander tend to focus on those examples of content that best support their case, while making less of examples of programming or television use which might be deemed more positive. Their focus on US television, meanwhile, leaves little space for consideration of the content and experience of television in different cultural contexts and, crucially, different regulatory systems. Many would argue for example, that early television content in most European countries was significantly different from that of their US equivalents as a result of public service regulations (see Chapter 8). Questions about how media are controlled, then, and about the broader cultural context in which technologies are placed, about tend to be brushed aside.

Because they regard technological features as having inevitable and predetermined social consequences, approaches such as those of Postman, Mander and McLuhan can be labelled *technologically determinist*. They assume that the inherent biases of media technologies dictate their use and impact in predictable ways, regardless of who develops and controls them, who uses them and what socio-cultural context they are placed within. Technologies, then, are *reified* – that is, they are transformed by the theorists into independent objects, when in reality they are developed, manufactured, controlled and used by humans in particular social contexts (Chandler, 1995). One of the consequences of this, according to Raymond Williams (1974), is that we are distracted from the human institutions and groups that bear responsibility for the development and use of technologies and the broader shape taken by society and culture, including inequalities of power. From this point of view, the techno-optimism of McLuhan plays into the hands of those groups and institutions that wield power in society by offering technology as the magic solution to social ills.

The techno-pessimism of Postman and Mander, meanwhile, is little better as it lets powerful interests off the hook by putting the blame for society's problems onto inanimate objects. In so doing, those who blame social problems on television sometimes are accused of veering close to the position of the *Luddites* – a working-class protest movement in nineteenth-century Britain that responded to job losses within factories by destroying the new textile machines it regarded as responsible. Like some critical medium theorists, the Luddites focused on the technologies, rather than on those who developed and controlled them, still less the broader socio-economic system. It is for this reason that pessimistic arguments about the impact of technologies are sometimes accused of being *luddite*.

Technologies and social contexts

The opposite view from that held by technological determinists is that, far from having predetermined socio-cultural impacts, technologies should be regarded as tools whose development and use is dependent on social contexts and human priorities. A garden spade normally is used to help us dig holes, but it may also lend itself to various other activities – a support for its user to lean on, a weapon with which to defend oneself, a means to smash windows and break into someone's house and so on. Similarly, it is sometimes noted that a knife may be used to cook, kill or cure.

The tool itself, then, does not determine its use. Use depends on the context and motivation of users – on their physical and social situation, on socio-economic conventions, regulations, cultural expectations and a range of other factors. Meanwhile, the very existence of a tool such as the spade – the fact that it was developed and manufactured in the ways it was – is itself reflective of social context. Far from being a primary driver of change, the spade, like other technologies, is a product of particular human needs, purposes and arrangements (see Williams, 1974).

Similarly, communications technologies may be regarded as having been developed as a result of socio-cultural circumstances and having been open to a variety of possible uses. Often, the eventual ways in which technologies are used can differ from the purpose for which they were originally envisaged. We tend automatically to regard the gramophone as a piece of equipment orientated towards the playing of recorded music, but it was originally intended as a means for individuals to record and play back speech. Similarly, during the initial development of broadcast technology, radio was envisaged not as a means for broadcasting content to mass audiences, but as a wireless form of interpersonal communication – a rival to the telephone.

Despite the extent of their expenditure on market research, those who develop and promote contemporary technologies continue to be unable to fully predict the ways in which they are used. That text messaging became one of the most popular uses of the mobile phone, for example, occurred not primarily by the initial design of the industry but as a result of largely unpredicted consumer enthusiasm for what was originally envisaged as a marginal application (Rettie, 2009).

Far from being predetermined by inherent technological biases, then, the purpose and social role of technologies is dependent on complex contextual factors, including the interests, capacities and priorities of industry, consumers and a variety of intermediaries. From this point of view, a technology such as television should not be seen as technologically predisposed towards either high-participation extensions of the senses or passive short-term escapism. Depending on the context of producers and users – as well as the details of the broadcast content – television may, in different circumstances, lend itself to both these types of usage as well as various others – a tool of information and education, for example, or a facilitator of social cohesion and political engagement.

So how do we break down and study the significance of the contexts in which technologies circulate? Paul Du Gay and colleagues (1997) offer one possible answer. They propose that, in order to understand the social and cultural significance of technologies, we must examine each of a series of interlinked processes – collectively termed the 'circuit of culture' – that all cultural artefacts go through.

Production refers to the institutional and social circumstances in which a technology is developed, manufactured and distributed, while *representation* concerns media discourse about the technology, which can play a crucial role in developing particular understandings of its purpose and meaning. This might include direct forms of marketing as well as broader popular representations in news, books, fiction or elsewhere. *Regulation* refers to the various forms of control imposed by government or other bodies, which can restrict and shape the ways in which technologies are used. Meanwhile, *consumption* emphasizes the importance of the contexts in which users engage with technologies and *identity* concerns the way in which such consumption practices are intricately connected with the development of individual and collective subjectivities.

Du Gay et al. illustrate the examination of these interconnected processes by offering an analysis of the Sony Walkman as a case study, but the model is intended to be applicable to the study of *any* cultural artefact or technology.

Capacities and constraints

Recognition of the importance of the institutional, discursive and consumption contexts in which technologies operate – whether through Du Gay et al.'s 'circuit of culture' model or another approach – ought not to result in the conclusion that technologies are entirely neutral. After all, as we saw, we could list a great many possible uses for the garden spade, but technical constraints relating to size, shape and density prevent it from being a useful means for people to cut grass, apply paint or eat food.

Although they are considerably more complicated than spades, communications media such as newspapers, radio and television also have particular capacities and constraints – sometimes referred to as affordances (Norman, 1988) – that have implications for the ways in which they are used and also for their social impacts.

Even though they underestimate the significance of crucial questions of context and use, then, we can still learn from medium theorists that technical features are important. While avoiding being overly prescriptive, it remains possible to develop ways of categorizing media with respect to similarities and differences that we feel might have social or cultural significance. The extent to which media facilitate communication through text, sound, still image, video or some combination of the four would be a good start, for example. We could then distinguish *mass* media technologies, which afford communication with a large group of people, from *interpersonal* technologies, which facilitate small-scale interaction between two people or, at most, a small group. Likewise, we might categorize media with respect to the extent to which they enable *one-directional* communication as opposed to *interactive* communication. *Synchronous* media, which operate in real-time, could then be identified as distinct from *asynchronous* media, which do not, and so on. Table 2.1 illustrates the ways in which these initial differentiators might work in relation to some long-established media technologies.

By categorizing technologies in these sorts of ways, we simplify their capacities, but, in doing so, enhance our understanding of their potential significance. For example, the audio-only nature of radio makes it reasonable to propose that, under the right circumstances, it may be better suited than

TABLE 2.1   Selected properties of traditional media

Household telephone	Interpersonal medium	Sound	Synchronous	Interactive
Newspaper	Mass medium	Text, still image	Asynchronous	One-directional
Radio	Mass medium	Sound	Synchronous	One-directional
Television	Mass medium	Video, sound, still image, text	Synchronous	One-directional

visual media to being used as a secondary activity accompanying things like driving or working. Meanwhile, because they are asynchronous physical objects based on printed text and images, we can probably conclude that newspapers are not especially well suited to the communication of live breaking news stories. In contrast, contemporary television, by enabling the instantaneous transfer of moving images and sound, has contributed to a situation in which we can watch and hear live events in real time. The development, use and consequences of this capacity are all dependent on human priorities and contexts, but the availability of the technology itself still alters what is possible.

Into the digital age

For many, recent developments in communications, dominated by the growth of satellite, digital and Internet technology, have heralded a societal transformation as significant as the transitions from oral to print communication and from print to broadcasting. The increasing use of satellite technologies by television companies during the 1980s and 1990s enabled the instant live transfer of moving images and sound across the globe. Live television coverage of international events has now become commonplace, enabling us to watch wars, disasters or famines as they happen. In the past, news of far-away happenings was carried physically by messengers or travellers and would take days or weeks to reach its destination. Contrast that with September 11th 2001, when millions of people around the world simultaneously watched live pictures of the collapse of the World Trade Center in real time. The shrinking of time and space into what McLuhan termed a global village would appear to have intensified dramatically since the time he was writing in the 1960s.

Meanwhile, as well as extending the capacity for instant global communication, the development of digital broadcasting and the Internet are bringing about the convergence of previously distinct forms of communication and precipitating a shift in the relationship between media producers and audiences.

FIGURE 2.2   An Internet cable
© Greg Horler

With its origins in the development of systems to improve military and scientific communications, the Internet comprised a single, decentralized network that enabled the transfer of information from and to any connected computer. By the 1990s, the creation and development of the World Wide Web had enabled content transferred from any point on the system to be publicly available and made it possible to organize and retrieve that content via hyperlinks and search engines. As the web was further developed and broadband introduced, it became feasible to upload or download high quantities of dense multimedia content, such as music and video files, as well as text and still images.

Convergence

There are various possibilities enabled by the digitalization of broadcasting and the development of the Internet that make these developments significantly different from the emergence of previous forms of mass media.

The first is *convergence*. Whereas previous media each tended to have their own distinct capacities and constraints, digitalization offers the prospect of bringing into a single sphere the technical possibilities of previously separate forms of communication. McLuhan claimed that, whereas print technologies privileged the written word, television served to reunite the human senses by bringing together text, moving images and sound. Processes of digitalization, however, offer the development of media environments even more inclusive and flexible by enabling text, images, music, speech and video *all* to be converted into a universal system of binary codes (1s and 0s) and then decoded by a single piece of receiving equipment.

Depending both on content and user priorities, then, websites may convey text or images, enable us to listen to sound or to watch digital video files. In some cases, these previously separate forms of communication are closely interlinked, so I may begin by reading the text of a news story and, then, halfway down the page, encounter opportunities to listen to related audio and video clips. And convergence is not limited to the bringing together of different mass communications processes. E-mail, instant messaging, discussion boards, online telephone services and, most recently, social networking sites all comprise examples of the ways in which the Internet incorporates interpersonal communication, too. As a result, distinctions such as those in Table 2.1 become rather more difficult to make.

Of course, the Internet is not the only contemporary medium of interest in discussions of convergence. Mobile phones increasingly bring together the telephone with personal music player, portable games machine, diary and personal computer, while games consoles double up as DVD or CD players and digital television platforms facilitate listening to radio stations, home shopping and playing games. Because they enable many different media forms to use the same kinds of digital code, then, processes of digitalization increase the cross-compatibility of previously separate technologies. Most of all, the boundary between the Internet itself and other forms of digital media is blurring, to the extent that television and radio programmes, as well as newspapers, increasingly are available to view or listen to on the Internet, while the Internet is itself becoming an integral part of technologies such as the mobile phone and games console.

Interactivity

The *interactivity* of digital media – particularly the Internet – is another socially significant feature. Leaving aside the disagreements between McLuhan and Postman, most accept that broadcasting and print technologies both afford a predominantly one-way relationship between a small number of producers and a large audience of readers or viewers. The only truly interactive media prior to the Internet were interpersonal technologies such as the telephone.

As well as incorporating a range of interpersonal means of communication, the Internet for the first time introduced the possibility of interactive *mass* communication. The capacity for millions of people to engage with the same content was combined with a level of interactivity previously only facilitated by interpersonal media. Ordinary people were able to distribute as well as receive content, whether by publishing their own website or blog, participating in communications on social networking sites, posting messages on public or community forums and uploading multimedia content such as home-produced videos, music tracks or photographs.

The Internet also offers users unprecedented levels of control over what content they interact with. Rather than merely switching on and flicking channels, we are faced with a choice between millions of sites, services and individuals. Similarly, digital broadcasting has facilitated a massive growth in the number of different channels on offer and the growth of +1 channels alongside developments in pay-per-view television, digital personal video recording technologies (PVR) and watch-on-demand Internet services are beginning to disconnect viewers from standardized schedules. Nevertheless, the experience of watching a television set, unlike that of using the Internet, continues to offer relatively few opportunities for users to contribute to or collaborate with programmes (Flew, 2003).

Mobility

A further feature of the contemporary digital environment is that, rather than being confined to particular, fixed locations, more and more of the media outlets we use are mobile, enabling us to communicate from all sorts of locations. The mobile phone enables us to have long distance conversations wherever we are, while digital music players, following in the footsteps of cassette- and CD-based personal stereos, enable us to take our entire music collection round the city with us, providing a personalized sound track to our movement through public spaces (Bull, 2007). Elsewhere, large desktop PCs increasingly are being replaced by laptops and an increasing range of functions, including the ability to surf the Internet, are now available on mobile phones and other ultra-portable devices. Ever more ubiquitous 3G and wireless networks, meanwhile, are making it increasingly possible to connect to the Internet wherever we are. As a result, whether on the train, in a café, at work, at home or walking between them, some of us are in what might be described as an 'always on' position when it comes to our connection to and engagement with media (Castells et al., 2006).

The Internet: a cure for social ills?

For some techno-enthusiasts, the digital revolution heralded fundamental cultural change and the creation of a better society. The apparent ability of Internet users to summon up information or culture on demand and make their own content available to a potential audience of millions prompted enthusiastic proclamations of a decentralization of power, a challenge to previously dominant organizations, a resurgence of political engagement, an enhancement of individual liberty and an improvement in global harmony.

Nicholas Negroponte (1996), for example, predicted that the technology would liberate individuals from the constraints of place, the operation and control of societies would be decentralized and community and global relations would be transformed for the better, while George Gilder (1992) predicted the transformation of education, decline of standardized television culture and draining of power from the established media industry. More recently, John Hartley (2009) has endorsed what he regards as the democratization of television as a result of the capacity on the contemporary Internet – and specifically via platforms such as YouTube – for ordinary people to become producers and distributors of content. Governments in various countries, meanwhile, have championed the potential of the Internet to enhance political engagement and improve educational achievement.

It is not difficult to see why theorists might take an optimistic view of the social impacts of the Internet. On the face of it, the technology places unprecedented control in the hands of users, freeing them from the structured hierarchical information agenda set by dominant mass media corporations, as well as from the broader constraints of space and time. Far more so than broadcast television, it resembles a cool medium, in McLuhan's terms, in that it offers the prospect of engaging a range of senses rather than just one and involves unprecedented levels of interactive participation.

As with McLuhan's celebration of television, however, some of the optimistic pronouncements about the Internet are open to justified accusations of technological determinism. Howard Rheingold is sceptical of what he regards as the blind optimism of theorists such as Negroponte, for example, suggesting such 'technophilia' replicates the enthusiastic proclamations that accompanied a host of earlier developments in communications technology:

> the same hopes, described in the same words, for a decentralization of power, a deeper and more widespread citizen involvement in matters of state, a great equalizer for ordinary citizens to counter the forces of central control, have been voiced in the popular press for two centuries in reference to steam, electricity, and television (2000: 307).

For Rheingold, we must bear in mind that, although the development of these previous technologies did have a substantial impact on society, 'the utopia of the technological millenarians has not yet materialized' (2000: 307). In other words, if the lofty ideals of techno-enthusiasts, including McLuhan's proclamations about television, have not been fulfilled by any of the succession of technologies on which their hopes have been pinned to date, then we would be wise to exercise caution regarding their proclamations about the impact of the Internet.

Rheingold is not saying that the technological capacities of the Internet are irrelevant or insubstantial. His point is that the ways in which the technology is controlled, disseminated and used are liable to reflect the economic, social and cultural relations into which it has become embedded as much as shape them. From this point of view, it is no great surprise that, just as they exerted control over the railways, the newspapers, radio and television, large-scale commercial organizations and governments have been able to exploit and dominate the Internet, using it as a means to consolidate their strength and influence (McChesney, 1999).

Beyond this, the social impact of Internet use is especially hard to determine because, especially when combined with the possibility of access from any location, its properties are more varied and flexible than those of any previous media form. Rather than being a *single* medium, the Internet is better understood as an integrated network of different communicative options: mass and interpersonal, one-directional and interactive, synchronous and asynchronous and image, sound, video and text-based. In combination with the enormous range of content on offer to users at any time and any place, this means that the range of different uses to which the technology could be put are quite mind-boggling.

In practice, then, the Internet may have as much potential to facilitate high-intensity, 'hot' forms of communication, in McLuhan's terms, as low-intensity cool ones, just as it may offer as many opportunities for reinforcement of existing social structures and relations of power as it does for their transformation. Marginal political groups might use it as a means to coordinate subversive protests, powerful corporations to bombard consumers with advertisements, bored workers to chat to their friends, families to watch mainstream films or television programmes, amateur musicians to gain exposure for their work, employers to facilitate communication between employees and governments to retrieve and store information on what the rest of us are doing. This list barely scratches the surface, of course.

The flexibility of Internet and digital technologies may, in itself, suggest particular socio-cultural outcomes, but it also makes it hazardous to predict what the overall impact of such technologies might be. This doesn't mean that we should give up on trying to assess the implications of the ways in which people use the Internet and other digital technologies and we'll touch on many such assessments during the pages that follow. Suffice to say, however, that the technical features of digital technologies are of great importance, but their social outcomes will depend on the interaction of these with existing relations of culture and power.

Conclusion: technologies in context

The development, control and use of communications technologies can have profound implications for everyday lives, individual identities and the broader social and cultural world. Such technologies offer capabilities and limitations that have important implications for how they can be used and their broader socio-cultural significance.

The study of media, culture and society, then, must always take into account the implications of the hardware through which media content is distributed. Yet, McLuhan's assertion that the 'medium is the message', along with his broader emphasis on media technologies as the primary driver of social change, affords too much power to inanimate objects, failing to recognize the range of uses to which each technology can be put and the extent to which their development and outcomes are shaped by industry and users operating within broader social contexts. This means that, as well as understanding the properties of technologies themselves, we must focus on the organizations that control them, the details of the content they are used to transmit and the activities and understandings of users.

QUESTIONS AND EXERCISES

1 a) What is it about McLuhan, Poster and Mander that makes them medium theorists?

   b) What does McLuhan mean by 'the medium is the message'?

2 On what points do McLuhan and Poster disagree in relation to the social impact of print media and television?

3 a) Into which of McLuhan's categories of hot and cool media would you place the following?

   Television. Book. News website. Radio. Games console. Personal music player.

   b) Are the categories hot and cool useful?

4 a) What does technological determinism mean and why has it been criticized?

   b) Apply Du Gay et al.'s 'circuit of culture' model to the technology of the iPod. Consider each of the different processes on the circuit – production, representation, regulation, consumption and identity.

5 a) In what ways are new digital media different from their analogue predecessors?

   b) Taking care not to be too deterministic, discuss the impact that widespread use of digital media might have on broader culture and society.

Suggested further reading

Du Gay, P., Hall, S., Janes, L., Mackay, J. and Negus, K. (1997) *Doing Cultural Studies: The story of the Sony Walkman*. London: Sage.
Practical illustration of the study of technology in its socio-cultural context via the example of the Sony Walkman.

McLuhan, M. (2001; 1967) *Understanding Media*. Abingdon: Routledge.
Classic analysis of media technologies, including elaboration of the author's famous argument that 'the medium is the message'.

Meyrowitz, J. (1985) *No Sense of Place: The impact of electronic media on social behaviour*. New York: Oxford University Press.
Theoretical discussion of the ways in which television is challenging social boundaries and transforming culture.

Postman, N. (1987) *Amusing Ourselves to Death: Public discourse in the age of show business*. London: Methuen.
Pessimistic account of the social impact of electronic media, particularly television.

Stevenson, N. (2002) *Understanding Media Cultures* (2nd edn). London: Sage: Chapter 4.
Accessible but detailed critical outline of McLuhan and medium theory.

3

Media Industry

Focal points

- *Political economy* as a macro approach that emphasizes media industry in context.

- Concentrations of media ownership, power and influence.

- Implications of the commercial imperative to maximize audiences and attract advertisers.

- Interventions by government and regulators to control media.

- Criticisms of *economic determinism*.

Introduction

It was famously asserted in the 1940s by German theorists Theodor Adorno and Max Horkheimer (1997) that, by the twentieth century, music, literature, art, film and other forms of culture – in the narrow, creative forms and practices sense of the term – formed part of a *culture industry*. What they meant was that, rather than being the product of autonomous artists or grass roots creativity, cultural goods were increasingly being manufactured and distributed on a massive scale by powerful organizations and had become little different from other industrial products, such as food, clothing or cars. For Adorno and Horkheimer, this industrial context had profound implications for the kinds of cultural products consumed by the population, as well as broader socio-cultural relations. Disappointingly, they did not provide a detailed empirical analysis of the complex ways in which media industries actually work (see Chapter 5). The concept of the culture industry draws valuable attention, however, to the importance of understanding the economic and organizational context in which media production takes place and it is this that we shall focus on in the coming pages.

The study of those who produce and distribute media and of the broader system in which they operate has become a key component of contemporary understandings of communication and society. For some theorists, such an approach is pivotal to the study of media. From this *political economic* point of view, media technologies and content, alongside the implications their circulation might have for audiences, ultimately are shaped by the structure of the media industry. In turn, the media industry itself is regarded as, to an extent, a product of the broader capitalist political economic system in which it operates.

While some political economic media analysts are conservative, many of the most well known within academic circles take a left-wing approach that is highly critical of the current media system. For Peter Golding and Graham Murdock (1991), what marks out the approach they term *critical political economy* is a specific interest in the ways in which inequalities of power embedded into the broader capitalist economic system are reflected in the ownership and control of media. For political economists, analysis tends to centre on the link between this control of media by the powerful minority and the reinforcement of the unequal system that gave rise to it.

This particular perspective on media draws on Karl Marx's analysis of the unequal, exploitative relations of the capitalist system – something that we'll pursue in greater depth in Chapter 6. It also can be regarded as a *macro* perspective, in the sense that its primary interest is in the broad media system, with the details of different texts, technologies and users regarded as structured by this. As Golding and Murdock suggest, the approach 'always goes beyond situated action to show how particular micro-contexts are shaped by general economic dynamics' (1991: 73).

In what follows, I'll consider a range of key issues and factors relating to the industrial context of media before briefly returning to some broader arguments about the place of political economic approaches within the study of media and society towards the end of the chapter.

Media organizations

Rather than referring to a single media industry, it is perhaps preferable to speak of a plurality, such is the diversity of media organizations. For example, we can identify distinct sectors of media connected to different formats, such as the music industry, the television industry, the newspaper industry and the various subsectors within each. Such *horizontal* distinctions, however, are becoming more blurry as a result of processes of media *convergence*. We can also note that, within each sector, there are different stages of the process of production and distribution, with companies often specializing in one stage or another. Within the film industry, for example, such *vertical* differentiation can be illustrated by the difference between studios, concerned with the development and production of content, and cinemas, which make that content available to consumers.

It is also important to distinguish between profitmaking and non-profitmaking media organizations. The latter can range from small-scale voluntary or charitable organizations, such as community radio stations, to all-powerful state-controlled media used by authoritarian governments to distribute propaganda and maintain power within countries such as the former Soviet Union or contemporary North Korea.

The most prominent non-profit media organizations in many developed countries, however, are often public service broadcasters, such as the UK's British Broadcasting Corporation (BBC), which is funded by a licence fee and charged by government with the specific goal of enriching society through the production of trustworthy, informative and high-quality content. Such organizations are crucial to the history of mass media and remain influential in some countries, but in more recent years have found themselves increasingly isolated within a media world dominated by corporations whose primary purpose is the pursuit of profit and satisfaction of shareholders. As Michael Tracey points out, while public media organizations 'acquire money to make programmes', commercial institutions 'make programmes to acquire money' (1998: 18).

Commercial ownership

Although individual companies vary in their size and influence, media industries invariably are *oligopolies*, which means that their markets are overwhelmingly dominated by a small number of powerful companies.

Concentration of ownership has been a key theme throughout the history of mass media. For example, after an early period dominated by small-scale, independent publications, newspapers became overwhelmingly controlled by large corporations run by so-called newspaper barons. Through a series of takeovers, for example, William Hearst established control over a vast portfolio of titles across the early twentieth-century USA, with *The San Francisco Examiner, The New York Journal* and *The Washington Times* among them. Meanwhile, the UK newspaper market at the time was dominated by three so-called barons – Viscount Northcliff and his brother Viscount Rothermere, who developed *Th e Daily Mail* and *The Daily Mirror*, and Baron Beaverbrook, who was responsible for the rise of *The Daily Express*.

Robert McChesney argues that the drive towards expansion and consolidation in the media industry has become even more concentrated in recent times, making it difficult for small or medium-sized firms to survive as such: 'a firm either gets larger through mergers or acquisitions or it gets swallowed by a more aggressive competitor' (1999: 20).

In some cases expansion involves the entering of new arenas by setting up new subsidiary companies. In the late 1980s, for example, global media giant News Corporation invested heavily in a brand new UK satellite television service called Sky (now BSkyB) – something that provided a substantial stake in the UK television market for the company. More often, however, companies expand by purchasing a controlling stake in other companies. Such takeovers involve less risk than setting up new operations because one can allow target companies to do the initial groundwork and risk taking before assuming control of the successful ones.

Takeovers and mergers are a constant feature of the media industry. They can be divided into the following different types.

Expansion within existing sector

Some take-overs and mergers simply involve expansion and/or elimination of competition within a single area of specialism. A local newspaper company might increase its sector dominance by taking over its local rivals or acquiring comparable publications elsewhere. In many countries, such consolidation has resulted in the domination of local newspaper markets by a small number of businesses. For example, Johnson Press owns over 300 local publications across the UK and Ireland. In another example, the ITV television network in the UK originally consisted of numerous independent regional companies, but a series of takeovers led to the creation in 2003 of a single company for the whole of England and Wales.

Expansion across sectors (horizontal integration)

Horizontal integration refers to attempts to take over other companies in order to broaden one's portfolio across different media sectors. For example, a newspaper company may acquire a stake in the television market by taking control of a broadcasting company. Also included within this category are strategic takeovers of Internet companies by multinational media corporations that had previously lacked a substantial stake in the online market. News Corporation's takeover of social networking site MySpace in 2005 is a good example of this.

One of the advantages of horizontal integration is the ability to simultaneously market single products across different sectors. Known as media synergy, this might involve a company releasing a blockbuster film with an associated CD soundtrack, computer game, book and television series. The products all promote one another and the commercial potential of the brand that unites them is exploited to the maximum.

Expansion up and down the production process (vertical integration)

As well as gaining a stake in different media sectors, media corporations have sometimes sought to control as many different stages of the production process as possible. A company that owns a record label, for example, might decide to buy a controlling stake in a music retailer, enabling them to control both development and distribution. Achieving control of the production and distribution chain was a key motivation behind Disney's takeover in 1995 of US television network ABC. To Disney, the television network offered a mass broadcast outlet for the huge amount of content produced by the company's famous studios. The takeover also entailed a horizontal element, in that a company with a substantial stake in the film and theme park industries was increasing its stake in the broadcasting sector.

Another merger that entailed elements of both horizontal and *vertical integration* was Internet company America Online (AOL)'s acquisition of multimedia giant Time Warner in 2000. Time Warner's extensive portfolio of traditional media content was combined with AOL's potential for online distribution of that content. It therefore offered AOL greater control of different stages of the production and distribution process (vertical) at the same time as offering a stake for the merged company in a range of different new and traditional media sectors (horizontal). However, a sharp decline in the value of Internet companies drastically affected the AOL side of the business soon after, forcing a reversal of the merger in 2002.

As a result of such trends towards consolidation, a substantial proportion of the global media markets are now controlled by a small number of transnational corporations whose assets are substantial. News Corporation, for example, owns hundreds of newspaper titles across the world, as well as global publisher HarperCollins, over 30 Australian magazine titles, extensive film and television studios, including Twentieth Century Fox and Twentieth Century Fox Television, numerous broadcast, satellite and cable networks, including Fox in the US, BSkyB in the UK and Star TV, which operates across Asia, and an increasing array of web companies, including MySpace, Photobucket and Fox Sports.com.

Occasionally, a combination of skill, innovation and timing enables a new company to take on the might of the established transnationals. Internet search engine Google, for example, managed to virtually monopolize its sector, generating extensive and sustained growth and allowing the brand to diversify into other services, such as e-mail, online maps and a web browser. Google avoided being taken over by an established transnational and it has begun to exert its own dominance, acquiring an extensive portfolio of services, not least through its acquisition of online video site YouTube in 2006.

Such a breakthrough, however, represents the exception rather than the rule in a market where the existing wealth and influence of the established transnationals usually offers the competitive advantages necessary to secure their dominance. In its early days, for example, Sky television sustained the kinds of losses that would have bankrupted many companies, but the extent of News Corporation's investment in the service, alongside its ability to heavily promote itself in the company's UK newspapers, enabled Sky to increase its subscriber base, acquire its main market rival and dominate the UK's subscription television market. News Corporation also has regularly instigated newspaper price wars, again using its wealth and power to sustain short-term losses in the interest of gaining competitive advantage.

Concentration of ownership = concentration of ideas?

For some theorists, the control of our channels of mass communication by such a small number commercial organizations has grave implications for the circulation of ideas and culture. Ben Bagdikian (2004: 3), for example, points out that each of the 'big five' transnationals (Time Warner, Disney, News Corporation, Viacom and Bertelsmann) has 'more communications power than was exercised by any despot or dictator in history' and that their tendency to cooperate with one another in the pursuit of mutually beneficial outcomes makes their influence over populations, governments and policies around the world immense. Many nation states find themselves dwarfed by such power and, as a consequence, have diminishing control over the distribution of culture in their territory (Malm and Wallis, 1993).

It is also specifically argued by some that the concentration of media ownership leads to a concentration of culture and ideas – that, instead of engaging with a diversity of competing perspectives and innovative forms of expression, populations are subject to a narrow and monolithic set of messages. 'The significant concern about such patterns of ownership', argues Bob Franklin, 'is that they diminish pluralism and choice, stifle diversity and empower owners to defend and advance their economic interests and political power' (1997: 207). In particular, some argue that the corporate interests of transnationals prompt them to support right-wing, pro-capitalist political ideas and that the content they distribute around the world can be expected to reflect this (Bagdikian, 2004; Herman and Chomsky, 1998).

Certainly there are examples to support this. It is often pointed out, for example, that News Corporation's news outlets, including the UK newspaper *The Sun* and US television channel Fox News, tend closely to mirror the views of the company's chairman and chief executive, Rupert Murdoch. More broadly, if we consider the range of media to which we are all exposed, it isn't difficult to identify common themes, such as a general endorsement of business and consumerism, and also to note the marginalization of other ideas, including anti-capitalist perspectives.

The notion of an automatic or exclusive link between concentration of ownership and concentration of ideas may oversimplify things, however. Although it is true that certain ideas are consistently emphasized and others marginalized, the overall contemporary media environment, including books, music and the Internet, offers a wide range of perspectives even if many of them are controlled by large corporations. For all the right-wing orientation of many of its news outlets, News Corporation also owns HarperCollins, a publishing umbrella responsible for books covering a diversity of perspectives. For example, it published Naomi Klein's widely read *No Logo* (2000) which offers a wholesale attack on the activities of multinationals.

It remains the case, however, that there is a very considerable imbalance in terms of the amount of exposure for different perspectives. For every *No Logo*, there are countless books, television programmes and films that explicitly or implicitly endorse the status quo. It is unclear, though, to what extent such disparity can be put down to the deliberate dissemination of the viewpoints of the powerful rather than, for example, the assumption that audiences are, for the most part, simply uninterested in anti-Establishment views. After all, when all else is said and done, the bottom line for media producers is the pursuit of profit.

The bottom line: sources of revenue

The achievement of an effective balance between minimizing costs and maximizing takings lies at the heart of all that profit-making media corporations do. Analysis of the core ways in which such companies make their money is of great importance to the development of an understanding of the motivations and priorities that ultimately determine the services and content they produce.

So, what are the most important sources of income for media corporations?

Advertising revenue

Since the early days of US radio, when programmes such as the *Eveready Hour* took the names of their sponsors, advertising, in the form of direct programme sponsorship or the interspersing of content with spot commercials, has been a pivotal source of revenue for media corporations.

According to McChesney (1999), the amount of advertising on television has increased significantly since the beginning of the 1990s, with each of the main US networks expanding the length and frequency of ad breaks. Meanwhile, new forms of advertising are emerging online, with precisely targeted pop-up and side-bar adverts and news or sports video clips prefaced by commercials.

As digital video recording technologies make it easier for audiences to skip past separate advertising slots, techniques such as direct sponsorship of programmes and product placement within film or television scenes have become increasingly important. For example the 2008 film adaptation of *Sex and the City*, included a constant stream of promotions for fashion labels, cars, mobile phones, notebook computers and other consumer goods.

The importance of advertising and sponsorship to media industry profits is such that advertisers, not audiences, often are the primary customers of media corporations. The underlying purpose of most content, then, is to garner our attention in order that the latter can be sold to those companies willing to pay the premium for it. As William Baker and George Dessart put it, 'the business of television ... is the buying and selling of eyeballs' (1998: 65). This reliance on advertising means that, in addition to the media organizations themselves, another set of corporate interests, often from outside the media sector, occupy an influential position with respect to the production and distribution of content.

Direct audience payments

Another key source of funding for media outlets comes from direct payments from consumers. These include 'per item' payments and broader or longer-term subscriptions to a particular body of content.

In the case of print media, direct payments are made in the form of a cover price or an annual subscription. Meanwhile, in the world of television, consumers increasingly pay subscription fees for pay TV services and premium channels, as well as additional pay-per-view fees for individual items, such as films or high-profile sporting events. This category of revenue also includes a range of other direct payments – for cinema tickets, CDs, books, computer games and Internet downloads, for example, or to access premium web services. While in some sectors direct payment from audiences is long established, in the case of television it only became possible for companies to restrict access to different levels of service with the onset of cable and digital set-top boxes.

Payments between media companies

For those involved in the production of content, direct payments from distribution outlets wishing to carry the content are of critical importance. For distributors or retailers of magazines, CDs, DVDs or books, such payments simply take the form of the wholesale price of the goods in question. In those cases where the content does not consist of distinct objects sold to consumers, however, distribution outlets pay content developers – who own the copyright for their work – for the *right* to screen, broadcast, print or in some other way reproduce the content. Thus, radio stations pay fees to record labels in return for the right to play songs or pieces of music. Similarly, newspapers and magazines pay agencies or individual photographers for the right to print images. Television channels also purchase the rights to broadcast films, dramas and other programmes or events. Often they negotiate exclusive rights deals, which prevent rival companies from being allowed to broadcast the content.

Sometimes, rather than paying to broadcast the exact same content or finished programmes, distributors will pay for the rights to a programme idea, format or brand. This enables the production of a new version more suited to the outlet's intended audience. In recent years, numerous UK programme formats and brands have been sold to broadcasters in the US, including *The Weakest Link*, *Pop Idol* and *The Office*. In each case, new versions were created, consistent with perceived differences in the expectations of the US audience.

As well as maximizing revenue from existing content by selling goods or rights, content producers in the broadcasting sphere often are commissioned to produce brand new programmes. For broadcasters who produce a proportion of their content inhouse, money is made from both direct distribution via their own outlets and the sale of rights to media companies elsewhere.

Maximizing audiences

Ultimately, the variety of forms of revenue outlined point to an underlying pressure to maximize audience size. Alongside the need to minimize costs, attracting and retaining sufficient numbers of consumers governs the ways in which commercial media companies operate and determines the types of content they distribute.

This certainly raises questions about suggestions that media simply act as a direct mouthpiece for the political interests of transnationals and, consistent with this, some commentators celebrate the importance of the likes and dislikes of ordinary people as a determinant of media content. Others, however, regard audience maximization as a negative influence, arguing that it encourages the distribution of whatever content offers the greatest instant stimulation and superficial appeal, to the exclusion of in-depth information and critical forms of expression. Such is the fear that we might change channel or turn to another outlet, they argue, that producers of content daren't lose momentum and intensity even for a short period (Baker and Dessart, 1998; Franklin, 1997). The situation is argued to have become particularly bad in recent decades as a result of sharp increases in competition caused by the increasing numbers of channels and outlets available to audiences. For McChesney, one of the results of this need to keep audiences stimulated and excited is likely to be ever more explicit emphasis, across formats and genres, on 'the tried and tested formula of sex and violence' (1999: 34).

According to Todd Gitlin (2000), meanwhile, the fear of losing money tends specifically to deter investment in innovative content and to encourage imitations of previously successful formats. Sure enough, successful television programmes tend to spawn numerous copycat versions on rival stations because the latter are deemed to represent a safe bet. Such priorities also explain the increasing importation of programme formats successful in other countries, where, again, the risks are lower because the format has already been tested (Moran, 1998). The ever-increasing number of sequels to blockbuster movies and movie adaptions of television series (and vice versa) constitute further examples of this. Such products offer a particularly risk-free route to commercial success because not only have audiences already indicated a liking for the basic theme and characters but also they are familiar with and attracted to the brand of the original. Generating comparable levels of box office success for new products is more difficult and has far higher chances of failure, despite the well-established practice of inducing audiences with familiarity in the form of well-known star actors and recognizable plot lines.

That the profit imperative has often resulted in a tendency to standardize, repeat, to copy and place emphasis on immediate stimulation over depth and detail is hard to dispute and it is a theme to which we shall return at various points during the book. Yet commercial organizations also have been responsible for the development of a range of innovative forms of content, some of which are undeniably high in their level of detail, complexity or challenge to audiences. In the realm of television drama, for example, Time Warner's US subscription television network HBO (Home Box Office) has specialized in such premium content, producing a string of critically acclaimed examples, including *The Sopranos*, *Sex and the City* and *The Wire*. Meanwhile, even the more broadly orientated Fox network, owned by News Corporation, has been responsible for highly respected and apparently innovative productions, such as *The Simpsons*, *House* and *Prison Break*.

The ultimate quality or usefulness of such productions is, of course, open to considerable debate – and this is also true for a range of other examples of commercially produced documentaries, films, music and other formats that are regarded by critics or others as innovative, socially valuable or sophisticated. As we shall see in Chapter 8, notions of quality are highly contestable. What is clear, however, is that there are a range of commercially produced or distributed forms of media content that, at the very least, seem hard to square with accusations of universal cheapness, sameness or superficiality. The production of such content by commercial media companies relates, in part, to an increasing diversification of media markets into different niches and segments. In some sectors, the sort of ultra-cheap copycat forms of content outlined by critics such as Gitlin and McChesney may become even more pronounced while, in others, companies will – to some extent at least – respond to audience demand for content that presents itself to us as more expensive, original or complex.

The role of sponsors

Needless to say, the greater one's overall audience, the larger the number of potential sponsors and the greater the premium they will be prepared to pay. In addition to fuelling general competition for audiences, however, advertisers can influence media content in more particular ways. As part of the service they provide to their sponsors, media companies seek to offer not just an audience of appropriate size but also one composed of the particular kinds of consumers advertisers are seeking to reach. Especially in the case of niche or specialist media, outlets must ensure that they consistently attract consumers of the appropriate demographic composition and lifestyle orientation.

The range of companies seeking to advertise means that most population groups with disposable income are of interest, but it remains the case that many advertisers have a preference for 'quality' audiences, which means wealthy, high-spending consumers. This has been argued to create a content bias against marginalized groups, such as the poor, the elderly and ethnic minorities (Herman and Chomsky, 1998). The scale of this problem has reduced a little as a result of expansions in the range of media channels and outlets and the increasing targeting of both advertising and programming towards specialist groups, including those traditionally marginalized, such as ethnic minorities.

If they advertise, companies will expect a discernable increase in sales as a result. It is therefore in the interest of media companies to favour content that is compatible with advertisers' desire to expose their products to willing consumers who are in the mood to spend money. Programmes with a light and cheery feel are particularly valued by advertisers because people are believed to be more likely to entertain the possibility of buying consumer goods if they are in a positive state of mind. According to Edward Herman and Noam Chomsky (1998), this means that an overemphasis on detailed, depressing or, worse still, guilt-inducing content about social or global problems is something to avoid.

In some cases, media will go further still, specifically orientating their content in a manner that encourages audiences to think positively about consuming products of the type being promoted by advertisers. The content of lifestyle magazines and television programmes for example, often is centred on the desirability of purchasing particular kinds of consumer goods in order to enhance one's quality of life. From motoring magazines to makeover television programmes, such content is not only designed to attract a suitable audience but also to soften them up for advertisers by capturing their imagination and enthusiasm for consumption before they're even exposed to the commercials themselves.

Media organizations also have to handle carefully any content that might have the potential to damage the commercial interests of advertisers. Decisions about news items, documentaries, columns, images or storylines that present prominent advertisers in a negative light can be the subject of substantial conflicts of interest. In an interview with Peter Jackson et al., Mike Cones, then editor of *GQ* magazine, referred to his publication's reliance on advertising as 'a marriage of dubious convenience'(2001: 62). To illustrate the potential power of advertisers, Cones described an incident some years earlier involving *Blitz*, a unisex style magazine. *Blitz* had published an article focused on the responses of members of the public to different perfumes and, as part of the article, included some negative comments, including (according to Cones) 'It smells like drain cleaner' and 'I wouldn't be seen dead anywhere near it'. Subsequently, several fragrance companies withdrew their advertising from the publication, prompting it to go out of business. Cones summed up the lesson from the story as follows:

> And that was it: a very painful, short, sharp lesson of the power of the advertiser. And so we to some degree preserve some editorial integrity. But in the end, if the advertiser looks at what we've put in the magazine and says 'Well this doesn't interest me. I can't see how this is going to enhance my product by being associated with whatever page it happens to be', then they may start looking elsewhere (Jackson et al., 2001).

While direct advertiser boycotts such as this are unusual, executives and media professionals instinctively know that they must think very carefully indeed before biting the hand that feeds them. According to Herman and Chomsky (1998), this can mean shying away from not only direct negative coverage of individual companies or products but also content that might conflict with the broader commercial or political interests of advertisers.

The onset of cable, satellite and digital media has further tilted the balance of power between media companies and advertisers in the direction of the latter. Multichannel television, alongside increasingly effective opportunities for online advertising, have left media companies in increasingly intense and desperate competition for a limited pool of advertising revenue, strengthening both the bargaining position and the expectations of advertisers.

According to McChesney (1999), advertisers are exerting greater and greater influence over the content of outlets in which their commercials appear, while the distinction between commercials and other content is becoming increasingly blurry. A growing emphasis on sponsorship of individual programmes implies a 'partner' status for advertisers, suggesting greater influence on content than the taking out of spot commercials. Some advertisers have gone further still, signing deals with media companies to co-produce content (McChesney, 1999). Meanwhile, the more general growth of product placement, alongside the development of 'hybrid' content, such as advertorials (advertisements that have the appearance of editorial content), serve to further illustrate what McChesney laments as the 'hypercommercialism' of contemporary media.

Governments and regulation

Despite their overall domination of global communications, corporate media organizations and their sponsors have not always had everything their own way. In different ways, national governments around the world have sought to exert their own influence.

At the extreme end of such intervention are those situations in which governments take on full operational control of core national media outlets. In China, for example, the main television broadcaster CCTV (China Central Television) forms a part of the communist government. In other cases, such as the UK's BBC, Canada's CBC and Australia's ABC, broadcasters were set up by governments and given statutory objectives and goals, but were operated at an arm's length from politicians.

While the Chinese government has regularly utilized CCTV as a tool for political propaganda, the more independent operation of broadcasters, such as the BBC, CBC and ABC, was intended to enable them to perform an impartial public service role, informing, educating and entertaining the public. The extent to which they are truly independent of government remains the subject of considerable debate, however (see Chapter 8).

Access restrictions

As well as setting up and/or subsidizing state or public broadcasters, governments have involved themselves in setting the parameters under which commercial media operate. Most importantly, they have attempted to control who has access to their national media networks.

In the early nineteenth century, the UK government utilized a stamp duty on newspapers, taxes on paper and heavy registration fees in order to attempt to restrict the ability to produce newspapers to the wealthy (Curran and Seaton, 2003). Today, the only real barriers to running newspapers are commercial ones.

The broadcasting situation in the UK has been far more tightly controlled. Until 1955, the government prevented access to broadcasting to anyone but the BBC and, prior to the onset of multichannel delivery platforms in the 1990s, UK homes still only had access to five channels. The BBC's *monopoly* on the radio airwaves lasted even longer – until 1973 – after which licences were awarded to a maximum of one independent local radio station per area (Franklin, 1997). Even in the 1990s, when competition was introduced into the sector, licences remained highly restricted and broadcasters had to satisfy a range of criteria to receive one. In the UK as elsewhere, 'pirate' radio stations – so-called because they were broadcasting without a licence – risked prosecution.

In the United States, regulation has tended to have a lighter touch than in the UK, but, nevertheless, access to the 'public airways' of broadcasting is restricted to those awarded a licence by the national regulator, the Federal Communications Commission (FCC).

Ownership restrictions

Governments also regulate how much of a country's communications outlets individual companies are allowed to control. Such regulation is designed to maintain competition, to prevent individual companies from gaining excessive power and influence across different media and, sometimes, to protect key national outlets from being purchased by international companies. Such regulations vary from country to country and can be quite specific. In the UK, for example, the rules established by the 2003 Communications Act state, among other things, that no company controlling a 20 per cent share of the national newspaper market may hold any more than a 20 per cent stake in the ITV broadcasting company and that the government may intervene in any proposed merger that would result in one company controlling a quarter or more of the national broadcasting or newspaper market. Despite these restrictions, the act will be remembered largely for its removal of previous obstacles to cross-media ownership, including a stipulation which had prevented non-EU companies from acquiring UK broadcasting companies and another which had prohibited prominent newspaper companies from acquiring a controlling stake in the FIVE television channel.

A similar relaxation of the rules has taken place in the USA, where the FCC recently raised the proportion of a given market that an individual

company could control from 35 per cent to 45 per cent, lifted a previous rule
which prevented companies from owning both a newspaper and a television
station within the same locality and raised from 2 to 3 the number of separate
television stations a company could own within a regional market.

Content regulation

Regulators also tend to take some interest in media content, although the
extent and purpose of such regulation varies from country to country and
for different media formats, with broadcasters often subject to stricter rules
than print media. Most countries require certain minimum standards of
broadcasters with respect to taste and decency and restrictions are often
placed on graphic violence, swearing and sexual explicitness. Even in the
USA, which often prides itself on the lack of interference in media content,
strict rules exist when it comes to decency and, in particular, sexual content. In recent years, the regulator attempted to underline its role as protec-
tor of decency, fining a number of networks for fleeting indiscretions
during live broadcasts. The most well-publicized of these was a huge fine
of $550,000 for CBS after Janet Jackson's bare breast was inadvertently
revealed during the half-time show of a prime-time Super Bowl broadcast.
The fine was subsequently overturned by a court of appeal, but the incident
demonstrates that content regulation is very much alive and well.
Regulators also regularly implement age classification systems in order to
inform consumers about the levels of adult content in films, DVDs, music
and other forms of content.

Sometimes, regulation of broadcast content goes considerably further.
All broadcast news or current affairs content in the UK, for example, is
required to show 'due impartiality', effectively banning news providers
from favouring any particular viewpoint. Meanwhile, the country's commercially funded terrestrial broadcasters – ITV, Channel 4 and FIVE – have
to fulfil what amount to quotas for particular kinds of content, such as
news, current affairs and children's programmes. Such 'positive' regulation
is intended to improve the overall quality and value of television to the
public, on the assumption that, left to their own devices, commercial media
will favour immediate stimulation and superficial entertainment.

In some countries, a further role for positive content regulation is the
development or protection of national culture. In Canada, broadcasters
must adhere to a quota system in order to nurture Canadian culture and
prevent the nation's airwaves from being dominated by imported content
from the powerful US industry. Content is measured against a complex
points system and can be designated as Canadian according to a number

of different criteria. In the case of Canadian radio, for example, a musical selection is designated as Canadian content if at least two of the following are Canadian: the composer, artist, place of production/performance or writer of the lyrics. Overall, at least 35 per cent of the music played on a Canadian radio station must be deemed Canadian content in order for it to comply. When it comes to film and television, in order to be designated as Canadian content, productions must achieve at least six out of a possible ten Canadian content points, based on factors such as the nationality of writers, directors, lead actors and others.

This quota system has been the subject of intense debate (Edwardson, 2008). Supporters argue that quotas have served as a vital way to protect and nurture Canadian identity, creativity and expression in the face of US cultural and financial dominance. Opponents, however, criticize the scheme for excessive bureaucracy and effectively forcing viewers to watch or listen to certain forms of content, rather than allowing them to decide what they would prefer in an open marketplace. Richard Collins sums up the dilemma between community and individual freedom nicely:

> Organized and self-conscious protective activity is necessary for a community to survive when ... exogenous culture [US popular culture in this case] is so attractive to community members that the boundary markers between communities are elided. In the latter case, the collective right of the community to continued existence may conflict with the individual right of its members to enjoy access and consumption of exogenous information (1990: 252).

Deregulation

There is also considerable debate about the broader issue of how much governments should interfere with the operation of media companies, involving fundamental questions relating to power and influence, freedom of speech and the overall purpose of media. What is increasingly clear, however, is that, in most countries, regulation is becoming more relaxed. We have already seen evidence that ownership restrictions are being relaxed and content regulation seems to be moving in the same direction, with the possible exception of restrictions relating to prime-time broadcasting of extreme violence, sexual content or bad language. Even in communist China, there are some signs of *deregulation*. Government subsidies to CCTV, for example, now are combined with advertising revenue, forcing CCTV to compete for audiences in a commercial marketplace with local television companies and pan-regional satellite networks, such as News Corporation's Star Television.

In part, the trend towards deregulation is due to the development of new technologies. Highly restrictive licensing regimes were partly created and justified on the basis that there was only a certain amount of broadcast bandwidth available within national airwaves and that this scarce resource had to be protected and used in the best interests of the public. The shortage of bandwidth was brought to an end by the onset of digital broadcasting, which enabled the simultaneous transmission of a multiplicity of channels.

Meanwhile, the Internet, by connecting users to sites across the world, has made national regulation a more complicated undertaking. The bringing together of previously separate media onto the same platform exacerbates the problem by making the application of different sets of rules for different media types unworkable. If an online 'newspaper' includes text, video and audio clips, should it be subject to relaxed newspaper guidelines or tougher broadcasting codes, for example?

The boundaries between private and public communication are also blurred on a medium which brings together anything from individual inter-actions on social networking sites to the core content of huge media corpo-rations. It might not be easy to impose restrictions on the latter without also impinging on the former.

Experience so far suggests that, with some exceptions, regulators will fall back on lighter touch regulation. China's extensive attempts to control use of the Internet by blocking access to various sites and monitoring users demonstrates that regulation *is* possible, but this case seems to be an excep-tion. The trend towards deregulation cannot just be attributed to new technologies however. It also reflects the broader ascendency of free market political ideologies, which regard government interference as an impedi-ment to good business and consumer choice. We'll consider such argu-ments, alongside those of advocates of regulation, in Chapter 8.

Supporting the industry: copyright

Not all forms of government intervention work to constrain the moneymak-ing potential of large media corporations. Copyright laws, which establish the right to claim legal ownership of and exclusively publish and distribute original ideas and culture, are essential to the ability of the producers or publishers of such works to make money. Without copyright laws, films, television programmes, pieces of music or other works would be allowed to be copied and either used or sold for profit by any individual or company across the world without any acknowledgement or payment to those who produced them. The prospect of having no control over who can use or sell their finished products would render it virtually impossible for those who invest in the production of original content to profit from doing so.

Not surprisingly, then, while they strongly oppose most forms of regulation and celebrate each relaxation thereof, media corporations have exerted all of their power and influence to lobby for the consolidation, enforcement and expansion of copyright laws. In particular, transnational companies have acted together to pressurize governments to ensure that copyright law is standardized and watertight across the globe and that every government prioritizes its effective enforcement.

The industry also has worked tirelessly to ensure that its profits are protected by governments and others in light of the massive expansion in the ease with which content can be illegitimately copied and distributed as a result of the Internet. As well as having the capacity to be made available to millions at the click of a mouse button, digital files can be copied an infinite number of times with no loss of quality.

High on the list of industry concerns, then, were so-called peer-to-peer file-sharing sites, pioneered by Napster in 1999, which facilitate the transfer of digital files, including music tracks, television programmes, movies and computer games, between the computers of users around the world.

Among other things, the industry responded by lobbying for amendments and clarifications to copyright law and the establishment by governments of effective ways of policing the situation. Napster was successfully sued for facilitating the infringement of copyright by an amalgam of recording companies, forcing it to shut down in 2001, and several other sites suffered a similar fate subsequently. Some individual users also have been taken to court.

Despite this, and the establishment of legal retailers of music downloads, such as iTunes and a legitimate version of Napster, the downloading of illegal files remains extensive. Among recent strategies used by the industry has been the lobbying of governments to pressurize Internet service providers (ISPs) to freeze the accounts of users repeatedly found to be participating in the illegal distribution of files. There are signs that the pressure may be beginning to bear fruit. In 2008, for example, the UK's six largest ISPs signed a memorandum of understanding, brokered by the government, in which they undertook to send warning letters to users whose accounts had been used for illegal file-sharing. Needless to say, arguments rage over the legitimacy of such tactics and the ethics and morality of file-sharing itself (Rojek, 2005).

Conclusion: economic determinism?

An understanding of media as an industry is of the utmost importance to any broader analysis of the relationships between media and society. By asking questions about how media are controlled, by whom and under what circumstances, political economic approaches to media not only rectify some of the problems with the technologically determinist accounts we encountered in the previous chapter but also provide a corrective to approaches that focus narrowly on the study of media content or audiences.

The answers to political economic questions tell us a great deal about why the media content and technologies we use take the form and character that they do and are essential to discussions about the extent to which and ways in which media could be changed or improved. As a consequence, we shall return to these macro questions of media production and regulation at a number of points in the rest of the book.

Nevertheless, it is important that the emphasis placed by theorists on the primacy of political economic contexts of production does not result in all other aspects of the media process, including technology, content and audience activities, being simply regarded as automatic effects of this. In the same way that those who overemphasize the impact of technologies are referred to as technological determinists, political economists sometimes are criticized for being economic or material determinists. This means that they sometimes assume, on the basis of a broad-brush analysis of the ways in which media industries work, that the details of media content and its impact on audiences are largely predictable and prescribed in advance. As we have seen, it is sometimes assumed, for example, that media are standardized as a result of the profit imperative or that concentration of ownership leads to the concentration of ideas without any real analysis of the content itself or the ways in which audiences engage with that content.

The notion that media are largely determined by their political–economic context remains a position worthy of consideration and readers should make up their own minds in this respect. Before doing so, however, they should also consider the approaches to media analysis outlined in the following chapters, which deal with the ways in which scholars have sought to understand the detail of media content and the ways in which audiences use and interpret media.

QUESTIONS AND EXERCISES

1 a) What is the difference between vertical and horizontal integration?

   b) Does the concentration of media ownership lead to the concentration of ideas?

2 a) Why are critics concerned about the pressure on commercial media organizations to prioritize audience maximization?

   b) Are their concerns well placed?

3 a) Bearing in mind that such episodes are rare, what does the withdrawal of advertisers from *Blitz* magazine (p. 51) tell us about the influence of advertisers over content?

   b) What sorts of content are liable to be most appealing to advertisers?

4 a) Is it right that the Canadian government should seek to mould the cultural identities of its citizens by imposing Canadian content quotas? How could we justify such an approach?

   b) Should governments and Internet service providers assist the recording industry by cracking down on file-sharing?

5 Given that media are dominated by powerful corporate organizations, to what extent is it inevitable that content will reinforce the powerful interests they represent?

Suggested further reading

Bagdikian, B. (2004) *The New Media Monopoly*. Boston, MA: Beacon Press.
   Critical discussion of the implications of the concentration of media in the hands of powerful corporations.

Edwardson, R. (2008) *Canadian Content: Culture and the quest for nationhood*. Toronto: University of Toronto Press.
   Outline of the ways in which the Canadian state has sought to regulate media content in order to protect and nurture national identity.

Gitlin, T. (2000) *Inside Prime-Time* (revised. edn). Abingdon: Routledge.
   Detailed account of the workings of the US television industry, uncovering the institutional priorities that underlie programming decisions.

Golding, P. and Murdock, G. (1991) 'Culture, communications and political economy', in J. Curran and M. Gurevitch (eds) *Mass Media and Society* (3rd edn). London: Arnold: 70–92.
   Theoretical outline of critical political economy as a perspective on media centred on industry and its broader capitalist context.

McChesney, R. (1999) *Rich Media, Poor Democracy: Communication politics in dubious times*. New York: New Press.
   Outlines the ways in which, according to the author, the current structure and organization of media industries is stifling democracy.

4

Media Content

Focal points

- Semiology as an approach that regards media texts as arrangements of signs.

- Narrative, genre and discourse analysis as related approaches to textual analysis.

- Differences between qualitative and quantitative forms of media analysis.

- Content analysis as a systematic, quantitative approach.

- The need to understand texts in their broader context.

Introduction

In the last two chapters, we have examined the technologies via which media communication is transmitted and the industry that controls them. Despite the importance of both these elements of the media process, a substantial amount of academic analysis has involved the detailed study of media 'messages' themselves – the very content that Marshall McLuhan regarded as so irrelevant.

Whether they take the form of novels, newspaper articles, radio broadcasts, television programmes or pieces of music, the units of content that carry such 'messages' are referred to as *texts*. This chapter is about the ways in which scholars have sought to analyse media texts, the motivations for their approaches and the kinds of conclusions they have drawn. We'll consider a number of different approaches, focusing in particular on two contrasting case studies: semiology and content analysis.

Although orientated towards media products themselves, the analysis of texts is not concerned with an understanding of content for its own sake. Rather, theorists seek to understand the broader social and cultural significance of media messages – their relationship with the social networks and cultural identities of the world in which they operate. As established in the Introduction, this involves an appreciation of the way that, rather than either reflecting society neutrally or shaping it through content invented out of thin air, media offer us highly selective representations of the world that have some capacity to influence or shape the future.

This circular understanding of content as representation helps to illustrate the potential importance of textual analysis. It shows that, in some cases, we might be able to come to tentative understandings of aspects of 'real' social relations by studying their representation in media. A study of changing representations of men and women in adverts over the last 50 years, for example, might tell us a great deal about shifting attitudes in broader society. More often, however, textual analysis tends to be used as a way of drawing attention to the particular ways in which media content selects and constructs the world and the ways selective representations might influence the future.

Media texts as arrangements of signs

One of the most well-known approaches to the study of media texts is *semiology*. Pioneered in the writings of Ferdinand de Saussure (1974) and Charles Peirce (1931–1948) and developed in relation to mass media texts by European structuralist theorists such as Roland Barthes (1968), semiology regards all communication – from speech to images to television programmes – as made up of signs.

The role of the semiologist is to decipher the ways in which different arrangements of signs generate meaning. According to de Saussure, all signs are made up of two core elements: a *signifier*, which is the means of representation, and a *signified*, which is a concept that is represented. For example, a smile acts a signifier and its signified is the concept of the happiness or amusement of its bearer. Particular forms of music have also acquired the role of signifiers in certain contexts, as in the case of emotional concepts such as fear, anger or joy.

Importantly, the word 'sign' should not be taken to mean the same as the term 'signifier'. Rather, 'sign' refers to the duality of signifier and signified – the relationship between the two. Equally important is that the signified in de Saussure's approach is not, as Barthes (1968) puts it, 'a thing' but rather a concept – an idea. Thus, smoke signifies not fire itself, as an external object, but the human concept of fire.

One of the most underlying systems of signs in society is language. In writing this chapter, I hope to convey meaning (signified) by means of particular arrangements of letters and words (signifiers) drawn from language, which is an ever-developing sign system. Successful communication requires a socially learned agreement between myself as author and you as reader as to the meaning of the signifiers that I am deploying. Semiological analysis, then, can be carried out on written texts or speech by deconstructing the ways in which arrangements of words generate meaning.

The premises and techniques of the approach are also used, however, to make sense of the construction of meaning in other forms of text, such as photographs, songs, films, adverts, news reports, magazine covers and so on. Written texts involve sequences of letters and words, images involve arrangements of shapes and colours and music involves compositions of sound, but, ultimately, they all can be regarded as amalgamations of signs. And just as the communication of messages via speech (parole) requires the establishment and learning of a shared language (langue), so the conveyance of meaning via images, music or film is reliant on the development and shared understanding of their own conventions. Thus, we understand particular arrangements of music, lighting, camera shots and so on in films, because we have learned and accepted the semiotic conventions via which this medium operates.

Signs as arbitrary?

The successful communication of meaning, then, is reliant on shared societal systems of understanding because, rather than being universal, the relationship between signifier and signified is culturally specific. In many societies we have become used to equating black with the concept of evil and white with good, but this is based on an historically established convention and in a different society with a different history, the associations between signifier and signified may well be reversed or there may be no semiotic connection at all between colour and morality. Nevertheless, signs are not necessarily entirely arbitrary. Often there is some initial 'relative analogy' (de Saussure, 1974) or 'motivation' (Barthes, 1968), behind the relationship between signifiers and signifieds. Peirce (1931–1948) elaborates on this through a distinction between icons, indexes and symbols.

Icons, he argues, are signs for which there is a physical resemblance between signifier and signified (or, as he put it, the sign and its object). Words such as 'splash' or 'crack' are iconic because their sound imitates the phenomenon they signify. In representing people, objects or events with analogous sets of shapes and colours, photographs also can work on an iconic level. The most well-known use of the word icon today is probably in relation to symbols on computer screens. Only some of these, though, are consistent with Peirce's sense of the term. A printer symbol that consists of an image of a printer is iconic, but some of the so-called icons used to open commercially branded pieces of software are not.

Indexes, Peirce's second type of sign, also involve a connection between signifier and signified, but, rather than there being a physical resemblance, the correspondence relates to a prior association between them of a sensory or causal kind. The most commonly cited example here is the use of smoke to signify fire. The two always accompany one another and this makes the use of the former to signify the latter far from random. Similarly, we could think about the use of images of dark clouds to signify rain or the use of tears to signify sadness. In each case, the culturally learned relationship between signifier and signified is based on an existing association.

In contrast to icons and indexes, Peirce's third type, *symbols,* are entirely arbitrary and there is no obvious initial connection. Because of this, such 'unmotivated' signs, as Barthes (1968) refers to them, are also liable to vary more from one culture to another. With the exception of words that imitate their object, language works on a symbolic, rather than iconic or indexical level, because there is no logical connection between the appearance or sound of words and the concepts to which they refer. The connection between the arrangement of letters 'fire' and the concept to which it refers, is reliant on an arbitrary historical agreement between English speakers to associate the two with one another. There are also all sorts of symbols outside the realm of language. The use of a green light to signify 'go' may have become commonplace across the globe as a result of cultural influence, but it is symbolic because there is no particular reason for it.

Levels of meaning

Whether arbitrary or not, when it comes to texts that consist of complex arrangements of signs, the connection between signifier and signified may not always be simple or one-dimensional.

By developing a distinction between *denotation* and *connotation,* Barthes (1968) elaborates the notion that signifiers may simultaneously convey meaning on different levels. *Denotation* refers to the most immediate level of meaning – the interpretation of what is represented at its most basic level of intelligibility. A photograph of a woman's face and upper body on the cover of a fashion and beauty magazine (see Figure 4.1) may refer, in the first instance, to the individual whose face and body are represented, the concept of womanhood and, perhaps, the significance of individual elements or features of the face, body and their decoration – the concepts of hair, eyes, skin, jewellery or make-up, for example.

It is important to remember here that denotation is not the same as signifier, even if sometimes the difference between the two can seem ambiguous. Rather, denotation is the signified in its most immediate, literal and obvious sense. Because of its immediacy, denotation, particularly in

FIGURE 4.1　Front cover of *Cosmopolitan* magazine, November 2009
© National Magazine Company

the case of visual images, has a strong chance of being recognized across cultures.

Of greater ultimate interest to mass media semiologists, though, are *connotations*, which Barthes refers to as second-order or 'associative' meanings.

Here we are in the territory of cultural inference and implication. Under the right cultural circumstances, the image on the magazine cover may convey not only the immediate meanings outlined above but also broader concepts that are further removed from the immediate representation. The expression on the face, the identity of its owner and the way it has been made-up and photographed, alongside various other features of the woman in question, may be taken to signify more abstract concepts, such as beauty, sexiness, satisfaction, confidence or success, for example, or even the notion of a connection between them. Because they are further removed than denotations from the signifier itself, connotations are, it is argued, more likely to be culturally specific – their communication is unlikely to be successful unless the audience is well versed in the particular cultural conventions by which they operate. Connotations, then, are more *polysemic*, or open to different possible meanings, than are denotations.

For some, the distinction between denotation and connotation is an ambiguous one (Hall, 1993). When one considers that even fairly immediate concepts such as 'face', 'woman' and 'make-up' are themselves socially constructed, then, arguably, there is no such thing as a 'literal' or absolute meaning. Even Barthes (1968), himself, recognizes that denotation might plausibly be regarded as the first and most immediate level of connotation. Nevertheless, for Stuart Hall (1993), once the culturally constructed nature of all meaning is recognized, the denotation/connotation distinction remains analytically useful in distinguishing between immediate and relatively uncontested meanings (denotations) and broader, more malleable inferences (connotations).

Signs as relational

Rather than operating in isolation from one another, signifiers generate meaning as a result of their relationships with other signifiers. We cannot understand the cover of a fashion and beauty magazines by means of an isolated examination of the image in the middle of it and neither can we make sense of an online news article by focusing only on the words in the headline. To analyse the ways in which meaning is conveyed, we have to understand how signs work in relation to one another. For semiologists, there are two relational axes on which to focus – *paradigmatic* and *syntagmatic*.

The *paradigmatic* axis concerns the relationship of each individual signifier in a text with a set of alternative signifiers that could have been used instead. The set of alternatives is known as a *paradigm*.

Paradigmatic analysis, then, involves breaking up the text into its components and assessing the significance of each element by considering how the meaning would have been different if alternative signifiers had been used instead. The idea is to compare what *was* selected by the producer of the text with what was *not* selected.

Barthes illustrates the point by reference to the garment system (1968). We can identify a number of different paradigms or types of clothing under headings such as headwear, footwear, above waist garments, below waist garments, underwear and so on. Having identified and isolated these, we can then analyse the significance of the choices a person makes by comparing them with alternatives within their paradigms. We can understand the significance of a long flowing skirt, for example, by imagining if it was substituted with a PVC mini-skirt or a pair of jeans.

The use of colour also provides plenty of opportunities for paradigmatic analysis. A predominance of red in a media text is liable to create a different impression than a predominance of green, blue or yellow. And colour can have specific impacts on meaning in particular situations. In order to demonstrate the absorbency of products such as nappies and panty liners, adverts often show blue liquid being absorbed by their products. Paradigmatic analysis may help us to understand why blue might be used rather than, for example, yellow, green, purple, red, black or clear. Meanwhile, in the case of the female face on the front cover of the magazine, we might identify a number of paradigms, including choice of model, use of lighting, hairstyle, direction of gaze, categories of facial expression and so on.

While paradigmatic analysis concerns the comparison of what is present with what is absent, *syntagmatic analysis* asks us to consider the ways in which the different signs present in a text interact with one another.

Having divided the text into pieces, then, we subsequently need to examine how its components fit together. The paradigmatic comparison of individual items of clothing with absent alternatives may be valuable, but we are unable to understand the significance of each component, or of the overall impression conveyed by the outfit they form, unless we examine their relationship with one another. A pair of jeans may convey a different message if worn with a T-shirt and trainers than if combined with a buttoned shirt, tie, blazer and smart shoes.

Until they are placed into a particular semantic context, individual signifiers can be particularly polysemic, or, open to interpretation. Red could signify danger, fire, heat, horror or sex, while yellow might imply heat, summer, happiness, cowardice or illness. The meaning is only clarified by the relationship between the colour and the other signifiers with which it is placed. In the context of a traffic light or warning sign, red conveys danger, but when used as the backdrop for footage of a couple gazing at one another, it may connote sexual desire.

For Barthes, images tend to be particularly polysemic, making it especially important to study the ways in which their meanings are *anchored* by other signifiers – particularly by headlines, captions or voiceovers, but also by sound, music and various other features.

In the case of our fashion and beauty magazine, the image of a confident, pouting female celebrity (Christina Aguilera) gazing out at the reader is anchored by the title of the magazine, *Cosmopolitan,* as well as a series of snappy textual references to fashion updates, style advice, perfume, sexiness, body confidence, happiness and 'hot sex' with men. The reader, we might argue, is prompted to regard the flawless, gazing woman in the centre as a sexy, sophisticated, confident and successful ideal of femininity, and encouraged, via the various references to self-improvement, to regard this image as something to be strived for, through being up to date with fashion, buying perfume or taking heed of tips about style, body confidence, sex and so on. Meanwhile, references to 'career crossroads' and to a successful rape prosecution work, among other things, to associate this particular version of glamorous femininity with independence and control.

In theory, the process of semiology involves the sequential completion of paradigmatic and syntagmatic analysis: 'What has to be done is to cut up the "endless" message ... into minimal significant units ... then to group these units into paradigmatic classes, and finally to classify the syntagmatic relations which link these units' (Barthes, 1968). In practice, however, it is difficult to fully separate the two stages because of the extent to which they both inform one another. To understand why red was used rather than blue or yellow (paradigmatic), I need to take into account the context in which the colour appears (syntagmatic).

Uncovering mythology

In addition to denotation and connotation, Barthes (1972) identifies a third order of meaning: *mythology* or *myth*. Myths are broad sets of cultural assumptions and beliefs evoked and reinforced by media texts. They help to shape the way in which we interpret denotations and connotations in media messages, but are themselves further developed and reinforced every time they are evoked.

Barthes illustrates this relationship in his analysis of a cover of the French current affairs magazine *Paris Match*. The cover depicts a young black man in French military uniform looking up proudly – probably at a tricolour flag. The connotations of this, argues Barthes, relate to the pride members of France's colonies have in representing, identifying with and defending the country. In turn, this taps into and develops a broader existing myth about the greatness of French imperialism: 'I see very well what it signifies to me: that France is a great Empire, that all her sons, without any colour discrimination, faithfully serve under her flag, and that there is no better answer to the detractors of alleged colonialism than the zeal shown by this negro in serving his so-called oppressors' (Barthes, 1972: 116).

Although his notion of mythology does not necessarily infer something that is false, Barthes is critical of the operation of myths, suggesting that they invariably serve powerful interests by making dominant ways of thinking appear to be natural and obvious. The primary purpose of semiology, for Barthes, is to deconstruct and expose the operation of myth through media content, and numerous cultural analysts have followed his lead in this respect. Studies of advertising, for example, have placed emphasis on the cumulative establishment of the myth that happiness is commensurate with the acquisition of consumer goods (Kellner, 1995; Williamson, 1995). Such themes also pervade our example of the magazine cover. The connotations of the text, which emphasize feminine fulfilment through fashion, style, cosmetics, self-confidence and sexiness, activate broader cultural myths, about the equation of happiness with particular kinds of consumerism, for example, and the association of even the most active, assertive forms of femininity with physical attractiveness to men (McCracken, 1992).

Limitations of semiology

Various questions have been raised about semiology as an approach to media analysis. Although he questions de Saussure's claim that semiology is a science, Barthes (1968) nevertheless asks us to accept that, if used properly, the approach can reveal the definitive meanings of media texts within a given societal context. But how do we know that semiological readings of adverts, films or images are accurate in their 'revelations' of meaning?

The problem, for some critics, is that, for all its technical-sounding terminology, semiology tends to be unsystematic (Strinati, 1995). Rather than comprising a clear and orderly set of step-by-step procedures that would result in similar conclusions if repeated by another analyst, the interpretation of meaning tends to be a messy undertaking, centred on individual interpretation. It is, in other words, *unreliable*.

Sometimes semiological readings lack even minimal levels of systematization. For example, in emphasizing his casual observance of the *Paris Match* cover and stating that 'I see very well what it signifies to me', Barthes (1972: 116) indicates that, far from emerging through the careful application of procedures, his conclusions apparently have emanated from some sort of intuition on his part – something presumably lacking in 'ordinary' readers. As well as making semiology unreliable, such emphasis on subjective interpretation raises questions about *validity*. Are semiologists measuring what they purport to be measuring – the definitive meaning constructed by a message – or are they, in fact, revealing their own unique personal response to it? And, as Dominic Strinati (1995) asks, how are we to know the difference between one and the other?

More fundamentally, perhaps, semiology risks reifying media content, implying that particular arrangements of signs operating within particular language systems generate definitive meaning all by themselves. Questions about the specific motivations and operation of media industries and regulators are bypassed, then, by a form of textual determinism. In fairness, Barthes recognizes the importance of media industries in his emphasis on the role of a 'deciding group' in the development of mass media sign systems, which, unlike language itself, are liable to be shaped by the few rather than the many (1968). However, he offers no means or prospect of analysing the media industry, prompting Chandler (1994b) to argue that semiology may be of some value in understanding *what* meanings are generated and *how*, but is not able to show *why* or what we can do about it.

Meanwhile, in assuming that there is such a thing as a definitive meaning that can be discerned by knowledgeable analysts, semiology neglects the engagement between media content and users. It is assumed that the connotations identified by the semiotician are definitive and, hence, liable to be received by audiences. Yet, research suggests that the range of different audience interpretations and responses to media texts can be considerable – something that has led some to suggest that there is no such thing as a fixed or pre-existing meaning and that meaning is produced only in the interaction of a text with its audience (Morley, 1992).

For John Fiske (1991a; 1991b), texts not only need to be understood in relation to the ways in which audiences engage with them but also in the context of their relationship with other texts and broader culture and society. From this point of view, the signs within an individual text have a syntagmatic relationship not only with one another but also with a range of other texts circulating in the present and past. The front cover of *Cosmopolitan,* then, needs to be understood in relation to the way its meaning systems connect with a host of other representations in films, adverts, newspapers and on websites. These *intertextual* relationships make it potentially hazardous to try to separate off any particular text. Texts, then, 'need to be understood not for and by themselves but in their interrelationships with other texts and with social life' (Fiske, 1991b: 4).

It would be unwise, however, to dismiss semiology entirely. The approach remains influential and continues to inform crucial debates about the kinds of meanings predominant within media and the ways they are constructed. In particular, we should be wary of rejecting it on the grounds that it is unsystematic. Overreliance on personal interpretation may be hazardous, but, as we shall see, this can be a feature of more systematic approaches, too. It is important to recognize, meanwhile, that a flexible, unsystematic approach may provide the only means by which we can hope to make detailed, contextualized sense of textual meaning. By focusing on such detail, semiology shows us how every element of a text is of significance, that no part of a message is coincidental or neutral and, most of all, that it is the complex relationships between signifiers which generate meaning rather than any individual elements in isolation. Sometimes people suggest that semiologists read too much into apparently simple texts. My response is that every detail of each media text has been painstakingly selected and positioned for a particular reason – very little is accidental or inconsequential.

Narrative, genre and discourse analysis

Semiology is not the only means by which scholars have sought to conduct in-depth or qualitative analysis of the content of media texts. A number of related approaches have emerged that each develop the analysis of texts in different ways. Importantly, rather than being mutually exclusive, particular elements of such approaches, together with semiology itself, often are combined in different ways.

Narrative analysis

Narrative analysis treats media texts as diverse as films, adverts, documentaries and newspaper columns as composed of different forms of storytelling and seeks to identify the conventions and devices with which such narratives are constructed (Fulton et al., 2005; Gillespie, 2006).

Semiology is of great importance here because many of the devices used by storytellers are reliant on the successful communication of meaning through signs – the use of music to infer emotion or hint at what may happen next or the use of clothing or an accent to signify particular character traits, for example. Narrative analysis is particularly concerned with understanding the narrative conventions on which stories draw and, in doing so, deconstructing the ways in which audiences are being asked to make sense of content.

One of the key focal points here is the order in which events are represented. For example, according to Tzvetan Todorov (1978), storytelling often activates a standard plot structure in which a state of *equilibrium* or normality is established at the beginning that is *disrupted* in some way by a causal event and eventually is *reinstated* in a slightly different form at the end as a result of corrective action. Films and novels often work in this way and so does the construction of plot in documentaries or news stories. Many of the accounts of the World Trade Center attacks of September 11th 2001 drew on this sort of disruption of normality structure and anticipated, in one way or another, a return to normality after America had taken appropriate corrective action.

Narratives also involve standard character types. Vladimir Propp (1968), for example, identifies seven character types that operated within Russian folk tales as follows:

- the villain, who disrupts normality

- the donor, who gives the hero a gift to enable normality to be restored

- the helper, who accompanies the hero

- the princess in need of rescue from the villain

- the dispatcher, who initiates the hero's journey

- the hero, who restores normality

- the false hero, who takes on the guise of hero and works to undermine the cause of the real hero.

While, to some extent, these are specific to the type of tales that Propp studied, they are also familiar in various different sorts of stories. If we take the original *Star Wars* film, for example, we have a clear villain and hero in Darth Vader and Luke Skywalker, a combined donor and dispatcher in the form of Obi Wan Kenobi, a princess in need of rescue in Leia and a number of helpers in Han Solo, Chewbacca, C3PO and R2D2. The only one of Propp's characters who is absent is the false hero – a variation of which arguably becomes a theme of the film's sequels (and eventual prequels), which focus on the fall from grace of Luke's father, Anakin.

Of course, the basic conventions and character types identified here barely scratch the surface of narrative analysis, which aims to understand in extensive detail the ways in which different stories are structured, the explicit and implicit devices used to convey different events and the ways in which different emotional responses are generated.

Genre analysis

A further variant, which relates closely to both narrative analysis and semiology itself, is *genre analysis*. Here, the curiosity of analysts is focused acutely on the relationship of different texts to one another and the ways in which they are clustered into particular types or genres (Solomon, 1976). Examples of genres include romance, comedy, science fiction, news and soap opera. They can also be thought of in terms of hierarchies, so the genre of comedy might be divided into stand-up, sitcom, romantic comedy and so on.

Genre analysis is concerned with looking at the establishment and operation of distinct conventions within each genre – conventions that relate to audience expectations about narrative structure, subject matter, setting, editing, music, visual features and so on.

For example, soap operas typically involve a series of overlapping and ongoing narratives about different members of a community that continue from episode to episode. They also seek to generate a broadly credible and mostly serious set of representations of relationships, dilemmas and personal crises. In contrast, sitcoms usually are centred on a particular family or small group of friends and focus on representations that are exaggerated for comedic value. They also have a simple beginning, middle and end narrative form in which, consistent with Todorov's standard structure, each episode begins and ends with a state of normalcy.

Generic conventions also apply to informational programming. 24 hour news programmes, for example, have developed a somewhat unique set of conventions of their own – the emphasis on fast-moving liveness, breaking stories, graphics, logos, on-screen tickers and two-way question and answer sessions between anchors and reporters 'at the scene'.

As well as being concerned with the characteristics of established genres, the ways in which they are constructed and their orientation to different sorts of consumers, genre analysts have taken a particular interest in the ways in which genres draw from and overlap with one another – something that, in some cases, results in the development of entirely new genres. Particular attention has been focused in recent years on the apparent merging of information-orientated genres with those associated more with fiction and entertainment. The now well-known genre of the docusoap is a primary example, the conventions of which are drawn from a mixture of drama, soap opera and sometimes even game show. Meanwhile, documentaries and news programmes themselves make increasing use of narrative devices and techniques associated with drama, including the use of reconstructions, graphic and emotive footage, dramatic music and allusions to traditionally fictional roles, such as the hero and villain.

Discourse analysis

Although semiology has its roots in linguistics, the former is probably more often associated with the study of image-based media than the in-depth examination of the minutia of language use. Subsequently, there has been a growth of interest among some theorists in the specific construction of meaning by means of the arrangement of words and sentences in media.

Commonly used in the analysis of news, but potentially useful for various kinds of media, *discourse analysis* (Fairclough, 1995; Kress and Hodge,

1979; Talbot, 2007) is concerned with the ways in which broader beliefs, world views and social structures are embedded in and reinforced in the use of verbal or written communication. The approach draws on linguistics and also on the post-structuralist theory of Michel Foucault (Hesmondhalgh, 2006). Foucault repeatedly emphasizes that the realities we experience are constructed by the discourses we use to describe and understand them and, crucially, that such discourses and the realities they construct are closely intertwined with relations of power.

Critical approaches to discourse analysis, as outlined by Norman Fairclough (1995), bring together Foucault's emphasis on discourse and power with a specific focus on the use of language in media. They are typically concerned with analysing the ways in which dominant ways of thinking and structures of inequality inflect and are reproduced and naturalized through speech and writing. The approach aims to explore the fine detail of both the content and structure of language use in media – something that involves both paradigmatic and syntagmatic dimensions. Focusing on various elements of vocabulary, grammar and syntax, analysts ask questions about how the particular formulations used position the speaker and the audience, what they include and exclude and how they invite us to understand events, individuals, groups and identities.

One example of a point of interest in discourse analysis has been the way in which different forms of words can attribute or obscure responsibility for events, emotions or reactions. The hypothetical headline 'Anger as Immigrant Workers Flood Britain' places the critical spotlight squarely on the actions of immigrant workers, who are the sole active agent in the formulation and thereby implied to be responsible for the situation. In contrast, the word 'anger' is not connected with any active agent. Instead of telling us who is angry using a verb (to be angry) and an actor, my hypothetical headline depersonalizes and passifies this aspect of the story by nominalizing the verb (turning it into a noun), so that those responsible for the anger are absolved of scrutiny and the anger itself is legitimated as a sort of universal (and natural) reaction among right-thinking people.

Another example of a common focal point for discourse analysis is the construction of communities through formulations of language and the positioning of speaker and audience in relation to these. Michael Billig (1995), for example, carried out a study of the construction of national identity in UK newspapers by means of the repeated use of words such as 'us', 'our' and 'we' in headline and article phrasing (see Chapter 9).

Crucially, rather than understanding individual texts in isolation, discourse analysis attempts to place them in context. One simple example of this is that, if one places my first example on immigrant workers within the context of the broader newspaper construction of a national 'us' that Billig identifies, then we might suggest that the 'anger' in the hypothetical headline implicitly, is being constructed as a natural emotion associated with this national 'us', which is implied to include both the journalists and their readers, while the immigrants are constructed as outsiders.

From quality to quantity: content analysis

Semiology, alongside related approaches such as narrative, genre and discourse analysis, is focused on providing an in-depth, or, *qualitative* explanation of the content of media texts and the implications of that content. As well as being the primary strength of semiology, this emphasis connects to the lack of systematization regarded as problematic by some critics.

The tradition that most contrasts with semiology in this respect is *content analysis*. Rather than focusing on qualitative interpretations and detail, content analysts are concerned with the identification of broad empirical trends across a range of texts. Proponents claim that, by using rigorous and systematic *quantitative* methodology, they can produce findings that are empirically verifiable – that is, capable of being proven or disproved by unbiased evidence.

'Systematic, objective and quantitative'

According to one of its early proponents, content analysis can be understood as an 'objective, systematic and quantitative' approach to the measurement of media content (Berelson, 1952: 18, cited in Gunter, 2000). More or less repeated in the definitions proposed by more recent theorists (such as Kerlinger, 1986), this threesome is worthy of explanation.

The notion of *objectivity* suggests that, rather than coming about as a result of the subjective biases of researchers, findings and conclusions should accurately reflect the reality of the phenomenon being studied. Results should be *valid*, then, in that they measure what they claim to measure, and *reliable*, in that a repeat of the procedures followed by a different research team would yield the same findings. This emphasis on the achievement of objectivity by applying systematic methods reflects the grounding of content analysis in *positivism* – an epistemology (or theory of knowledge) that regards social research as analogous to the natural sciences and, as a consequence, prescribes the replication in the social sciences of scientific rigour and standards of proof.

The positivist emphasis on objectivity is often associated with research methodologies that seek to *quantify* the frequency with which particular phenomena occur. Consistent with this, content analysis involves the prior identification of particular types of content and the counting of their occurrences across a sample of texts.

Rather than analysing the detailed semiological construction of particular versions of femininity in a particular advertising campaign, then, I might count the number of times female characters are presented doing housework or looking after children, as compared to a range of other roles, across a large and randomly selected sample of adverts. The idea is that, if I follow the appropriate procedures, such an approach would enable me confidently to generalize my results – to come to a definitive conclusion as to what proportion of television adverts present women in domestic roles. I may then be able to compare my conclusion with earlier studies or with comparable work in different countries in order to measure changes over time or global variations. I may even be able to compare my results with data about the actual distribution of women's time in the social world in order to discover whether or not media are exaggerating the importance of domestic roles in women's lives.

It is by being *systematic* that, according to proponents of content analysis, we can produce findings that are objective, generalizable and comparable with other studies. Systematization means that we reduce the potential for bias through the rigorous application of a carefully devised set of parameters, definitions, techniques and procedures. The idea is to leave as little as possible to chance or to the subjective judgements of researchers.

Systematization also creates the possibility of studies being repeated by other research teams, either for purposes of direct verification or to enable meaningful comparison from place to place or time to time. There are various examples of systematization in content analysis and we'll illustrate them here by focusing on some of the most important ones.

Categories and coding

Rather than beginning with a media text and describing it in whatever way the analyst deems most appropriate, content analysts code content into predefined categories. Such categories, alongside the systems of classification of which they are a part, must be defined precisely and applied consistently. If I want to measure the number of 'acts of violence' within a sample of content, then I must first define what counts as an act of violence for the purpose of the study. Does a gentle push count, for example, does someone need to be visibly hurt and do I include verbal intimidation? Also, what will count as an individual unit of violence? In the case of a prolonged gang fight, do I count every individual blow struck or do I record the whole encounter as a single unit? Such decisions make a radical difference to the findings and therefore must be prescribed and systematized in order to ensure rigour. I may wish to further categorize acts of violence recorded – whether according to descriptive types (kicking, punching, striking with a weapon and so on), levels of extremity or other factors.

Roger Wimmer and Joseph Dominick (2006) stress that, in order to avoid confusion, each category set must be *mutually exclusive* – they should not overlap with one another – and *exhaustive* – they should cover the full range of possibilities. If I am seeking to measure the frequency of different story types on news websites, it would not be wise to attempt to code each story into one of the following five categories: 'international stories', 'crime stories', 'sports stories', 'celebrity stories' and 'other'. First, the international stories category clearly has the potential to overlap with the other three and, second, the category set as a whole is far from exhaustive. Where would I place a story about a local politician or one about a lost cat, for example? These and many other stories would have to be coded within the 'other' category, which means they would effectively be excluded from the analysis.

Population and sample

Another crucial area for systematization is that of defining the *sample* of content on which analysis is to be carried out. Qualitative approaches such as semiology are often unsystematic in this sense because there is a tendency for analysts to focus on examples of content that happen to interest them or most effectively illustrate trends they already believe to be taking place. Although there may be some advantages to such selectiveness, it means that we cannot know for certain how typical or widespread the outcomes of the analysis are.

In content analysis, this would be unacceptable. Samples are expected to be generated according to a consistently applied set of principles designed to ensure representativeness. To be representative, the make-up of a sample must be such that it can accurately and fairly stand in for the broader *population* of content a study is trying to draw conclusions about. Examples of populations for content analysis studies might be 'advertisements on Canadian television', 'national UK newspapers' or 'Russian social networking site profiles'. It is by having a sample that is likely to be typical of their population that content analysts are able to generalize their findings.

Content analysis sampling often takes a multistage form. A study of UK newspapers may establish rules for including, first, a set of publications, second, a series of dates and, finally, a selection of content from each edition. Such parameters must be carefully designed in order to avoid sample bias. If my sample of national UK newspapers consists of the front page content of *The Times*, *The Guardian* and *The Daily Telegraph* every Saturday during the period 15 December to 2 January, for example, then it would be far from typical of its population as it would exclude all non-front-page and weekday content, it would favour 'quality' newspapers over the popular press and it would over-represent a non-typical time of year, dominated by Christmas. To avoid such biases, I might include a greater range of newspaper types, days of the week and content from each paper, as well as a less abnormal period of the news year. Also, rather than rely on my own judgement, I might introduce some element of randomization in the selection of dates, newspapers, pages and so on.

Case study: Gerbner and television violence

George Gerbner and colleagues' annual studies of US television violence from 1967 onwards provide a particularly well-known and influential example of content analysis in action (Gerbner and Gross, 1976).

The population for the studies was limited to 'dramatic programming', with non-fiction such as sport, game shows and news excluded. The sample consisted of drama transmitted during every weekday evening and weekend morning for a single week during each year the study was carried out.

Violence was defined as 'the overt expression of physical force (with or without a weapon) against self or other, compelling action against one's will on pain of being hurt or killed, or actually hurting or killing', with a single unit defined as 'a scene of some violence confined to the same parties' (1976: 184). The studies placed emphasis on the level and type of violence in each individual programme, the involvement in violence of each individual major and minor character and the coding of each specific violent act. The approach enabled the categorization of violence into different types, as well as an analysis of factors such as the kinds of characters involved and the consequences of violence in the plot.

The studies demonstrated that a high proportion of dramatic programming contained violence. In 1975, for example, 78 per cent of the programmes analysed contained violent episodes and 64 per cent of lead characters were involved in an episode of violence. The average hour of viewing contained 8 violent episodes, a figure that rose to 16 per hour in children's weekend daytime television. Over the years, findings also illustrated consistent patterns relating to types of violence and, fascinatingly, the profile of those involved. For example, violence was committed as often by characters with a 'happy fate' as those with an unhappy one, but the former – who tended to be young, white, American males – were killed and injured less, their violence presented as more efficient and their characters as more attractive (Fiske and Hartley, 1988). Young male characters were most likely to be perpetrators of violence, while females and the elderly were more likely to be victims. Female characters, for example, were as likely to be killed as to be a killer, while males were almost twice as likely to be a killer than to be killed. This effect was concentrated even further if gender was combined with ethnicity and other factors: 'old, poor and black women,' it is pointed out, 'were shown only as killed and never as killers' (Gerbner and Gross, 1976: 190).

By focusing on the profile of characters, Gerbner and his colleagues' work measured not only violence itself but also the ways in which different social groups were represented in media. It also illustrates a range of comparative ways in which content analysis can be used. As well as comparing results from one year to the next in order to illustrate changes over time, Gerbner compared his findings with statistics on crime within society itself – something that led him to argue that television representations exaggerated and distorted the level of crime and violence in society.

Limitations of content analysis

Among the various ways in which scholars have sought to study media texts, content analysis has possibly been the most influential with respect to the general public, the media industry itself and policymakers. The approach has clear potential value as a means of facilitating broad assessments of the quantitative character of media representations and, in particular, enabling meaningful comparisons – whether across time and space, between media outlets or between media and 'real' society. Despite the tendency of its proponents to emphasize the superiority of their systematic numerical approach over qualitative approaches such as semiology, however, content analysis has significant weaknesses of its own.

While it carries advantages with respect to reliability and the ability to generalize, the quantitative emphasis in content analysis leads to findings that can be simplistic and lacking in depth. Rather than being carefully understood as part of the very particular context in which they present themselves to viewers, selected segments of media texts are extracted from the narratives of which they are a part and simplified into instances of abstract categories such as 'episodes of violence' or 'representations of women in domestic roles'. Usually, attempts are made to incorporate elements of context by recording certain additional aspects of the characters or narrative, but these are inevitably superficial. Gerbner is able to differentiate between violent episodes committed by characters with happy and unhappy outcomes, for example, but such categories are themselves simplified abstractions and barely scratch the surface with respect to the diversity and complexity of the contexts in which violence is given meaning for real audiences. Meanwhile, such contextualizing variables as do exist are often ignored in the headline figures of studies. Gerbner makes a great deal, for example, of figures such as the number of violent episodes per hour of viewing, which fail to make even basic distinctions between different types. An appreciation of the relationship between the parts and the whole in the construction of meaning is largely bypassed in content analysis, then, as a result of an overriding emphasis on reducing, categorizing and quantifying.

The claims to objectivity of some proponents of content analysis are highly questionable, meanwhile. For all of the emphasis on being systematic and reliable, the outcomes and conclusions are still shaped by subjective agendas and judgements. The formulation of research questions, design of samples, devising of categories and identification of units of analysis are all reliant on human judgements and all liable to affect results. In defining a single unit of violence in his 1970s studies, for example, Gerbner stipulates that if a new agent of violence enters into an existing violent episode, then that moment should be recorded by his team as a separate violent episode – in other words, what could conceivably be construed as a single fight would be recorded as two separate violent episodes (Gerbner and Gross, 1976). Whether we think this approach sensible or not, it is a subjective judgement call that is liable to have had a substantial impact on the overall quantity of violent acts recorded in the studies. While this does not mean that we should ignore such studies or dismiss content analysis altogether, such decisions ensure that the findings reflect the particular approach the researchers chose to take as much as they do the 'reality' they were seeking to shed light on.

As with other approaches to the analysis of media texts, content analysis also is subject to the limitation that the context in which such texts are produced and consumed is neglected. There is a danger that the role and motivation of producers in selecting and emphasizing particular kinds of content may be overlooked, then, and also that it will be assumed, without any evidence, that the prevalence of particular forms of content will shape the outlook or behaviour of audiences. In fairness, some content analysts, including Gerbner, have recognized that content analysis alone cannot support assertions about the impact of media on society and they have sought to combine their analysis of media content with direct research on users. We'll come back to this in Chapter 5.

Conclusion: putting texts into context

The approaches outlined in this chapter are united in their focus on the details of media content as a means of learning about the relationship between media, culture and society. Yet, as we have seen, such approaches can differ significantly in their motivation, focus and methodology.

In particular, it has been illustrated that there is a stark contrast between *qualitative* and *quantitative* approaches – the former offering detailed analysis of the ways in which meaning is produced in a handful of examples and the latter taking a large-scale systematic approach in order to ascertain broader trends. While both semiology and content analysis have their specific weaknesses, both have also offered those seeking to understand the role of media in society a range of useful tools and insights.

Likewise, the range of related approaches to the analysis of content, including narrative, genre and discourse analysis, each have the potential to offer valuable clues as to the connections between the forms of culture we consume via media and the broader socio-economic context in which we live. There may be a case, then, for the development of dual or multi-method studies that combine elements from different qualitative or quantitative approaches in order to maximize the benefits of each.

The notion that media selectively represent the broader social and cultural world and, in so doing, offer the prospect of influencing the future of that world provides a broad framework within which we can make sense of the role of media content. It also illustrates the importance of observing and understanding what media content consists of and how meaning is constructed. However, only as part of an overall analysis that includes an understanding of the role of technologies, institutions and media users, can the analysis of media texts provide an effective contribution to our understanding of the relationships between media, culture and society. In particular, we cannot hope to gauge the ultimate significance of what we may observe within the content of media texts without the development of an understanding of what real audiences and users do with such texts. It is this that we turn to in the next chapter.

QUESTIONS AND EXERCISES

1 Distinguish between the following terms associated with semiology:

a) signifier and signified

b) icon, index and symbol

c) denotation, connotation and myth

d) paradigmatic and syntagmatic analysis.

2 Select an example of a magazine cover, newspaper article or web advert and carry out a detailed semiological analysis of the ways in which it conveys meaning. Try to break the text down into its components, focusing on each element individually as well as the relationships between them.

3 a) In terms of their approach to narrative, what are the differences and similarities between the conventions of news stories, Hollywood films and soap operas?

   b) Think of an example of a Hollywood film and see how closely Propp's character types can be applied to it.

4 a) What are the strengths and limitations of Gerbner's use of content analysis as a means to tell us about violence on television?

   b) Would a qualitative approach to the study of violence on television be more or less useful do you think?

5 If we don't know how audiences will respond to it, is there any point in analysing media content?

Suggested further reading

Barthes, R. (1968; 1964). *Elements of Semiology*. London: Cape.
Detailed account of the workings and significance of semiology by the theorist with whom it became most associated.

Fulton, H., Huisman, R., Morphet, J. and Dunn, A. (eds) (2005) *Narrative and Media*. Cambridge: Cambridge University Press.
Collection of chapters focused on the role of narrative in different genres of film, broadcasting and print media.

Fairclough, N. (1995) *Critical Discourse Analysis: The critical study of language*. Harlow: Longman.
Influential outline of critical discourse analysis as an approach to the study of media content.

Gerbner, G. and Gross, L. (1976) 'Living with television: the violence profile', *Journal of Communication*, 26: 173–99.
Presents the results and conclusions from Gerbner and his colleagues' annual measure of television violence using content analysis.

Williamson, J. (1995: 1978) *Decoding Advertisements: Ideology and meaning in advertising*. London: Marian Boyars.
One of the most well-known critical applications of semiology to the study of media texts.

5

Media Users

Focal points

- Approaches that try to measure the effects of media on individual attitudes and behaviour.
- Studies focused on the personal uses and functions of media.
- Developing understandings of media users as active, oppositional or subversive.
- Ethnographies of audiences, fans and users.
- Criticisms of different kinds of 'effects' and 'active audience' approaches.

Introduction

Analysis of the habits, practices and identities of those who use media forms a vital part of the development of an understanding of the relationships between media and the broader social and cultural environment. As we have seen, technological, industry-orientated and content approaches have faced the criticism that they attribute too much power to the medium, producer or text, respectively, in determining the significance and impact of media. Though they differ in various other respects, such approaches all sometimes assume that media users form a passive element in the communications process whose role is limited to receiving pre-existing meanings and being affected in predetermined ways.

In contrast, a substantial number of media researchers have explicitly made it their business to develop a detailed understanding of what happens when individuals, families or communities come into contact with media texts and technologies. These approaches to 'audience research' vary considerably in terms of their methodology and theoretical approach. Most notably, perhaps, while some have sought to measure or theorize the extent to which media audiences are affected by pre-existing media meanings or stimuli, others have attributed to them a considerably more active role in the selection and use of media for their own purposes. Although there are considerable points of overlap between the two, the study of media audiences can also be usefully divided between approaches originating from US empiricist research traditions and those emerging from European cultural studies.

US empirical traditions of audience research

Systematic research on media audiences was initiated by researchers in the United States in the first half of the twentieth century. It was prompted by a variety of factors, not least the increasing use of media by politicians, advertisers and others as a means of influencing people and a sense among researchers that existing approaches to the question of media influence were inadequate.

Theories emanating from the neo-Marxist Frankfurt School (the prominent members of which had emigrated to the USA during the Nazi era) and from US mass society theorists, such as David Riesman (1953), presented what subsequently has been labelled a 'hypodermic syringe' model of media, whereby standardized messages were assumed to be automatically 'injected' into a passive audience, resulting in a culture of mass ignorance and manipulation.

Existing empirical studies of influence, meanwhile, had been largely confined to 'audience measurement' approaches, which measured the effectiveness of advertising or political campaigns by counting how many people their materials had reached (Nightingale and Ross, 2003).

Alongside the lack of research evidence for the pessimistic claims of the Frankfurt School and others, the deficiencies of such early empirical work prompted a drive for specific analysis of the influence or 'effects' of media. From the 1940s onwards, extensive audience research was carried out, leading to intense debate about the influence of media on the attitudes and behaviour of audiences. In the following pages we'll examine some of the most important of these, grouping them according to perspective and approach.

Effects research

As its name suggests, *effects research* is concerned with attempting to measure the influence or impact of media. It has been particularly dominated by an interest in the ideological or political influence of media such as political propaganda and by the concern that media may have negative impacts on individuals' behaviour.

We'll start with the latter area, in which interest has been particularly focused on questions of criminality and violence. Analysis of the influence of media in this respect became particularly prominent among US research-ers during the 1960s and remains a key point of research and debate among academics and within news media to this day.

Bobo dolls and short-term behavioural effects

Speculation by newspapers, campaigners and academics about the negative impacts of media violence on consumers – and children in particular – has been a key feature of discussion about the influence of media for several decades. Partly as a result of this, extensive research has been carried out in order to try and ascertain the existence and extent of any such negative influences on viewer behaviour. Much of this research has taken the form of laboratory experiments, carried out by behavioural psychologists.

The most well-known and influential of these were are a series of so-called 'bobo doll' experiments led by Albert Bandura during the early 1960s. Influenced by social learning theory, which focuses on the capacity of indi-viduals to learn behaviours by observing others, Bandura and his colleagues sought to ascertain the extent to which children are prone to imitate the violent behaviour of adult role models. The interest of the researchers was not solely in media and the first of their experiments focused on children's imitation of the behaviour of an adult who was in the same room as them (Bandura, Ross and Ross, 1961). Nevertheless, later experiments did focus on the role of television and, in order to illustrate these, we'll examine an example in a little more detail.

In one particular experiment, Bandura Ross and Ross (1963) divided a sample of infant subjects into three experimental groups and one control group. Each of the three experimental groups was exposed to an individual violently attacking an inflatable 'bobo doll'. The doll was hit with a toy mallet, punched, kicked and sat on – all of which accompanied by shouts such as, 'Sock him in the nose!' and, 'Hit him down!' For the first experi-mental group, these violent acts involved an adult in the same room as them, while for Groups 2 and 3 they were viewed on television. Group 2 watched a film of an adult attacking the bobo doll, while, for Group 3, the violence was perpetrated by an adult dressed as a cartoon-style cat.

In the second stage of the experiment, all the groups were subjected to 'aggression arousal' by being refused permission to play with toys. The idea was to ensure that the children were feeling frustrated in order to recreate the kinds of circumstances in which one might expect violence or aggression to occur.

The final stage of the experiment involved placing the children in a room containing a variety of toys, including a bobo doll and a mallet, and this time allowing them to play. The children's play was carefully observed, particularly with respect to their general levels of aggression and *imitative aggression* – that is, the similarity between any acts of aggression exhibited and those they had observed earlier.

All three experimental groups exhibited higher levels of aggression and higher levels of imitative aggression than the control group. The group exposed to the adult attacking the doll on television exhibited the highest levels on both measures, while the group exposed to the violent cat character exhibited the lowest of the experimental groups.

On this basis, Bandura claimed to have demonstrated not only that children had exhibited clear social learning, by imitating the behaviour of role models, but also that this was particularly concentrated if the behaviour was viewed on television rather than within the same room as them. Meanwhile, the lower aggression scores for the group exposed to the violent cat seemed to indicate an ability to distinguish between realistic and unrealistic role models and a greater propensity to imitate the former.

Bandura, Ross and Ross' influential work forms part of a much broader and ongoing body of experiments designed to measure immediate media effects. Such experiments vary in terms of their precise structure. While the Bandura experiment described above took a *post-test-only* format (the behaviour of the subjects was tested only *after* exposure to the stimulant), for example, other work has tested subjects' behaviour both before *and* after exposure (Gunter, 2000). The idea of such *pre-test-post-test* designs is to further isolate the stimulant as the sole cause of behavioural or attitudinal change, though there is a danger that exposure to the pre-test could, in itself, affect post-test responses (Wimmer and Dominick, 2006).

While many studies are laboratory-based, others take the form of field experiments, whereby researchers measure the responses of individuals to particular stimuli within their own environments, often over a period of days or weeks rather than hours.

Importantly, the results of experimental studies have been varied and, while many have appeared to demonstrate problematic media effects, others have not. In one post-test only experiment, Seymour Feshbach (1961, cited in Gunter, 2000) even claimed to have demonstrated that the watching of violent media had a cathartic effect on angry subjects, making them *less* rather than *more* hostile.

Long-term 'cultivation' effects

In contrast to the emphasis on immediate behavioural influence in most experimental studies, other researchers have focused on the long-term impact of media use on people's overall attitudes and outlook.

George Gerbner argues that television dominates the symbolic environment of those who view it heavily, becoming central to the milieu in which they form their understandings of the world. As a consequence, television is deemed to gradually cultivate an attitude to the real world based on the distorted version of society it presents to us. Gerbner was particularly concerned about this because, as we saw in Chapter 4, content analysis studies that he had carried out appeared to demonstrate that the 'television world' was dominated by crime and violence. Not satisfied with measuring content alone, Gerbner also sought to assess the long-term impact on viewers of their repeated engagement with the violent world of television.

In a series of surveys in the late 1970s, representative population samples were categorized as either light, medium or heavy television viewers. Their answers to a series of questions about their attitudes towards crime and violence were then analysed. Many questions related to things like general opinions, personal experiences and fears, while others were factual, relating to the prevalence and significance of crime within society, for example.

The primary finding was that those respondents categorized as heavy viewers were far more likely than the other groups to respond to these questions with 'TV answers', which means responses commensurate with the bleak, violent view of society presented by television. Heavy viewers, for example, were more fearful of becoming victims of crime and more likely to have an exaggerated view of the proportion of the population working in law enforcement or of the proportion of reported crime that is violent than the other groups (Gerbner et al., 1977).

Gerbner's conclusion is that heavy television viewing cultivates a fearful attitude to the world, something that may induce 'second order effects', such as supporting political parties that campaign on a 'tough on crime' platform, distrusting one's neighbours or refusing to allow one's children to play outside. Gerbner explains:

> if you are growing up in a home where there is more than say three hours of television per day, for all practical purposes you live in a meaner world – and act accordingly – than your next-door neighbour who lives in the same world but watches less television. The programming reinforces the worst fears and apprehensions and paranoia of people (1994: 41).

Methodological problems

Studies that appear to demonstrate significant short- or long-term effects of media violence on viewers have been enormously influential, not only within academia but also within broader public and political discourse. Yet, there are doubts about the methodological approaches used to demonstrate such 'effects'.

Laboratory experiments allow researchers directly to isolate and assess the impact of the factor in which they are interested (in this case, exposure to particular forms of media) by engineering situations in which the circumstances of subject groups are identical but for their different levels of exposure to that factor. Thus, Bandura and colleagues could conclude that it was exposure to different forms of aggressive activity which prompted the behavioural differences between their experimental groups because everything else about the way they had been treated was identical.

Yet, the artificiality that enables this manipulation of variables is also the most significant weakness of experiments. Although they may offer useful clues, they cannot prove that children will imitate television violence in a similar way when placed in the context of their normal, everyday lives. Furthermore, there is a substantial conceptual difference between violence as a form of play and seriously attacking a fellow human being. A further issue is that laboratory experiments are only capable of measuring the short-term effects of a small number of stimuli, whereas in everyday life, media influence must surely relate to the cumulative impact of multitudes of content. Field experiments move a step closer to studying people within everyday contexts but they too place people into situations that are artificially engineered, making it difficult to assess their findings.

Focusing on the long-term cultivation of attitudes by measuring self-reported attitudes via surveys, Gerbner avoids the short-termism and artificiality of behavioural experiments. Yet, there are difficulties with aspects of his approach also.

Although he identified *correlations* between heavy television viewing and the expression of fearful attitudes about crime and violence, he did not prove that the television viewing was the *cause* of those attitudes. It is also possible that a fearful outlook contributed to a tendency to stay in and watch lots of television or that a different variable relating to the characteristics of heavy television viewers might have explained the correlation. Although Gerbner employed statistical controls to show that the correlation had not been caused by sex, age, class or education levels, Gunter (2000) notes that the impact of other factors, including ethnicity, income and working hours were not tested. We should be cautious, then, before drawing too many conclusions about causality from this sort of survey research.

Limited effects and two-step flow

The style of effects research pioneered by Bandura and colleagues can be described as employing a reasonably straightforward stimulus–response model of learning, not entirely dissimilar to what some have described as the hypodermic syringe model. In contrast, effects researchers at the University of Columbia were more sceptical about the notion of a direct and inevitable chain of influence between media and individual attitudes or behaviour.

Research they carried out on the impact of media on voting behaviour during US presidential elections appeared to demonstrate that exposure to newspaper- and radio-based political campaigning had a minimal impact on audiences (Lazarsfeld et al., 1944; Berelson et al., 1954). The research, which involved repeated interviews with a panel of individuals and one-off interviews with random members of their local community, concluded that political allegiances were more strongly influenced by factors such as religion, social class, family ties and localized social networks than by media. Indeed, most individuals displayed little knowledge of candidates or issues, let alone any indication that their voting behaviour might be altered by media exposure. In the case of most ordinary people, then, the role of media seemed limited to the reinforcement of existing intentions rooted in tradition and community:

> The ordinary voter, bewildered by the complexity of modern problems, unable to determine clearly what the consequences are of alternative lines of action, remote from the arena, and incapable of bringing information to bear on principle, votes the way trusted people around him are voting (Berelson et al., 1954: 309).

The possibility of media influence is not entirely ruled out by the researchers, however. It is argued that media coverage and campaigns are liable to have some influence on a relatively small number of politically engaged and influential individuals within each community. These individuals, it is argued, may pass on their opinions to those around them, creating an indirect form of media influence, or, the 'two-step' flow, as the researchers called it. Influence is only possible, then, because it is transmitted via interpersonal contact within trusted social networks.

Paul Lazarsfeld further developed the two-step flow model of media influence in his subsequent collaborations with Elihu Katz (1955). This included examination of the significance of interpersonal networks as an intermediary of media use and influence in relation to popular culture. In a survey-based study of young women's habits and opinions relating to moviegoing, for example, they identify certain respondents as discerning 'movie leaders', who were looked to by others as a source of expertise in the selection and interpretation of such media.

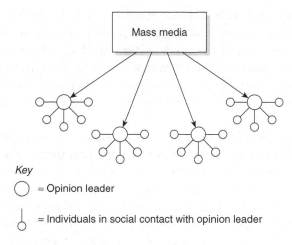

Key

○ = Opinion leader

⎺ = Individuals in social contact with opinion leader
○

FIGURE 5.1   Two-step flow model (Katz and Lazarsfeld, 1955)

Uses and gratifications

Having worked with Lazarsfeld on the two-step flow model, Katz later became a key exponent of an alternative approach to the relationship between media and audiences. Instead of focusing on whether or not audiences are affected by media messages, the *uses and gratifications* approach seeks to understand the ways in which audiences actively select and utilize media for their own purposes. The difference between this 'uses' perspective and 'effects' work is summed up nicely by UK theorist James Halloran (1970), who asserts that 'we must get away from the habit of thinking in terms of what the media do to people and substitute it for the idea of what people do with the media' (cited in Morley, 1992: 51). Indeed, according to the uses and gratifications approach, it is futile to investigate media influence on individuals until you understand the motivations and uses of the latter:

> even the most potent of the mass media content cannot ordinarily influence an individual who has 'no use' for it in the social and psychological context in which he lives. The 'uses' approach assumes that people's values, their interests, their associations, their social roles, are pre-potent, and that people selectively 'fashion' what they see and hear to these interests (Katz, 1959: 2).

Uses and gratifications reversed traditional communications models such as that of Harold Lasswell (see Chapter 1), which started with media encoders and ended with audience reception and effects. The varied needs and uses of audiences were now deemed pivotal features and media content was relegated to a set of resources that gratified such audience goals.

The model is essentially a *functionalist* one, in the sense that it regards mass communications content as a resource that emerges to fulfil individual needs and goals and, in turn, enables society as a whole to function more effectively.

Uses and gratifications research involves surveys or interviews with individuals in order to ascertain the functions different forms of media have for them. Reliant on the 'self-reporting' of uses and motivations by consumers themselves, such research has resulted in elaborate typologies of needs and uses. Distinctions have often been made between short-term escapist gratifications, which consists of immediate relief or entertainment, and longer-term educational functions, which relate to lasting forms of knowledge and understanding. Katz et al. (1973) identify 14 needs in 5 different categories, while Denis McQuail et al. (1972) distinguished between the following:

- diversion, a short-term escape or emotional release, enabling suspension of everyday routines and problems

- personal relationships, a substitute for face-to-face social companionship, a facilitator of relationships or a source of community belonging

- personal identity, a resource for the development or reinforcement of personal values, meanings and a sense of one's place in the world

- surveillance, a source of knowledge, information and engagement with the world.

There remains a somewhat unresolved question about the extent to which different kinds of content or medium should be regarded as differentially suited to particular needs. In other words, to what extent does the structure or content of media prescribe that it can only result in particular outcomes? Karl Rosengren and Sven Windahl (1972: 27) suggested that there had emerged 'a growing consensus that almost any type of content may serve practically any type of function', while Katz, Blumler and Gurevitch were not so sure, calling for greater investigation of 'the attributes that render some media more conducive than others to satisfying specific needs' (2003: 42).

Functionalist and complacent?

Having instigated and pioneered the detailed study of media influence, researchers associated with the University of Columbia, alongside colleagues elsewhere, played a significant role in a shift away from the study of direct media effects and towards an interest in the place of media within individual lives and identities. Lazarsfeld and colleagues' conclusions on political influence emphasize that we cannot begin to understand people's relationships with mass communication without an awareness of their broader social context. In focusing on the purposes of active media users, uses and gratifications perhaps represents a logical development from this. Both models remain influential – the latter proving popular with some researchers of Internet use, for example (Ruggiero, 2000) – but neither is without its problems.

The research of Lazarsfeld and colleagues was based only on the issue of media's influence on voting behaviour itself. Subsequent research, which focused not on voting itself but on which political issues voters thought were the most important, demonstrated a close correlation between what respondents said and the issues most strongly emphasized in newspaper coverage, suggesting that media might play a role in setting the public agenda (McCombs and Shaw, 1972). More importantly, perhaps, Lazarsfeld et al.'s research is unable to provide us with an understanding of the kind of long-term influences with which Gerbner's work is concerned. In the short term, an individual may resist or ignore media messages, but it remains possible that, over a longer period, both they and those around them may gradually incorporate greater amounts of knowledge and experience derived from media. Lazarsfeld's conclusions also rest on the observation that individuals were subject to the comparatively stronger influence of religion, local communities and families. Many theorists believe that, in recent times, individuals have become less firmly rooted within such tight-knit localized communities, social class affiliations having become more fragile, families more complex and religious participation less universal (Bauman, 2001). With the weakening of these alternative sources of influence, might the influence of media become more substantial?

Uses and gratifications, meanwhile, can be criticized for assuming that individuals always have a clear rationale for media consumption. In some cases, clear motivations or functions may be of less importance than factors such as the force of habit. The reliance of researchers on surveys that require audiences to self-report the role of their media use may contribute to an exaggeration of the importance of active, rational choices. People may be unlikely to admit to being mindless couch potatoes or having no particular reason for their actions when filling in a survey that explicitly requests clear reasons.

The focus of uses and gratifications research on individual psychological needs, meanwhile, prompts David Morley, to argue that the approach neglects the role of sociological categories such as class, ethnicity, locality and gender in patterns of media use and interpretation. As he puts it, 'Uses and gratifications is an essentially psychologistic problematic, relying as it does on mental states, needs and processes abstracted from the social situation of the individuals concerned' (1992: 48). In this respect, some 1970s uses and gratifications work represented a move away from the greater focus on sociological context of earlier University of Columbia research.

Finally, the functionalist premise of uses and gratifications theory results in an overall perspective that comes across as complacent and uncritical. It is assumed that media exist to satisfy the demands and needs of audiences and that media consumption is an active process which, with the exception of occasional 'dysfunctional' uses, is beneficial to individual everyday life and the smooth functioning of a pluralist society. This rosy picture seems to omit the possibility of manipulation or propaganda and, in so doing, renders mass media beyond any serious critique, whether in relation to the kinds of content from which audiences can choose or the structures of ownership, funding and control. Theories of mass culture may have overestimated the passivity of audiences (see Chapter 6), but uses and gratifications approaches risk taking things too far in the opposite direction.

Cultural studies: dominant and oppositional readings

Encoding, decoding and preferred meanings

Counterposed to the US tradition, with its emphasis on behaviourist effects research and functionalist audience models, is a perspective on media audiences rooted, at least partially, in European cultural theory and centred on questions of discourse, meaning and power. Pivotal to the approach is Stuart Hall's work at the University of Birmingham's Centre for Contemporary Cultural Studies (CCCS).

Drawing on semiology, Hall places emphasis on the 'encoding' of meaning into media discourse by producers. 'The discursive form of the message', he argues, 'has a privileged position in the communicative exchange' (1993: 98). A neo-Marxist thinker influenced by the work of Antonio Gramsci, Hall also argues that these encoded meanings 'have the institutional/political/ideological order imprinted in them' and are liable to reinforce this prevailing order by reinforcing dominant, or, *hegemonic* ideas (1993: 93).

Yet, at the same time as recognising the role of media encoders in influencing audiences, Hall's model, which was developed in the 1970s, breaks away from semiology by recognizing that what he terms the *preferred meanings* encoded into media texts will only be realized if they are *decoded* appropriately by audiences. There is a possibility, then, that audiences might actively challenge the meanings of media messages in the process of interpretation, rather than passively accepting them. Rather than understanding such active interpretations as the manifestation of a plethora of individual psychological needs, as uses and gratifications theory has tended to, Hall argues that audience responses to media are related to socio-economic context and are clustered within the following three categories.

- The *dominant hegemonic* position, which refers to audience interpretations that are commensurate with the meaning encoded into the text and, hence, with the dominant cultural order within which the media industry is assumed to operate.

- The *negotiated* position, which refers to acceptance of the overall view encoded into a text, but disagreement with specifics. Dominant premises are largely accepted, but specific 'exceptions to the rule' may be insisted on (1993: 102). Audiences might, argues Hall, accept the broad premise of a media report that suggests workers pay must be frozen to control inflation, but may insist that certain sets of workers deserve higher levels of pay.

- The *oppositional* position, which occurs when the preferred meaning is identified and rejected by audience members. Here, a news report about the need to reduce pay might be rejected as a distorted message that serves to reinforce dominant interests and perpetuate inequalities. For Hall, such oppositional readings act as a crucial site for contestation of the dominant order.

Despite continuing to place considerable weight on the role of preferred meanings and dominant interpretations, Hall's discussion of differential audience responses helped to precipitate a shift of European approaches away from semiological interpretations of texts and towards an interest in the decoding of meaning and, specifically, the possibility of subversive audience interpretations.

Social context and differential readings

Also a former member of the CCCS, David Morley shares Hall's view that semiology underestimates the importance of audiences, arguing that Barthes and others were guilty of 'an endless quest for a mythical object – the "real" or "ultimate" meaning of the message' (1992: 76).

Morley also rejects the individualistic and strongly audience-centred approach of uses and gratifications, preferring to draw on Hall's emphasis on dominant, negotiated and oppositional readings and to concentrate on the role of socio-economic context as an arbiter of such readings. What are important are 'the differences between the cultural frameworks available to different individuals,' he argued, 'so that I, say, as a Durham coal miner, interpret a message about government economic policy differently from you, say, as an East Anglian bank manager – that is not a difference which is simply attributable to our different psychologies' (1992: 80).

Morley investigated such differences by carrying out research on the 1970's UK current affairs television programme *Nationwide*. Having identified what were regarded as right-wing, pro-Establishment preferred meanings of the programme in an initial textual analysis stage of the project (Brunsden and Morley, 1978), Morley went on to show episodes to 29 different audience groups, taken from different segments of society (Morley, 1980). Each group was then invited to discuss the programme and their perspectives were mapped in relation to Hall's typology of dominant, negotiated and oppositional readings.

The study concludes that responses to media content were not determined by social class alone but were strongly related to discourses and assumptions people had access to as a result of more particular social and occupational positions. A group of politically conservative bank managers are deemed to have exhibited a dominant reading because they barely noticed *Nationwide*'s perspective on current affairs, accepting its dominant premises without question and preferring to talk about matters of presentation. In contrast, a group of left-wing shop stewards formed a highly critical appraisal of the programme, which they deemed guilty of presenting a façade of inclusivity while promoting middle-class, right-wing perspectives.

Limitations of Hall's model

Morley's study also highlights some limitations with Hall's typology, however, as not all the groups proved as easy to classify as the bank managers and shop stewards. The response of a group comprising inner-city college students was dominated by a refusal to engage with the discourse of the programme at all, on the basis that it was of no interest to them. Although he tentatively identifies this as an oppositional reading, Morley recognizes that such disengagement is substantively different from conscious opposition and is not really accounted for by Hall's model. There were also difficulties categorizing the responses of a group of print management trainees, who were sharply critical of what they regarded as the *left-wing* bias of *Nationwide*. This is classed as a dominant reading, on the basis that the group clearly were not conscious of the right-wing, middle-class bias that Brunsden and Morley's analysis of the programme had pointed to. But how can we be certain that Brunsden and Morley's interpretation was 'right' and the print manager trainees' interpretation 'wrong'? Despite his criticisms of semiology, Morley himself perhaps places too much emphasis on what he and Brunsden – from their own particular social position – had taken to be the 'real' meanings of the text.

Even if we accept that it is possible for analysts to identify the preferred meanings encoded into individual media texts, the case of Morley's print manager trainees highlights an ambiguity in Hall's dominant, negotiated and oppositional typology. The model seems to attempt simultaneously to classify *both* the extent to which an audience accepts the coding of a particular media text *and* the positioning of the audience's response vis-à-vis broader dominant meaning systems. The implication is that the preferred meaning of media content automatically embodies broader dominant understandings of the world and that acceptance of the former automatically equates to acceptance of the latter. The model entails a degree of ambiguity then, when it comes to the analysis of audience responses to texts the preferred meanings of which are themselves oppositional. If I view a series of websites that have been coded with an unremittingly anti-capitalist view of the world and I respond by accepting such messages, then is my interpretation dominant because I accepted the preferred meaning or oppositional because I took resistant stance towards dominant capitalist ideology?

Partly as a result of this problem, Hall's model remains rather too inflexible to enable a detailed understanding of range of audience responses to different media texts. More fundamentally, although it acknowledges the potential for different readings and responses, it continues to regard audiences primarily as receivers or decoders of messages. The value of this in enabling Hall to retain an emphasis on the ideological role of media ought not to be underestimated (see Chapter 6), but such an approach does not get us particularly far in terms of the question of what audiences actually do with media.

Audiences as cultural producers

If Hall and Morley raise the possibility of audiences interpreting messages in oppositional ways, then many of the theorists who have followed in their footsteps dispense with the notion of audiences as receivers of existing meanings altogether, preferring to see the activities of everyday media users as active, creative and productive. As was the case with the uses and gratifications approaches, but with greater emphasis on the social and political significance of consumption, one-way transmissions models are turned on their head and audiences afforded the role of central instigators rather than passive recipients.

Of particular note here is the work of John Fiske. Though he draws on elements of neo-Marxist theory in emphasizing the forces of dominance, social control and homogenization within which contemporary communication takes place, his primary focus is on the ways in which these forces are resisted by the everyday cultural practices of ordinary consumers. The economic power of the culture industry may be great, argues Fiske (1991a; 1991b), but its cultural influence is limited to an ability to provide a variety of texts from which consumers will actively choose on the basis of whether or not they have any potential relevance to their lives. Products are successful or unsuccessful, according to this view, not on the grounds of economic muscle or manipulation, but on the basis of whether or not they offer a suitable range of potential meanings and uses. Contrary to the teachings of semiology and Hall's notion of the preferred meaning, the products put on offer do not have fixed, a priori meanings that are waiting to be 'decoded'. Rather, meaning is produced by consumers themselves in their interaction with texts. This prompts Fiske to proclaim that 'popular culture is made by the people, not produced by the culture industry' (1991a: 24).

Such is the importance of user creativity, according to Fiske, that texts will only become popular if they offer a suitable 'excess' of potential meaning for audiences to develop their own understandings. The global popularity of pop stars such as Madonna can be explained by the capacity of such texts to generate a range of meanings of significance to different groups of consumers. The product is sufficiently flexible that it allows itself to be transformed into both repressive and empowering sets of symbolic meanings: 'Madonna is circulated among some feminists as a reinscription of patriarchal values, among some men as an object of voyeuristic pleasure, and among many girl fans as an agent of empowerment and liberation' (1991a: 124). We might add that Madonna has also become a significant symbol of affection in many gay and queer communities.

In emphasizing the political significance of creative acts of consumption, Fiske draws on de Certeau's use of the metaphor of cultural guerrilla warfare to describe the everyday refusal of consumers to submit to powerful structuring forces (1984). Forces of homogenizing power are met, it is argued, with ongoing grass roots cultural resistance, in the form of small-scale practices of 'poaching' and 'trickery' (1984). Fiske illustrates his own development of this argument, using the example of 1980s consumers ripping their jeans to generate a new set of distinctive grass roots meanings for a popular, standardized commodity: 'it is a refusal of commodification', he argues, 'and an assertion of one's right to make one's own culture out of the resources provided by the commodity system' (1991a: 15). For Fiske, what can be applied to jeans can also be applied to newspaper articles, television programmes, films and popular music. Such products are all continually 'ripped' or adapted by consumers and such adaptations each amount to small-scale challenges to the forces of power and control.

Ethnographies of audiences, fans and users

For all his emphasis on the importance of audiences as producers of meaning, Fiske's analysis of examples tend to be disappointingly reliant on his own readings of textual content rather than on audience research (Stevenson, 2002). Fortunately, however, the development of an ethnographic tradition of research, centred on in-depth interviews with and observations of media users and audiences, was already well underway by the time his most well-known pronouncements were made and has continued to develop since. Studies of romance readers (Radway, 1987), soap opera fans (Ang, 1985) and magazine readers (Hermes, 1995), alongside elaborations of the use of domestic media technologies by an increasingly audience-focused David Morley (1988) and by Ann Gray (1992), are among a plethora of projects offering detailed qualitative accounts of the ways media fit into the everyday lives, identities and symbolic worlds of audiences. To differing degrees and in different ways, such studies emphasize the contexts, competences, choices, interpretations and understandings of audiences. Consumers are regarded as active agents who incorporate media into their existing contexts.

A particularly celebratory approach is taken by Paul Willis in his work on the symbolic creativity of consumers (1990). On the basis of extensive interviews and ethnography with young people in Wolverhampton, Willis directly contrasts his findings with passive models of consumer behaviour. From creative engagements with adverts, to the incorporation of soap plots into real-life dilemmas and critical readings of magazine advice columns, he repeatedly emphasizes the control exerted by respondents over their media use. Emphasis is also placed on the productive social activities of consumers, including the creation and exchange of popular music mix tapes (which we might perhaps compare to contemporary swapping of MP3 playlists), whereby individuals become self-appointed filters and manipulators of the music world. On the basis of the detailed accounts of young people, themselves, then, the study concludes that ordinary cultural consumption tends to be discriminating, skilled, active and creative.

While Willis and Fiske celebrate the creativity of consumption across the board, studies of 'fan cultures' focused on the intense engagement of particular groups of highly committed consumers (Hills, 2002; Sandvoss, 2005; Gray et al. 2007). On the basis of an ethnographic study of a community of film and television fans, Henry Jenkins (1992) not only emphasizes the ways in which participants actively integrated cultural narratives into their individual everyday contexts, but also focuses on their tendency to reflect, in depth, on the meaning and significance of content as part of their exchanges with other enthusiasts.

Such reflective engagement is argued frequently to have extended towards their creative production of DIY texts – in the form of stories or videos, for example – that offered extensions or alternative versions of the official product. Jenkins makes sense of such activities by extending de Certeau's notion of 'poaching'. The fan cultures he studied are deemed to have appropriated those sections of media products that interested them, transformed them in ways appropriate to their interests and used them as the basis for developing an active, autonomous community. Such communities also had an activist element, attempting, for example, to influence official versions of the products they enjoyed by mounting campaigns for the inclusion of new character types or the revival of favoured series.

The ability easily to connect with one another, converse and share ideas or products on the Internet is deemed by Jenkins (2002) to have transformed fan cultures. If previously ideas were traded by post, at conventions and over the telephone, today fans can instantaneously engage with a vast range of individuals and interpretations from the moment they consume the latest instalment of their favourite texts.

In an ethnographic study of an online forum for soap opera fans, Nancy Baym describes the facilitation by this online space of extensive interpersonal interactions and ties centred on mutual enthusiasm for soaps: 'Being a member of an audience community', she says, 'is not just about reading a particular text in a particular way; rather it is about having a group of friends, a set of activities one does with those friends and a world of relationships and feelings that grow from those friendships' (2000: 215). Baym argues that the Internet has enhanced the possibility for participation in such fan communities and also made the perspectives and creations of fans more visible, to the extent that the boundary between media producers and audiences may be blurring.

More generally, the development and deployment of new digital technologies has been argued to have the potential to alter the relationship between 'producers' and 'consumers'. Not only have ordinary people become increasingly able to create and distribute content of their own making via discussion forums, blogs, social networking sites, YouTube and so on, but they also enjoy potentially greater levels of control in their capacity as users of content. Multichannel television, mobile technologies and the Internet offer the capacity to actively select from an ever greater range of content and shape the time, place, format and order in which they consume it. Ethnographic work on uses of the iPod by Michael Bull (2007), for example, emphasizes the ability to have one's entire, hand-picked music collection, complete with customized playlists, on instant demand as one traverses the city. Individuals are able to transform the public environments they travel in and through by the ongoing active selection and ordering of music suited to their mood or environment. Consumer/producer distinctions are also rendered ambiguous by facilities that combine the provision of content with the capacity for audiences to respond, including reader comment facilities on news websites, for example. Such developments further emphasize the status of those who engage with media as active users rather than passive recipients.

Conclusion: an uncritical celebration?

In focusing the microscope squarely on the complex ways in which people use and understand media as part of their existing social backgrounds and contexts, ethnographies such as those outlined above shift attention away from the notion of media users as receivers who are passively influenced or affected by media to a greater or lesser degree. Meanwhile, the tendency, following Fiske and de Certeau, to regard the activities of users as politically significant acts of cultural subversion against the dominant order represents a substantial break from the functionalist and psychologically orientated uses and gratification approach. Despite this tendency to emphasize cultural struggle rather than cosy consensus, however, some audience ethnographies are open to the criticism that they rather uncritically celebrate the power of consumers to forge their own meanings. In its most extreme form, this 'active audience' position implies that it makes little difference what kinds of technologies and content are made available to people or by whom because audiences will generate meanings and uses of their own anyway.

Although he makes regular mention of forces of power, control and homogenization, Fiske's account, by attributing the ultimate production of all meaning to audiences, seems to afford little real influence to the industry or broader structures of dominance. The version of events presented by Fiske and those who share his approach, arguably constitutes less a struggle between the forces of control and those of resistance and more an inevitable series of triumphs by the latter. For Golding and Murdock, such a version of events constitutes a 'populist romance in which the downtrodden victims caricatured by economic determinists [that is, theorists who assume that audiences are manipulated] are revealed as heroic resistance fighters in the war against cultural deception' (1991: 86).

The possibility of media industries acting as an (effective) instrument of ideology is entirely foreclosed by such an approach (Stevenson, 2002), as indeed is the notion that their operations are responsible for any substantive influence or impact. The effect of this is to let the industry off the hook in terms of its potential negative impacts or, worse still, unwittingly celebrate its current commercial structure as the facilitator of a playground of consumer creativity and empowerment. The potentially problematic impact on media of concentrations of ownership, profit imperatives, the influence of advertisers, pressures to compete for audiences and numerous other factors ceases to matter as a result of the assurance that audiences are selective, knowledgeable, creative and subversive. Critiques of media, alongside attempts to regulate or improve them, are rendered redundant.

Not all ethnographies of audiences and users are quite so sweeping with respect to the power and agency they afford to consumers, however. Many seek to balance their emphasis on audience activities and understandings with a recognition of the influence of the media industry and broader social structures. Meanwhile, those focusing on particular fan cultures sometimes confine claims about audience productivity and subversiveness to groups of unusually committed audiences rather than generalizing them to all consumers (Jenkins, 1992), though the implied distinction here between creative fans and passive ordinary consumers is itself open to accusations of elitism (Hills, 2002).

More generally, audience ethnographies of various kinds have offered invaluable insight into the significance of media in the everyday lives of individuals and communities. The continuation of such work in the age of digital, online and mobile media technologies is of great importance. What is important is that such ethnographies of users, alongside other approaches to the study of audiences, are understood in the context of an awareness of the constraints and limitations on use which are built into the structure of texts and technologies and of the role of industry and broader relations of power in shaping such constraints.

As will hopefully have become clear, this book urges readers to understand media from a rounded point of view that encapsulates the role of technologies, industrial context, content and users, maintaining that an overemphasis on any one of these to the exclusion of the others is liable to result in a distorted and partial picture.

QUESTIONS AND EXERCISES

1 a) Can a laboratory experiment involving the hitting of an inflatable doll tell us anything about the social impact of media violence? What are the strengths and weaknesses of Bandura et al.'s approach?

b) Does Gerbner's combination of content analysis and survey research prove beyond doubt that media cultivates a fearful attitude to crime and violence?

2 a) Is the 'two-step flow' approach a useful way to understand questions about media influence?

b) Produce your own uses and gratifications typology by identifying as many motivations and functions of media use as you can think of and arranging them in categories.

c) In what ways has uses and gratifications research been criticized?

3 In what ways did Morley's *Nationwide* project develop Hall's dominant, negotiated and oppositional model of audience interpretations? What are the strengths and weaknesses of Hall's approach?

4 a) What does Fiske mean when he says that 'popular culture is made by the people, not produced by the culture industry'? Is he right?

b) What is the difference between his approach and the uses and gratifications perspective?

5 Are audience ethnographies in danger of uncritically celebrating the active creativity of media users?

Suggested further reading

Fiske, J. (1991a) *Understanding Popular Culture*. London: Routledge.
   Argues that consumers produce active and sometimes subversive meanings in their interactions with cultural texts.

Gunter, B. (2000) *Media Research Methods*. London: Sage.
   Outline of approaches to the study of the impact of media, orientated particularly towards psychological and effects approaches.

Hall, S. (1993; 1980) 'Encoding, decoding', in S. During (ed.) *The Cultural Studies Reader*. London: Routledge: 90–103.
   Develops a model of the media process that emphasizes the industry as encoders of meaning as well outlining different forms of audience responses.

Jenkins, H. (1992) *Textual Poachers: Television fans and participatory culture*. London: Routledge.
   Classic study of the practices and identities of avid television fans.

Katz, E., Blumler, J. and Gurevich, M. (2003; 1974) 'Utilization of mass communication by the individual', in K. Nightingale and A. Ross (eds) *Critical Readings: Media and audiences*. Maidenhead: Open University Press.
   Reflective outline of the uses and gratifications perspective from authors involved in the development of the perspective.

PART TWO

MEDIA, POWER AND CONTROL

6

Media as Manipulation? Marxism and Ideology

Focal points

- Media as a purveyor of mass ignorance and distraction.
- Identification and critique of dominant meanings in media content.
- Case study of ideologies of consumerism in media.
- Cultural imperialism theories and the global circulation of ideology.
- Distinctions between culturalist and political economic approaches to *Marxism*.

Introduction

Marxist approaches to questions of media and society argue that the prevailing socio-economic order is exploitative and that media form an integral part of this system, both reflecting and bolstering the interests of established wealthy and powerful interests through content saturated with Establishment ideology. This chapter examines such critical approaches to media in greater detail, focusing in particular on Marxist notions of media as ideology.

We will begin with an introduction to Marx himself, before examining key neo-Marxist approaches, including the early Frankfurt School, European cultural studies perspectives and critical political economy. We will also consider arguments between different Marxist approaches and broader criticisms of the assumptions across their perspectives.

Importantly, Marxist approaches contrast with many of the perspectives on the question of media users examined in Chapter 5. In particular, functionalist uses and gratifications perspectives and cultural studies notions of subversive audiences paint users, rather reassuringly, as active agents in control of their own destinies. Even the strands of effects research that endorse the notion that media could shape audiences, meanwhile, have tended to focus either on measuring the immediate influence of particular stimuli (adverts, political campaigns) or on identifying longer-term effects of selected 'problematic' features, such as violence.

According to Stuart Hall (1982), such perspectives are pluralist, in the sense that they focus on various details about particular forms of influence but fail to address broader questions of media control or to offer a critical analysis of the prevailing system of power and the role of media content in reinforcing it. Such approaches have largely assumed, in other words, that the current system is essentially a good thing and that, with the exception of certain problematic aberrations, media form a potentially valuable component in its efficient operation. In contrast, Marxist approaches, including that of Hall himself, reject the broader capitalist system and regard media as purveyors of dominant ideology.

Marxism and ideology: basics

It is not possible to capture the sophistication of Karl Marx's complex broader theory here, but a reminder of some basic tenets of his critique of capitalism is of importance in order to understand subsequent developments of the approach as a means of understanding media.

For Marx, capitalism is characterized by the ownership of wealth and property by a small but all-powerful class group – the *bourgeoisie* – and the exploitation of the non-wealth-owning majority – the *proletariat*. The capitalist system perpetuates the power of the bourgeoisie, who control the means of production (factories, machinery) and ensure the subversion of the proletariat, whose labour is hired in order to produce objects that generate wealth. Such workers are alienated, argues Marx, because they put most of their life into the production of objects, only to see such objects appropriated and sold by their bourgeois employers.

Lacking control over the purposes or products of their labour, workers are reduced to a commodity object themselves, their labour being sold to the bourgeoisie in order that the latter might profit from it. The only way the proletariat can own any of the objects they have devoted their lives to producing is to buy them by paying their wages back to the bourgeoisie.

For Marx, capitalism is defined by this class relationship – the power of the bourgeoisie depends on their exploitation of the proletariat and the more the proletariat sell their labour to the bourgeoisie, the greater their *alienation* and subordination. So, why would the proletariat majority put up with such exploitation? Marx's answer reflects his materialist approach to the relationship between dominant economic relations – which he refers to as the mode of production – and the realm of culture, politics and ideas.

For Marx, the dominant ways of thinking in a society will always reflect the prevailing mode of production and the interests of the ruling class. Writing in 1859, he put it in the following way: 'the mode of production of material life determines the general character of the social, political and spiritual processes of life' (2000: 67). What this suggests is that capitalist economic relations are accompanied by a corresponding set of dominant cultural values, ideas and beliefs – ideology in other words. The circulation of this dominant ideology – via institutions such as the family, the political system and religion – acts as a support for the material situation from which it emerged by making the proletariat happier to accept the situation in which they find themselves. More specifically, ideology promotes *false consciousness*, blinding workers to the true nature of their exploited position by inverting capitalist arrangements so that they appear natural and inevitable rather than historically specific and changeable. Religion, for example is famously deemed to act as 'the opiate of the people' (1844: preface), a sedative that numbs the pain of workers by presenting their man-made and historically specific situation as inevitable and induced by God's will.

Marx famously predicted that the proletariat eventually would overcome their false consciousness and overthrow the capitalist system. The failure in much of the world for such a proletariat revolution to take place was a significant point of debate for a range of variants of *neo-Marxism* that were to emerge in the twentieth century. Another key focus for neo-Marxists was the massive growth of mass media, which increasingly were attributed a role as significant as that which religion had afforded for Marx in the nineteenth century.

The culture industry as mass deception

Of great importance to neo-Marxist analysis of media are a group of theorists collectively known as the Frankfurt School, whose work was mostly completed in the United States after their escape from Nazi Germany in the 1930s. The rise of fascism was to influence the work of scholars such as

Theodor Adorno, Max Horkheimer and Herbert Marcuse, but their primary concern was with the apparent triumph, within the West, of capitalism, which had apparently seen off a range of potentially destabilizing moments, not least the Russian revolution, world wars, general strikes and the Great Depression of the 1930s. Despite all these, capitalism had managed to develop and thrive, its logic so firmly embedded that the prospect of significant working-class opposition in countries such as the United States appeared to have faded significantly.

The result of this continual growth of the system Marx had predicted would be overthrown was that the ability of individuals to think and act freely, imaginatively and creatively – to be human, as the Frankfurt theorists saw it – was being crushed by a relentless all-encompassing capitalist machine. People were *reified*, or, reduced to objects – cogs and pulleys in the system. Lofty enlightenment ideals about expansion of the mind and enhancement of the human condition had failed to materialize, it was argued. Instead of liberating humans, the project of reason and rationality had been incorporated into capitalist economic relations, taking on a pragmatic, *instrumental* logic focused on maximizing efficiency, profit and control – something that was suffocating critical thought, creativity and human subjectivity. In seeking to understand how the population had been induced to accept such objectification, the Frankfurt School theorists turn to the ideological role of consumerism and mass media.

While Marx regarded ideology as a discernable set of ideas that emerged from capitalist relations, the Frankfurt School's analysis of the ideological role of media and culture envisages something more all-pervasive. Describing the rise of what they term *the culture industry*, Adorno and Horkheimer (1997) argue that, like everything else, human expression and creativity had been subsumed into the capitalist logic and surrendered to its relentless processes of instrumentality and rationalization. From their point of view, art in its pure form represents everything important about human subjectivity, including creativity, freedom and independent critical thought.

Under capitalism, however, art becomes a mass commodity, little different from the range of other industrial products on the market. For Adorno, culture ceases to be a creative social relationship between artist and audience and becomes reified into a set of anonymous consumer objects exchanged for money. This emphasis is developed further by Marcuse (1964), who argues that the superficial lure of such objects generates '*false needs*' in the minds of workers. The attractions of meaningless, superficial consumption, then, provide motivation to work ever harder for the system, while distracting people from their true needs, which, for the Frankfurt School, involve their release from oppression and their ability to develop and flourish as individuals. In contrast, the momentary release provided by cultural consumption serves to incorporate consumers further into the capitalist machine:

> We may distinguish between true and false needs. 'False' are those which are superimposed upon the individual by particular social interests in his repression ... Their satisfaction might be most gratifying to the individual but this happiness ... serves to arrest the development of the ability ... to recognize the disease of the whole and grasp the chances of curing the disease. The result then is euphoria in unhappiness (Marcuse, 1964: 4–5).

The Frankfurt School also specifically criticize the content of culture industry products which, as a result of profit maximization, is deemed to be wholly standardized. Rather than challenging, inducing creativity or stimulating independent thought, the predictability of such products makes the process of consumption simple, repetitive and effortless. Predigested in order to slip down easily with minimum fuss, such products can be compared to baby food, argues Adorno (1991). 'No independent thinking must be expected from the audience', he and Horkheimer explain, 'the product prescribes every reaction' (1997: 137).

In his best-known case study, Adorno argues that popular jazz hits were structurally indistinguishable from one another – to the extent that sections or components of one tune could be transferred to the equivalent position within another. Like the listeners who consumed them, such components are judged as being little more than interchangeable cogs in a system, lacking any significance or consequence: 'Complications have no consequences,' argues Adorno, for, 'regardless of what aberrations occur, the hit will lead back to the same familiar experience and nothing fundamentally novel will be introduced' (1990: 256). The result of this standardization, according to Adorno, is the inducement of mindless modes of listening, dominated by enslavement to rhythm or escapist forms of emotional identification.

What is true of music is deemed equally so in an array of other media formats. If in popular music, 'the whole is pre-given and pre-accepted before the actual experience of the music starts' (1990: 257), then so in the Hollywood film, 'as soon as the film begins, it is quite clear how it will end, and who will be rewarded, punished, or forgotten' (Adorno and Horkheimer, 1997: 125).

Another key phenomenon identified across formats is *pseudo-individualization*, whereby standardized commodity objects are presented with an illusory veil of difference and diversity. This veil might take the form of unexpected twists within standardized film plots or passages of apparent originality within formulaic songs. Pseudo-individualization might also relate to the construction of apparently distinctive stylistic identities for artists through the cultivation of an image and identity, for example. For Adorno, it is this appearance of difference that makes standardization acceptable to people: 'concentration and control in our culture hide themselves in their very manifestation. Unhidden they would provoke resistance' (1990: 307).

The Frankfurt School's contention, then, is that media and culture have been incorporated into an all-encompassing socio-economic system dominated by instrumentalism, rationality and objectification. The result is an industrialized version of cultural expression, the enticing, standardized form of which numbs the minds of the population, crushing their capacity for independent thought and distracting them from the development of real solutions to their alienation. The culture industry acts as a conduit for the incorporation of the masses themselves into the system and helps to bring about an apparent end to any realistic prospect of mass opposition.

Unsupported elitism?

The immediate response of many students is to reject the Frankfurt School's approach and, in particular, its implication that they themselves are mindless consumers, stupefied and blinded by predigested cultural texts. Many theorists, too, find uncomfortable what they regard as a patronizing attack on the cultural tastes of ordinary people.

The approach ought not to be dismissed too quickly, however – not least because many of the arguments have a quite remarkable level of fit with elements of contemporary media and culture. In fact, most would accept that the commodification of culture identified by the Frankfurt theorists has expanded very considerably since the time of their writing. There surely is no shortage of contemporary examples of cultural artefacts to which we might plausibly apply a Frankfurt School-style cultural critique.

It is hard to dispute, for example, that most contemporary popular music has a predictable, standardized structure or that lyrical themes, the cultivation of stars and the format of performance often are formulaic. The notion of pseudo-individualization also has potential application. We watch countless television programmes and films, whose basic narrative and structure are extremely similar, yet we often think and speak of such texts as though they were substantively distinct or original. Similarly, we argue vehemently about the merits of the different songs, bands or genres stored on our computers or iPods despite them having the most striking similarities in song structure, lyrical themes and performance convention.

The Frankfurt School's broader emphasis on the lure of cultural consumerism and its provision of temporary, superficial forms of enjoyment also seems at least as applicable now as it was over half a century ago. If theories sometimes go rapidly out of date as society changes, then, in this case, we might plausibly suggest that the opposite is true.

This does not mean, however, that the work of the School is without significant problems. Much of the approach rests on a belief that the essential condition of humanity revolves around a particular version of individual self-determination, imagination and creativity. Distinct from Marx's (also questionable) materialist emphasis on the human importance of meaningful labour, this idealist Frankfurt School assumption is debatable and rather ill-defined. How do we know self-determination and creative subjectivity are indeed what is most naturally human and who decides what counts as creative or human and what doesn't? On what basis does Marcuse, for example, know that certain 'needs' or experiences of enjoyment are more legitimate or genuine than others? We cannot accept the Frankfurt School theorists' critique of capitalism in its entirety unless we are sure about their understanding of how human life *should* be.

Despite its relevance to examples across media culture today, the Frankfurt School's dismissal of mass culture was probably overgeneralized at the time and would certainly be too sweeping if applied across the board to the more complex, fragmented and interactive media system of today. In labelling every cultural industry product as standardized and dismissing all apparent variants as pseudo-individualization, the Frankfurt scholars underestimate the possibility that the pursuit of profit might in certain circumstances encourage innovation and difference. In a culture dominated by multichannel television and iTunes, in which consumers can instantly access a vast array of content, their work provides a valuable reminder that more does not necessarily mean different. Yet it is difficult to accept that there are no meaningful distinctions at all between cultural industry products.

For all their emphasis on the industrialization of culture, the Frankfurt School theorists carried out little analysis of how the institutions that produce and distribute culture actually work (Thompson, 1990). Such analysis may have confirmed some of the trends they allude to, but would probably have revealed a set of motivations, decisionmaking procedures and ways of working rather more complex than they allowed for. They also failed to provide evidence for their claims about the negative impact of mass culture on audiences. Their appraisal of mass cultural content may have been detailed at times, but it is a significant leap to infer, from such textual analysis, confident conclusions about how audiences can be expected to respond. As John Thompson puts it, 'Horkheimer and Adorno try to read off the consequences of cultural products from the products themselves' (1990: 105).

Moreover, their certainty about the universally passifying impacts of mass culture sits uncomfortably with the ability they bestow on *themselves* to criticize it. On the one hand they insist that the whole population has been incorporated by the all-encompassing rationalist machinery of the capitalist system and its culture industry, crushing any capacity for independent thought or critique, but, on the other, they claim for themselves the unique ability to see how the system works and respond to its cultural products in a different way from everyone else. This has prompted some to claim that the Frankfurt School theorists are essentially elitist as they assign to themselves a penetrating discernment and taste deemed to be lacking among ordinary people.

Ideological meanings

For Thompson (1990), the Frankfurt School present a 'social cement' version of the concept of ideology. Rather than persuading people to support the status quo by propagating a particular set of dominant ideas, the culture industry directly binds or cements people to the system by crushing their capacity to think critically or independently at all. Other theorists, however, have focused greater attention on identifying the propagation via media texts of specific perspectives, meanings and modes of representation that are deemed to serve ideological purposes.

Beyond Marx's materialism

The development of attempts to critique the presence of such ideological messages within media content rested on challenges to Marx's materialist insistence that the realm of ideas automatically mirrors the material situation of a given society. Marx's position afforded little possibility that the proletariat could escape false consciousness through the exposure of ideology by theorists or, indeed, through any sort of struggle in the realm of ideas. For Marx, in order to change dominant ideas, you had to change the economic system, not the other way around.

This deterministic stance was softened in the theory of Louis Althusser (1971), who suggests that, although an economic base determines culture and ideas 'in the last instance', the latter nevertheless have 'relative autonomy'. In order to survive and reproduce itself, the economic system relies on control of dominant thinking by *ideological state apparatus* – a category that includes media alongside religion, schools and the family among other institutions. The principle of *relative autonomy*, however, introduces the possibility that there might be a degree of diversity, disagreement and struggle within these spheres and that dominant ideology might be challenged. Under the right circumstances, then, culture and ideas may have the capacity to be changed independently of the underlying material or economic system.

Antonio Gramsci (1971), writing some years earlier, had gone further still in emphasizing the importance of independent struggle and change within the realm of culture and ideas. Gramsci coined the term *hegemony* to refer to the predominance of taken-for-granted ways of understanding the world that strengthen the interests of the dominant political group. In order to maintain their position of economic and political power, argued Gramsci, the dominant group must achieve hegemony by dominating the realm of ideas and culture. Yet, rather than automatically submitting to dominant interests, civil society is characterized by ongoing struggle between hegemonic and counter-hegemonic ideas.

The dominant group may have significant advantages, given the resources at its disposal, but the maintenance of hegemony, in Gramsci's view, is constantly subject to challenge. Rather than being predetermined by the economic or material situation, struggles for influence over the everyday commonsense understandings of the population are deemed pivotal to the conservation or overthrow of a prevailing system. And, in Gramsci's account, intellectuals, broadly defined, play a crucial role in these ideological struggles.

Taken together, Gramsci and Althusser open the way for the possibility that, by exposing and challenging the operation of dominant sets of ideas within media content, social theorists might themselves play a role in social change.

For Stuart Hall, media constitute the primary site for the playing out of the kinds of struggles over meaning outlined by Gramsci. As we saw in Chapter 5, Hall recognizes that some audience groups may not fully accept the messages encoded into media texts. This does not prevent him, however, from regarding media as a highly effective means of establishing hegemony. Television is deemed particularly powerful because of the way it presents itself as an impartial 'window on the world' for viewers, making ideological representations look objective and natural (1982: 75). For Hall, whether it emits deliberate bias or not, media discourse rarely steps outside of a set of underlying, unquestioned frameworks and assumptions that serve dominant interests. 'Broadcasters', he argues, 'may not be aware of the fact that the frameworks and classifications they were drawing on reproduced the ideological inventories of society' (1982: 72).

Despite the best intentions of news providers, then, the regular reporting of economic crises or industrial disputes as damaging to the economy or 'the national interest' is deemed to have activated commonsense, ideological assumptions – that the strengthening of capitalism is a good thing, that the effective functioning and survival of this system is in our best interests, that we should all identify with our country and so on.

Hall also focuses on the ways the dominant system would respond and adapt in the face of challenges. In *Policing the Crisis* (1978), he and colleagues argue that sensationalized and racialized coverage of violent crime during the 1970s functioned as part of a re-establishment of hegemony in the face of a variety of threats to the system, including the rise of rebellious youth subcultures and increasing moral permissiveness. Focused on 'muggings', the coverage stigmatized racial minorities and evoked more general themes of a society out of control – something that paved the way for new forms of political authority in the form of Thatcherism. Through adapting and responding to challenges, hegemony was restored.

Roland Barthes, whose contributions to the development of semiology were examined in Chapter 4, is also of great importance to the development of a tradition focused on the deconstruction of ideological messages within media texts. Through his emphasis on 'mythology', he emphasizes that semiology should not be limited to the isolated analysis of particular texts but should identify the repeated activation and reinforcement in such texts of broader prevailing ways of understanding the world.

Like Hall, on whom he had been an important influence, Barthes suggests that ideology 'transforms history into nature' (1972: 129), that the circulation of myths serves to make assumptions that are historically specific appear to be natural and inevitable. One of the primary focuses in Barthes' work, and that of more recent critics of ideological media content, has been the operation of myths relating to consumerism. Using this theme as a case study to illustrate the way theorists have sought to uncover the operation of ideological meanings within media, let's briefly elaborate.

Case study: consumerist myths

Contemporary culture is saturated with messages that promote consumerism and the desirability of commodities. An average trip around town will involve encounters with commercials via billboards, shopfronts, in-store television, the inside and outside of buses and trains and all manner of other locations. And we should not expect any respite if we choose to go to the cinema, a café or a bar either. Commercials have even become a feature of workplaces and educational establishments. Many people carry exposure to further advertisements around in their bags or pockets, whether in the content of newspapers and magazines or on web-enabled mobile phones or portable games consoles.

Back in the 'private' sphere of our homes, we are also bombarded by commercials via television, radio, games consoles and, of course, the Internet, where engagement with adverts accompanies the use of social networking sites, the reading or watching of online news and the use of e-mail and instant messaging software. Sometimes, 'viral adverts' are even circulated in a grass roots fashion by consumers themselves.

Cultural theorists have sought to uncover the particular ways in which commercials convey ideological meanings. Such critics are interested not in the individual success of particular adverts in generating sales, but the way each advert taps into and reinforces broader sets of dominant assumptions.

For Douglas Kellner (1995), the central basis of such shared meanings is that buying or consuming is to be aspired to, that the identity of each of us is, first and foremost, as a consumer and, that in order to achieve happiness and fulfillment, we should strive to buy as many commodities as possible. Because of the relentlessness of this underlying message, a questionable set of ideas on the status of members of society and the achievement of human fulfilment begins to seem natural, acquiring the status of 'common sense'. This works in the interests of the prevailing capitalist social order by encouraging individuals to work hard and enhance their capacity to consume and by enabling capitalists to maximize their wealth accumulation and retain their material dominance.

Alongside other analysts such as Judith Williamson (1995), Kellner's analysis of commercials particularly emphasizes the ideological role of the construction of *symbolic values* with which products are associated. Rather than selling clothing purely on the basis of its *use value* – its capacity to keep us warm, for example – advertising and branding by fashion labels places emphasis on establishing products as symbols for culturally desirable concepts such as being up to date, confident, edgy, sophisticated, youthful, independent or radical. Advertisers, then, use carefully put together arrangements of signs to associate their products with particular human qualities, implying that consumers can associate themselves with such qualities if they choose to buy. They offer us the chance to purchase not only an object but also an identity. As Williamson put it, 'they are selling us ourselves' (1995: 13).

Kellner illustrates the workings of symbolic value in commercials by means of an analysis of cigarette advertising. Marlboro's use of the symbol of the cowboy associates smoking its cigarettes with tradition and rugged masculinity, while Virginia Slims' female-orientated campaign associates the use of its product with female liberation and independence. In the case of the latter, representations of a past in which female smoking was frowned on are contrasted with today's confident, glamorous, daringly dressed and, hence, 'liberated' Virginia Slims woman, anchored by the slogan 'You've come a long way baby' (Kellner, 1995: 336).

FIGURE 6.1   Shiseido advert (2001)
© Shiseido Company Limited, sourced from The Advertising Archives

Commercials for cosmetics have also associated products with the concept of liberation. In 2001, for example, magazine adverts for Shiseido make-up depicted elaborately and artistically made-up female faces, juxtaposed with the caption 'Be Radical' in one case and 'Empowering' in another, associating the brand with the notion of difference, boldness and female independence. Such symbolic associations with progressive politics may be argued to play a particularly glaring ideological role, co-opting idealistic notions such as empowerment and radicalism so that, rather than inferring activism or political change, they become traits that one can acquire by smoking the right cigarette or adorning oneself with the right brand of make-up or perfume.

Crucially, in the course of presenting the consumption of objects as the primary means to happiness and liberation, advertising masks the ways in which the production of such goods is premised on capitalist exploitation. Thus, in his analysis of the cultural construction of wine in France as a blissful substance, whose consumption symbolizes belonging to a great nation, Barthes (1972: 61) reminds us that such a myth masks the alienative relations of production on which the nation's consumption of wine is dependent.

Part of the ideological message of advertising, then, is the promotion of *commodity fetishism*: the symbolic separation of commodities from the social conditions in which they were produced. Naomi Klein's (2000) analysis of the global cultivation of brands highlights various instances of this, not least the huge investment by Nike in the construction of an image associated with individual human achievement and excellence. Klein argues that, while consumers in the West were persuaded to pay a premium for Nike products in order to buy into such symbolism, the exploitative conditions in developing-world factories in which many of them were produced were rendered invisible.

It is not just in adverts themselves that we might identify ideologies of consumerism, however. Partly because of their own interest in attracting advertisers but also as a result of the universalization of the consumer myth, magazines, news, television programmes, films, popular music and all manner of other media forms place emphasis on buying, buying and more buying. Makeover programmes, for example, present the transformation of individual appearances, homes or gardens through the purchase and combination of appropriate consumer goods. Narratives typically connect such transformations with the prospect of dramatic improvements in the happiness and fulfilment of the individuals featured. We aren't supposed to always agree with the particular approach taken by the 'experts', and argument over details is part of what makes such programmes enticing, but underlying all this is a reinforcement of the notion that we should all, at regular intervals, look to transform our individual lives and identities through consumption (Redden, 2007).

There are endless other examples, of course. The celebrity industry, which pervades a range of media texts, presents us with something of a consumerist fantasy or utopia, comprising hugely attractive, successful and wealthy individuals whose clothes, jewellery, make-up and cars are the subject of extensive column inches (Marshall, 1997). This fascination is frequently drawn on as a direct means of selling consumer products to consumers via the frequent emphasis on celebrities in advertising campaigns. Not all coverage of celebrities is positive, of course, and we're often invited to take enjoyment from wardrobe failures or questionable behaviour. Far from dampening enthusiasm for the consumerist myth, however, such individual 'failures' merely illustrate the importance, for both celebrities and the rest of us, of consuming effectively.

Political economy and ideology

While the approach of some ideology critics has been to expose the operation of dominant meanings in media content, others have placed greater emphasis on the commercial structures of media ownership and control. As we saw in Chapter 3, critical political economy seeks to carry out the kind of detailed analysis of the workings of the culture industry that the Frankfurt School theorists failed to provide. To a degree, the approach bypasses the Frankfurt School's variant of neo-Marxism and, indeed, those of Althusser and Gramsci, preferring the more materialist emphasis in Marx's own work. Proponents are critical of what they regard as culturalist approaches to Marxism that, from their point of view, overestimate the autonomy of the sphere of culture and ideas and too frequently study media content in isolation from the economic and material relations in which it is produced (Golding and Murdock, 1991). In contrast, critical political economists concentrate on the economic dominance of the wealthy and powerful and the way this translates into ownership, influence and control over the dissemination of ideas (Murdock and Golding, 1995). They replace the culturalist emphasis on meaning as a site of intellectual struggle, then, with a materialist stance that locates ideology as something centred on the context of media production and control.

Manufacturing consent

Alongside the writings of Graham Murdock and Peter Golding, the best-known example of this approach is perhaps Edward Herman and Noam Chomsky's book *Manufacturing Consent* (1998), in which it is argued that the extent of corporate control over communications leaves little possibility of any sustained critique of the prevailing capitalist order. Five institutional 'filters' in the set-up of the media system are identified, each of which serves to make counter-ideological forms of content less likely.

Filter one is the ownership and profit orientation of media and cultural institutions. Media are overwhelmingly controlled by a small number of highly powerful corporate institutions and, although these corporations often compete with one another, they also have common political interests because of their shared corporate status. Notably, they each stand to benefit from global capitalism itself and from government approaches that are conducive to profit maximization. They therefore are likely to oppose regulations that constrain their commercial operations and to dislike forms of content which raise doubts about the capitalist system or those who maintain it.

Filter two relates to the imperative to attract and retain advertisers, most of whom also constitute large-scale moneymaking corporations that share the interest of media companies in the promotion of deregulated global capitalism. Such advertisers are unlikely to be enthusiastic about content that is critical of the capitalist status quo or exposes problematic corporate activities, for example, something that provides media companies with a further incentive to filter out such content. More generally, advertisers are deemed to have a preference for light, entertaining and superficial forms of content because these are deemed most conducive to the positive reception of commercials by audiences.

Filter three concerns the extensive influence on media of a range of other wealthy and powerful groups. Including governments, mainstream political parties, high-profile pressure groups and large-scale corporate interests, such groups are able to use their wealth and power to manipulate flows of information to media. The organization of press conferences, the release of information, comment, images or footage and the cultivation of beneficial relationships with journalists enables such groups to wield disproportionate influence on media organizations only too pleased to be provided with regular sources of cheap content.

Filter four, 'flak', refers to the negative consequences that are liable to result from any substantial coverage by a media organization of counter-ideological messages. In the unlikely event that any such messages should manage to make it through filters one, two and three, then, the media organization(s) in question can expect to face a barrage of high-profile criticism and labelling, alongside the threat of legal challenges and the possible withdrawal of advertisers.

Linked closely to this is the fifth and final filter, which comprises a broader ideology of anti-communism that is deemed to dominate US society. An atmosphere that associates critical content with the US' cold war enemies, Herman and Chomsky argue, serves as a further barrier to the media exposure of such content. More recently, the operation of flak in the United States has taken the form of a broader rhetoric around the notion of 'anti-Americanism' – something levelled regularly against opponents of the Bush administration in the early 2000s. In 2003, the BBC found itself subject to such accusations, from Fox News presenters among others, regarding aspects of its coverage of the Iraq war.

The cumulative effect of the five filters operating together, according to Herman and Chomsky, is to ensure that media are thoroughly dominated by ideological forms of culture that serve the interests of the status quo.

Cultural imperialism as globalization of ideology

Approaches associated with critical political economy have been particularly evident in the development of Marxist approaches to the increasing globalization of media and culture. In contrast to Marshall McLuhan's optimistic discussion of a technologically driven *global village* that would foster mutual understanding between previously unconnected cultures (see Chapter 2), *cultural imperialism* theories focus on the globalization of culture as a highly unequal process dominated by powerful capitalist interests based in wealthy countries. The drive to minimize costs and maximize profits is deemed to have prompted media and culture industries, with the help of global communications technologies, to operate in a thoroughly international manner.

Operating globally enables large, integrated corporations to maximize the *supply* of materials and labour available to them and thereby minimize costs by sourcing the cheapest. Why produce branded clothing in the USA when you can contract a company in Haiti to do it for you with far cheaper labour (Klein, 2000)? Even more importantly, from the point of view of cultural imperialism theorists, companies maximize *demand* for their products and services by attempting to sell their cultural goods to consumers all around the world. Such is the importance of maximum exploitation of global markets to the success and growth of companies that most media products – from television series to popular music – are now produced with global appeal in mind. This is deemed to have encouraged an emphasis on simplicity and standardization so that locally specific complexities are minimized.

Cultural imperialism theories contend that the globalization of media and culture involves the systematic exploitation and cultural domination of small countries by powerful transnational companies based in wealthy parts of the world (Boyd-Barrett, 1977; Schiller, 1976; 1992). Standardized forms of international media culture are distributed by transnational companies to as many countries as possible. Unable to compete with the wealth, influence and market dominance of the transnationals, domestic media in smaller countries are forced to rely on cheap, imported products rather than developing a distinctive home-produced cultural sphere.

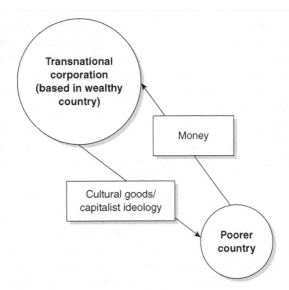

FIGURE 6.2   Cultural imperialism (adapted from Malm and Wallis, 1993)

Reliance on such imported products also means that, rather than being invested in local economies, money is transferred out of such countries and into the coffers of the transnationals. We might add that cultural resources sometimes are also appropriated from smaller countries by transnationals, as in the exploitation of musical influences or talent by the international recording industry.

Cultural imperialism theorists liken this situation to the exploitation and cultural indoctrination of indigenous populations by Western colonial powers in the nineteenth and early twentieth century. The difference is that, instead of being imposed by military rule, cultural domination is attributable to overwhelming financial muscle and the use of communication technologies. Either way, the result, it is argued, is likely to be the swamping of indigenous cultures by an increasingly monolithic global mass culture originating in powerful countries. What the Frankfurt School referred to as the culture industry, then, is deemed to have gone global. For Richard Peet, previous global diversities are fast disappearing as an entertainment-orientated mass culture originating in the West comes to dominate ways of life around the world:

> The tendency is towards the production of one world mind, one world culture and the consequent disappearance of regional consciousness flowing from the local specificities of the human past ... the new gods of entertainment are worshipped around the globe in one big fan-club (1989: 195–6).

While part of the criticism is of the process of homogenization and the erosion of distinctive local cultures per se, cultural imperialism theories, in keeping with their Marxist roots, also focus specifically on the role of global mass culture as a form of Western, capitalist ideology. Thus, for Peet, the export of mass culture is intrinsically linked to the global spread of capitalism itself as a material and social system: 'mass production and consumption have meant standardized, programmed ways of thinking with little room for regional variation ... global capitalism evolves as a single way of life gradually incorporating ... the majority of the world's population' (1989: 193).

While cultural imperialism theories are usually centred on a macro political economic analysis, support has also come from theorists using textual analysis to identify what are deemed to be Western capitalist ideological messages within widely exported media texts. In the 1970s, Ariel Dorfman and Armand Mattelart (1971) carried out an analysis of Disney comics, which, at the time, had been sold in some 47 different countries and translated into 21 different languages. Dorfman and Mattelart's analysis suggested that the narratives in the comics, featuring characters such as Donald Duck, were riddled with dominant meanings and served to normalize capitalist social relations and the American way of life. Characters, for example, are deemed to have exhibited a constant obsession with making money, becoming rich and indulging in compulsive consumerism. Narratives also demonstrate regular engagement in ruthless competition in order to achieve such goals. There are even references, it is argued, to imperialism itself, in the form of stories in which the characters compete to exploit resources such as oil and gold in exotic and far away lands. Dorfman and Mattelart conclude that the global circulation of products such as Disney comics is a vehicle for the spreading of ideologies that make capitalism and consumerism seem natural and inevitable.

Arguments and criticisms

Political economic versus cultural approaches

As we have seen in the cultural imperialism case above, sometimes textual analysis and political economic approaches to media are used in support of one another in the development of arguments about the role and impact of ideological communications. Nevertheless, there continues to exist something of a schism between the two approaches, each of which tends to be connected to different interpretations of Marxism. Ideology critique via textual analysis is often associated with a culturalist or cultural studies approach, influenced by the emphasis on the relative autonomy of the cultural sphere in the work of theorists such as Althusser, Gramsci and Hall, while critical political economy takes a materialist approach closer to that in much of Marx's own work.

Political economists have often criticized the likes of Barthes, Hall and others for focusing all their attentions on the detail of the ways in which dominant meanings are conveyed via media texts without providing any substantive understanding of the material structures of media ownership and control (Garnham, 1995). This, it is argued, relates to an overestimation of the autonomy of the sphere of ideas and culture from forces of material determination. For political economists such as Nicolas Garnham, the cultural sphere is subject to 'ultimate determination by the economic' (1995: 219), something which means that it is the operation of the structures of ownership and control which provides the most fruitful site for analysis.

For their part, those associated with the culturalist approach criticize what they regard as the deterministic stance of the political economists who, from their point of view, too often draw simplistic conclusions about the content and ideological impact of media on the basis of a macro analysis of structures of control. Herman and Chomsky, for example, assume that oppositional messages inevitably are filtered out of media by the systems and structures they describe, but provide little detailed analysis of media content to demonstrate the operation of such ideological bias in practice.

Likewise, despite exceptions such as Dorfman and Mattelart, theories of cultural imperialism tend to draw bold conclusions about the swamping of local cultures by standardized, ideological mass cultural products from the West, largely on the basis of a macro analysis of the functioning of the media industry and global capitalism (Tomlinson, 1991). In contrast, *culturalist perspectives* suggest that, even if communications are materially dominated by powerful, globalized capitalist interests, the dominant ideas that this is liable to give rise to will always be accompanied by the potential for marginal forms of culture to emerge. From this point of view, even if hegemonic meanings tend to predominate, academic analysis and intervention should be focused, in detail, on the ways in which struggles over meaning are played out.

Complex communication flows and consumer resistance

While the notion of the cultural sphere as relatively autonomous and a site of struggle initially was deployed as part of the project dominated by exposing the workings of ideology or hegemony within media texts, culturalist perspectives have in recent times become associated with greater doubts about the value of Marxist approaches to ideology. Such doubts relate to both the diversity and multidirectional flow of meanings within modern culture and to the capacity of media audiences and users to develop active and subversive uses for media.

For many, the sheer range of ideas circulating in the contemporary cultural sphere renders an exclusive emphasis on mind-numbing mass culture or dominant meanings, overly simplistic. Just as the Frankfurt School theorists overgeneralize their critique of the culture industry, so theorists like Hall are sometimes criticized for their implication that, despite the occasional presence of counter-discourses, ideological or hegemonic meanings pervade the vast majority of media content. Likewise, in focusing on the global circulation of a monolithic mass culture, theories of cultural imperialism arguably underestimate the range and complexity of cultural products that are transferred around the globe (Tomlinson, 1991). For every *Dallas*, *Star Wars* or Michael Jackson, there are numerous smaller-scale, more narrowly targeted global products, from marginal music genres to independent film. *Cultural imperialism theory* is also ill-equipped to account for the resilience to global imports of strong local media industries in countries such as Mexico, Brazil and India, less still the increasing role of such countries as media exporters who create counter-flows of culture to populations based in North America and Western Europe (Hesmondhalgh, 2002).

Emphasis on the diversity and multidirectionality of flows of culture has become particularly influential in light of recent shifts towards a digital media climate, with increasing numbers of channels and messages, as well as greater possibilities for ordinary media users to distribute their own content. As we shall see in Chapter 9, however, we should be cautious of assuming that an increase in the number of different messages, channels and 'senders' automatically renders the world of communications democratic and Marxist understandings of power and ideology irrelevant. First, powerful media organizations continue to control a substantial proportion of the culture we consume. Second, an increase in the quantity of content does not automatically equate to an increase in the circulation of counter-hegemonic culture or ideas. The Frankfurt School's notion of pseudo-individualization may still be of some use in reminding us of this.

Perhaps the biggest and most sustained challenge to Marxist theories of ideology, however, has come from an emphasis on the capacity of audiences to actively produce their own meanings and uses from media content. The implication of such arguments is that, even if media are dominated by large-scale profitmaking interests and/or standardized or ideological content, we ought not to assume that audiences necessarily will be manipulated or homogenized.

In response to criticism of the global ideological impact of US soap *Dallas*, research by Elihu Katz and Tamar Liebes (1985), illustrated that, rather than having their culture and ideas swamped by US ideology, audiences in different countries each drew on different sets of local understandings to from their responses to the programme. A plethora of other audience studies and theories (such as Fiske, 1991a; Willis, 1990) have raised equally strong questions about the implicit assumption in many Marxist approaches that audiences are passive victims of media manipulation (see Chapter 5).

Conclusion: avoiding easy dismissals

The arguments against Marxist notions of media, power and ideology are enticing, persuasive and often difficult to disagree with. It is heartening to think of members of society – ourselves included – as active, critical users, drawing creatively from a vast range of content and even producing some of our own. In contrast, it is profoundly uncomfortable to take the opposite approach and suggest that ordinary people are manipulated, ignorant or suffering from false consciousness. Such an approach is often labelled as patronizing and elitist – sometimes justifiably so. Yet, there is a danger that the desire to avoid being regarded as patronizing, together with the convenience of legitimating our own popular cultural tastes, might lead us towards a complacent celebration of a status quo in which media around the world are, whichever way one looks at it, thoroughly dominated by powerful corporate interests.

Marxist approaches may be open to criticism, then, but we would be well advised not to dismiss their critical approach to questions of media, power and control altogether.

QUESTIONS AND EXERCISES

1 a) To what extent can Adorno and Horkheimer's criticisms of popular cultural products be applied to contemporary media? Are there any examples of contemporary music, film or television that you would argue are *not* standardized and could *not* be construed as pseudo-individualization?

   b) In what ways might Marcuse's notion of 'false needs' be applied to the example of contemporary advertising?

(Continued)

(Continued)

2 a) In what ways do Althusser and Gramsci move away from Marx's deterministic approach to the relationship between material relations and dominant ideas?

  b) Why is this important to the development of a tradition focused on identifying and critiquing ideological meanings in media content?

3 Select an example of a media text (such as a magazine, a website, a television programme, an advert or a film) and try to subject its structure and content to ideology critique. In what ways might it reinforce dominant understandings of the world?

4 Should we regard the transnational circulation of media and consumer goods as cultural imperialism? List the strengths and weaknesses of such an interpretation.

5 a) What is the difference between culturalist and political economic versions of Marxism when it comes to questions of media and ideology?

  b) Are Marxist approaches to media rendered entirely redundant by assertions that audiences are active?

Suggested further reading

Adorno, T. (1990; 1941) 'On popular music', in S. Frith and A. Goodwin (eds), *On Record: Rock, pop and the written word*. London: Routledge.
Famous critique of the standardized structure of popular jazz music, deemed to induce passivity and conformity in listeners.

Hall, S. (1982) 'The rediscovery of "ideology": return of the repressed in media studies', in M. Gurevitch, T. Bennett, J. Curran and J. Woollacott (eds), *Culture, Society and the Media*. London: Routledge.
Criticizes pluralist approaches to media and sets out a critical cultural studies approach to the question of ideology.

Herman, E. and Chomsky, N. (1998; 1988) *Manufacturing Consent: The political economy of the mass media*. London: Vintage.
Political–economic analysis of the filtering of media content by structures of ownership and control.

Kellner, D. (1995) 'Advertising and consumer culture', in J. Downing, A. Mohammadi and A. Sreberny-Mohammadi (eds), *Questioning the Media: A critical introduction* (2nd edn). London: Sage.
Critical analysis of the ideological implications of advertising content.

Tomlinson, J. (1991) *Cultural Imperialism: A critical introduction*. London: Pinter.
Offers a strongly critical account of theories of cultural imperialism as an approach to the globalization of media.

7

The Construction of News

Focal points

- News as manufactured representations of the world.
- News values as criteria for the selection and construction of stories.
- Deconstruction and analysis of news stories.
- Questions of bias and news as ideology.
- Infotainment and criticism of the 'dumbing down' of news.

Introduction

Most people would probably agree that, sometimes, the news falls short of presenting a balanced and truthful reflection of the world. Accusations of bias or lack of balance in coverage sometimes come from academics, but they just as frequently are expressed by members of the public, politicians, interest groups and, indeed, journalists themselves. In the years following the September 11th 2001 World Trade Center attacks, for example, Fox News was subject to frequent criticism that its hawkish coverage failed to live up to the channel's own claim to be 'fair and balanced'. Meanwhile, during the same period, the BBC, whose charter specifically requires impartial in coverage of current affairs – found that its coverage was subject to accusations from some observers of bias against the foreign policies pursued by the UK and US governments. Newspapers are also a regular target for accusations of unbalanced coverage, with 'red-top' UK tabloids such as *The Sun* and *The Daily Mirror* often singled out for criticism.

The annoyance of viewers about what they perceive to be biased news coverage often reflects a belief that such examples constitute a betrayal of what news can and should be. Outlets or reports deemed to be biased are contrasted with ideals of news as a form of media that should perform an invaluable public service by providing us with neutral information and truthful facts about the world. Consistent with notions of media as a mirror on society, this view suggests that news can, should and sometimes does offer us an undistorted reflection of the world.

Such a view of what news should be also informs the way in which it is regulated in some countries. While UK newspapers are allowed to be overtly biased if they wish to be, television broadcasters are subject to a statutory public interest requirement to 'ensure that news, in whatever form, is reported with due accuracy and presented with due impartiality' (Ofcom, 2009). The qualifier 'due' here recognizes the impossibility of covering 'every argument and every facet of every argument', but, never-theless, the aspiration to have essentially unbiased news is clear.

It will become apparent in this chapter, however, that, no matter how well intentioned it is, news can *never* constitute a neutral, unbiased or impartial mirror on the world. Although it is based on real events and controversies, the content of newspapers and bulletins – like that of all media texts – is manufactured and constructed in particular ways, accord-ing to particular viewpoints, cultural values and institutional priorities. What we read, view or listen to is not a neutral account of the world, but one or more particular versions, or, *representations*. It may be that some of these versions are more detailed, better substantiated and more accom-modating of different viewpoints than others – and we may wish to sup-port and encourage these – but none are unbiased. The content of news, therefore, tells us as much about the practices, values and priorities of those who produce and consume it as it does about the world it purports to represent.

When considering the ways in which news is manufactured, it is valuable to envisage a filtering process to illustrate how the plethora of events and issues that take place on a given day are streamlined into an eventual bul-letin, newspaper or website agenda (see Figure 7.1). The processes involved are complex, but, in order to simplify them, we can distinguish between

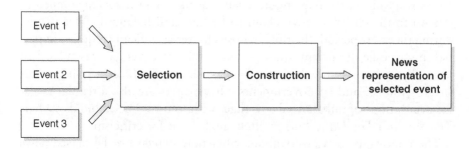

FIGURE 7.1   News filtering

two sequential stages – the *selection* of events and issues on which to base news stories and the subsequent *construction* of such stories.

Selection, gatekeeping and agenda setting

Discussions about bias often focus on the ways in which particular stories are presented by news providers. Before any decisions about the construction of a given story are made, however, journalists and others must select which events to cover and which to exclude – a process largely invisible to the public and one that has substantial implications for the version of the world presented to us. By making such decisions, news organizations act as *gatekeepers*, with the capacity to affect what we know, care and talk about and what passes under our collective radar.

This apparent power to shape public awareness and priorities is known as *agenda setting* – a term associated with research by Maxwell McCombs and Donald Shaw (1972), who identified a correlation between the amount of coverage devoted to an issue in the media and the level of importance attributed to it by the public. Such findings appear to provide empirical evidence for the plausible assumption that news gatekeeping has a strong influence on what people know about and what they think is important, although it should be noted that the direction of causality is ambiguous as news providers may claim that the stories they include reflect *existing* public priorities rather than shaping them.

So what are the factors that influence whether or not an event will be included in the news? My writing of this paragraph is an event, as is your reading it. Yet, except in the most exceptional of circumstances, none of us would expect these things or any of the other little events in our daily lives to be reported by journalists. But what is it about such events that makes them unsuitable for the news compared with the kinds of stories that are regularly included?

Detailed consideration of the criteria used by journalists and editors in evaluating newsworthiness provides greater understanding of the priorities of news media and the versions of the world they place before us. As well as excluding a host of undeniably trivial events, these criteria – known as *news values* – also result in selections and exclusions that are more controversial.

News values

There are differences of priority and emphasis between news providers in terms of the precise blend of stories they cover on a given day. Yet, analysis has suggested that they also share a number of core criteria, or news values, which determine story selection.

The best-known attempt to outline these shared news values is provided by Johan Galtung and Mari Ruge (1973), who identify eight criteria that they present as universal and a further four that are deemed more specific to developed, capitalist countries. The criteria are intended to be cumulative rather than independent of one another – that is, the more of them that apply and the greater the extent to which they apply, the more likely an event is to be covered. Let's look at each of the criteria in turn.

Frequency

For an event to make the news, argue Galtung and Ruge, its timespan should be compatible with the frequency with which news is published or broadcast. Criminal or violent incidents tend to be ideal because they play themselves out in the short timespan between one edition of a newspaper or bulletin and the next. In contrast, gradual improvements in a country's education system are unlikely to make the news, unless highlighted by a discrete event, such as the release of a report or a high-profile school visit by a member of the government. Similarly, the slow process of repairing a war-torn country is liable to receive less coverage than the bombing that damaged it. The rebuilding of Lebanon in the 1990s and early 2000s, for example, was ignored by Western media until the project was set back by the discrete, short-term event of Israel bombing the country in 2006.

Some commentators have connected the notion of frequency with an increasingly prominent specific role for *immediacy* or *recency*, which refers to the particular emphasis placed by websites and television news on breaking brand new stories as quickly as possible, to the extent that the most recent stories sometimes are prioritized even if they aren't particularly strong with respect to other news values (Bell, 1991).

Amplitude

Amplitude refers to a threshold of noticeability. In order to be deemed newsworthy, a fire, for example, must be of a sufficient size or a crime of a particular level of seriousness. The more extreme or dramatic an event is within its category, the more likely it is to receive prominent coverage. In the age of television news, many have argued that the role of spectacle and drama in the selection of news stories is becoming ever more important (Baker and Dessart, 1998). A story is particularly likely to be covered if the drama is captured directly through sound, image or film. A dramatic police car chase, may be covered if caught on video, but not if the news provider would have to rely on a verbal description alone.

Clarity

The more clear or one-dimensional an event is, in terms of the ways it can be interpreted, the more appealing it is likely to be for news providers. Events make good news copy, it is argued, when ambiguities with respect to their cause, meaning or significance are at a minimum. Stories that involve the clear attribution of right and wrong and obvious victims and villains fit well within this category. Acts of criminal violence, for example, can easily be centred on clear individual perpetrator(s), who can be blamed, and individual victim(s), with whom audiences can empathize. In contrast, arguments about political policy tend to be complex, messy and uncertain.

Cultural proximity

News providers tend to favour stories that involve practices, places or people familiar or relevant to the audience. News is ethnocentric, argue Galtung and Ruge, in that it is biased towards that which is closest to us. Thus, in UK news, disasters in the UK itself or in countries regarded as culturally close to the UK tend to receive greater levels of coverage than similar events in other parts of the world. Nevertheless, events in culturally and geographically distant places may still sometimes be newsworthy if they have some other form of relevance. A disaster in Africa may receive more coverage in the UK if British citizens were among the casualties, while a change in the Iranian government might receive US news coverage as a result of ongoing diplomatic tensions between Iran and the USA.

Predictability

Newsworthy stories often tend to fit with our expectations and cohere with the way in which we believe the world to work. Predictability is related to clarity as the more a story can be presented in a way that fits in with our expectations, the less the potential for ambiguities. Sometimes this may relate to specific anticipated events. Media speculation about the possibility of violence at big football tournaments or protest marches often leads to the prioritization of coverage of any actual violence, even if it is minor. The expectation generated by the speculation renders the story newsworthy all by itself (Hartley, 1982). In other cases, stories are rendered newsworthy because they confirm broader social expectations or *stereotypes*. News stories about young people causing a nuisance, for example, activate stereotypical expectations about youth delinquency.

Unexpectedness

In emphasizing cultural proximity and predictability, Galtung and Ruge do not mean to imply that news prioritizes everyday mundanities. Rather, these criteria operate in tandem with a tendency to emphasize events that are in some way extraordinary or unusual. A story about the disappearance of an infant within the country of a news provider may be liable to fit with various sets of established expectations (about the danger of paedophiles, for example), as well as to satisfy the criteria of cultural familiarity (it happened to a family near us or like us), at the same time as attaining its newsworthiness primarily because of the rarity of such an event.

The unexpectedness news value is of great importance and, more than anything, explains why all the details of each of our everyday lives are unlikely to become news – they are simply too unremarkable.

Continuity

Once a story has entered the news agenda, it may gain sufficient public interest to give it the momentum to *continue* to be newsworthy in the future. Individual stories can become like soap operas, in the sense that people become keen to find out what happens next. This can prompt news providers to allocate significant space to ongoing stories, even if there have been no significant developments.

An excellent example of this news value was provided in 2007, when the disappearance of Madeleine McCann dominated the headlines of television and print news in the UK and elsewhere for several months, despite a paucity of developments in the case. In the absence of the latter, newspapers were sold and viewers enticed by coverage based on the behaviour and public statements of McCann's parents and a mixture of speculation and hearsay. The interest generated by the initial coverage made it imperative for outlets to continue to find something to say about the story.

Variations on this news value have been emphasized by other commentators. Paul Rock (1973) emphasizes the way in which, once a story has been ratified as news by being preserved by one provider, it will often be picked up by others, reflecting the professional influence of journalists on one another and the desire not to miss out on a story that has momentum. Today, television and Internet news providers often are influenced by which stories their rivals are covering, but their agendas also pick up stories from the mornings' newspaper front pages.

Meanwhile, Allan Bell (1991) argues that the desire to continue to feed the public appetite for existing stories sometimes prompts the co-opting of smaller stories onto the agenda purely because they relate in some way to the bigger story.

Composition

Galtung and Ruge's final universal news value emphasizes the need for bulletins or newspapers to fit together as a whole. Providers may seek to complement stories with others that connect to the same theme or, conversely, to achieve a balance of types of story within each edition, which may mean including some domestic stories on a heavy foreign news day, for example, or slotting in something light and trivial after a big political story.

Galtung and Ruge go on to outline four further criteria that are especially significant in developed capitalist countries. The implication is that state-controlled media in communist countries might have different priorities, as might media in less developed nations. The authors are speculative about such differences, however, and, given the subsequent collapse of communist regimes around the world and the broader globalization of media, the extent to which these additional values are indeed unique to Western countries is unclear.

Elite nations

Quite simply, events that relate to the most powerful nations in the world are of greater consequence and therefore more likely to be covered than those taking place in poorer, less influential places.

Elite people

Similarly, stories about powerful or famous people are more newsworthy, on the whole, than those about poor or unknown people because the actions of the former are liable to be of greater consequence and interest than those of everybody else. Celebrity stories are particularly valuable because they encapsulate extraordinary levels of wealth, power and influence at the same time as having proximity and relevance to the lives of ordinary people (from relationships to babies to weight loss, for example), engendering identification and empathy.

Personification

A further key criterion for news selection within capitalist developed countries, for Galtung and Ruge, is the extent to which a story can be represented by focusing on the intentions, actions or emotions of individuals. Rather than emphasizing the determination of individual lives by structural forces such as the distribution of wealth, news tends to present us with a world dominated by individual morals, decisions and behaviour. Stories that can easily be presented by focusing on individuals, therefore, are more liable to be selected than those which cannot. Individual actions fit in with the criterion of frequency, can easily be represented using photographs or film and can engender identification and emotional responses in a way that discussion about the broader structures of society cannot.

Of particular importance to the contemporary news age, this emphasis on personification explains the increasing emphasis on so-called *human interest* stories, including those about crime, celebrities and disasters. Personification even plays a significant role in the selection of political stories, with increasing emphasis being placed on those relating to the character and lifestyle of politicians rather than policy arguments.

Negativity

Finally, Galtung and Ruge argue that negative news stories are liable to dominate the news agenda because they tend to fit better with other news values than positive stories. Negative stories often concern discrete short-term events, they are easier to present in an unambiguous manner and tend to involve rare or unexpected phenomena. In July 2008, the publication of the UK's annual crime figures demonstrated a significant fall in violent crime. On the same day, a teenager was stabbed in London. Not surprisingly, perhaps, headlines were dominated by the latter, which, as well as being a negative rather than a positive crime story, also fitted better with established expectations, offered greater potential for personalization and formed an immediate, self-contained story with easily discernable villains and victims.

Case study: September 11th 2001

One of the biggest news stories around the world in recent decades was that of the terrorist attacks on New York and Washington on September 11th 2001.

The newsworthiness of the story may seem obvious, but it nevertheless serves as a valuable case study with which to illustrate the operation of news values. A clear set of events unfolded in a manner compatible with the frequency of publication of newspapers and with the desire for immediacy that characterizes television and online news coverage. The amplitude and unexpectedness of the events were enormous, as was their potential for negativity – the tallest buildings in the world were destroyed, the most powerful country in the world was being attacked, the explosions, fires and falling buildings were as dramatic and spectacular as one could imagine, the human costs were extensive. The event could easily be presented in simple, unambiguous terms and it also had a clear personal angle, in terms of the presentation of violent, destructive attackers and helpless, distraught victims. The event involved an elite nation, a variety of elite people and offered cultural proximity for some nations and relevance for others. September 11th as a story also involved elements of predictability, cohering with some Western stereotypes of extremist Arabs or Muslims, for example. And it had extensive continuity – the slightest new developments or speculation dominating the news agenda for days, weeks and months afterwards.

Perhaps the only factor that it failed to satisfy is composition, as the story was so big that its relationship to other stories was of little consequence. It became what Tamar Liebes (1998) terms a 'disaster marathon', in that real-time news providers devoted 100 per cent of their time to a single unfolding story.

Constructing stories

According to Bell, journalists are 'the professional storytellers of our age' (1991: 147). Having selected particular events on the basis of their story potential, they make a series of decisions about how to turn them into a good story, arranging headline, commentary text, images, illustrations and/ or film and/or audio footage accordingly. Each element connects to the broader *angle* on the story the news provider is seeking to achieve.

As well as determining what will make a good story in the first place, news values influence the particular version of events that is constructed. An event selected on the basis of its potential as a human interest story will be represented with a particular emphasis on that angle. Conversely, a story that does not fit well with some news values may be constructed in a manner which compensates for this. Bell (1991) demonstrates that coverage of global warming in New Zealand activated the values of clarity and cultural proximity by exaggerating the certainty of negative scientific predictions and linking the abstract notion of global warming to recent local weather or impacts on local cities, for example.

Approaches such as semiology and discourse analysis (see Chapter 4) offer valuable ways to better understand the ways in which different elements of news stories work together to create a particular angle or impression. Headlines, images, footage, music and commentary all can be viewed as sets of signifiers that invoke particular connotations and those elements involving written or spoken language can be analysed in terms of their vocabulary, syntax, grammar and other features. It can be particularly helpful to think about news content as sets of paradigmatic selections and syntagmatic combinations (Hartley, 1982).

Focused on comparing each element of a news report with alternatives that might have been used, paradigmatic analysis reminds us that, for every headline, caption, photo or interview quote included, numerous others were considered and rejected. Let's take the example of images. One of the best-known media clichés is that the camera never lies, yet photography captures selective images of events from particular points of view and, after the photos have been taken, editors choose one or two images to illustrate their version of the story from an extensive range on offer to them.

Paradigmatic analysis can help us to understand such decisions and the impacts they have on how readers are encouraged to interpret the story. If a murder story were to include a large black and white close-up of the scowling face of the perpetrator, we might ask why a close-up rather than a medium or distance shot, why a scowling face rather than a smiling one, why black and white rather than colour and why a photo of the perpetrator rather than, for example, the police officer who headed up the investigation?

The use of language in news stories is equally important. Headlines identify the news provider's main angle and can colour how we interpret the content which follows. They can also be analysed using a paradigmatic approach to discourse analysis focused on the selection of words. If presented with the headline 'Surgical strikes limit collateral damage' in the context of a war story, we can better understand the likely connotations by comparing the words present with possible alternatives that are absent. Why not 'bombs' instead of 'surgical strikes' for example, and why not 'civilian deaths' instead of 'collateral damage'?

Syntagmatic analysis, meanwhile, involves an assessment of the semantic impact of the ways in which components of a story have been arranged and combined. Therefore, we need to examine each of the words in our headline separately and then consider how they work together (see Figure 8.2).

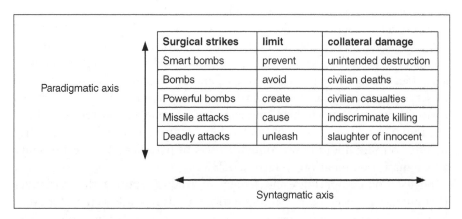

Surgical strikes	limit	collateral damage
Smart bombs	prevent	unintended destruction
Bombs	avoid	civilian deaths
Powerful bombs	create	civilian casualties
Missile attacks	cause	indiscriminate killing
Deadly attacks	unleash	slaughter of innocent

Paradigmatic axis

Syntagmatic axis

FIGURE 7.2   Simplified illustration of syntagmatic and paradigmatic news analysis

With respect to our example, terms such as 'surgical strike' and 'collateral damage' are frequently used by military spokespeople to create an impression of clean, skilful, systematic, high-tech and precise warfare in the hope of avoiding media emphasis on messy, bloody consequences for innocent civilians. In the context of this headline, the two terms connected by 'limit' syntagmatically reinforce one another, generating an impression of warfare as clean, highly skilled, civilized and without undesirable consequences. It is being suggested to audiences that the blood and pain of civilians will be spared without the need even to mention the notions of blood or pain.

This example headline is a hypothetical and simplified one, but there is little doubt that, during the Gulf Wars of 1990 and 2003, US and UK authorities actively sought to promote and encourage the use and normalization of such terminology in media as a means of maintaining public support (Allen and Zelizer, 2004).

On a broader scale, syntagmatic analysis emphasizes the ways in which meaning can be influenced by the context into which individual components are placed. A piece of video footage may be open to a range of interpretations if viewed alone, but simultaneous audio commentary or onscreen text may significantly reduce such ambiguity. The presence of onscreen captions such as 'Striking back' and 'War on terror' that accompanied footage of US military action in Afghanistan in 2001 helped to frame such pictures as a depicting a just response to terrorist provocation, rather than, for example, an aggressive attack on a sovereign nation. Similarly, the potentially ambiguous connotations of a still image on a newspaper's front page may be *anchored* by the caption underneath it, the main headline above it or other images. If a black-and-white close-up of a perpetrator of violent crime is juxtaposed with a colour picture of the victim with her family, then the combination may help to generate a powerful narrative involving an innocent fun-loving, family-orientated victim slain by a ruthless, heartless villain – something likely to be further reinforced by the captions, headline and main commentary.

Because news representations of events revolve around storytelling, narrative analysis (see Chapter 4) can also be valuable in making sense of them. News stories often approximate elements of the character and structure of fictional stories. When reporting crime stories, media often strive to construct a particularly idyllic representation of the victim, whose normal, happy family life is cruelly disrupted or ended by a perpetrator represented as cruel and villainous to the bone.

Such a depiction activates news values of clarity and predictability by drawing on deeply embedded conventions of fiction running through countless fairy tales, children's cartoons and movies. The ability to replicate elements of familiar fictional plots is part of what makes stories attractive to media as well as an influence on the version of such stories we are presented with. In addition to the victim and the villain, the hero is another favoured character, part of what makes rescue stories – especially if they involve women, children or cute animals – particularly newsworthy.

Differences between news providers

A possible criticism of Galtung and Ruge's approach to news values is that, by focusing on *shared* news values, it glosses over some potentially significant *differences* between one provider and another that can affect both the selection and construction of stories.

Medium

News on outlets that allow greater frequency of update tend to be dominated by recency and immediacy as news values. Covering breaking stories faster than one's competitors and being as up to date as possible is an increasing priority for news radio stations, websites and television news channels. In the case of the latter, the synchronous (real-time) nature of the medium also prompts an emphasis on concise, fast-moving coverage with an urgent feel. In contrast, daily newspapers tend to provide a more structured, tightly prepared, reflective and detailed presentation of news. Although the generation of exclusive stories remains an important means of securing circulation, up to the minute immediacy is clearly not possible. As a result of being asynchronous (not in real time), newspapers can cover a considerably larger overall number of stories than television or radio news and many have responded to declining circulation figures by increasing their overall size through the development of new sections and supplements (Franklin, 1997).

News coverage on outlets which allow visual communication, meanwhile, tends to place particular emphasis on this. The move to colour printing affected the agenda and presentation of newspapers in this respect, while the prioritization of both still images and video clips increasingly dominates news websites. Television news has been most overtly affected, however, with the availability of enticing footage of dramatic or emotional events often resulting in prioritization of a story. Even apparently non-visual events are illustrated by footage of related activities or animated graphic sequences. A story about inflation, for example, might be accompanied by archived pictures of people shopping or an animated sequence featuring images of consumer items expanding in cost.

Style and market position

Even news providers which use the same medium differ in terms of their style and approach. In the UK, for example, distinctions are often drawn between populist 'red-top' newspapers, such as *The Sun* and *The Daily Mirror*, and highbrow or 'quality' publications, such as *The Daily Telegraph*. The former adopt an informal, overtly opinionated style, place strong emphasis on illustrations and are orientated towards personalized human interest stories, celebrity gossip, sport and the construction of sensation and emotion. Arguably this amounts to a particularly strict and intensive application of the news values outlined by Galtung and Ruge. In contrast, 'quality' newspapers have been able to apply such news values somewhat more loosely, placing emphasis on in-depth coverage of politics, financial and international stories and adopting a more formal and sophisticated tone.

The differences between these two categories are sometimes stark. On a single day in May 2009, for example, the front pages of the qualities, including *The Telegraph*, *The Guardian*, *The Times* and *The Independent*, all were dominated by a story about the possible resignation of the speaker of the House of Commons, while those of popular newspapers, such as *The Sun* and *The Star*, centred on the break-up of Peter Andre and Katie Price. In between 'popular' and 'quality' newspapers are 'middlebrow' titles, such as *The Daily Mail* and *The Daily Express*, which encapsulate elements of both approaches.

Such distinctions in style and approach connect strongly to the target audiences of the providers. In order to deliver consistent, clearly defined and loyal audiences to advertisers, providers each tend to be associated with particular status categories, to the extent that they even become badges of identity for their readers.

Broadly, the more populist news providers tend to be associated with audiences of a lower social class and, consistent with this, they often go out of their way to orientate their presentation, style and subject matter towards their particular construction of 'ordinary people' rather than social elites. Nevertheless, readers of popular formats are demographically much more diverse as well as being more numerous than those of highbrow providers, who tend to be dominated by narrower groups of highly educated professionals. James Curran and Jean Seaton (2003: 96) explain that this reflects long-standing differences in funding, with quality papers reliant on delivering narrow, high-spending, elite audiences to advertisers and the popular press more focused on 'catering for the lowest common denominator' in order to maximize direct revenue from sales and attract advertisers by means of the sheer quantity of their readers.

Political stance

With the exception of those operating under statutory requirements to be balanced (UK television news, for example), news providers often are associated with a particular political orientation and this, too, affects news values. A pro-Republican news provider in the USA may devote greater space and adopt a more critical tone for a story about a Democrat political scandal than a Republican one, for example.

Editorial positioning forms an additional element of the targeting of a loyal readership, but it can also be influenced by the views and interests of proprietors. Few would regularly adopt a position at odds with their readers, but as we saw in Chapter 3, a succession of media barons, from William Hearst to Rupert Murdoch, have used their newspapers as a means of promoting their own political agendas (Eldridge et al., 1997).

Similarities: back to bias and ideology?

Despite the importance of the differences outlined above, if we consider the vast range of conceivable versions of news on a given day, then, arguably, it is the *similarities* between news providers that remain more noteworthy. Compare several providers serving the same country or region and one is liable to notice extensive overlaps in terms of the events covered and the ways in which such stories are represented.

For this reason, the efforts of Galtung and Ruge and others retain considerable value in mapping out the shared priorities that underlie these similarities. The approach reminds us, not only that each provider of news is biased in itself but also that shared priorities can lead to a collective bias. Arguably, no matter what newspaper or television bulletin we consume, we are all liable to be confronted with a strikingly similar overall view of the world.

Galtung and Ruge's approach, however, does not go as far as that of Marxist thinkers, who argue not only that news collectively presents a selective version of the world but also that this representation is systematically orientated towards a bourgeois, pro-capitalist perspective. While they lament the 'distorted' view of the world created by news media, Galtung and Ruge interpret this as a complex set of biases attributable to a mixture of journalistic procedures and commercial priorities. For Hall (1973: 182), such identification of what he terms 'the formal elements in news making' is a useful step, but one that fails to identify the ways in which news values trigger, reinforce or 'index' the circulation of specific dominant or hegemonic ways of thinking about the world.

News values, from this viewpoint, are rooted in and inseparable from ideology; they emanate from, represent and so reinforce an existing consensus controlled to a significant extent by the powerful (see Chapter 6). We might argue, for example, that an emphasis on personalization in news is rooted in pro-Establishment ideas about individual choice, sovereignty and responsibility and that it serves to obscure the ways in which existing structures of inequality constrain and exploit individual lives. Likewise, it might be suggested that prevailing ideas and assumptions are liable to be strengthened by a tendency to prioritize cultural proximity and tap into what is predictable, as well as by a constant focus on spectacular negative events. Arguably, our engagement with extraordinary murders, explosions, crashes and disasters serves to reinforce the normality and desirability of the everyday status quo within our living rooms.

Class bias

In the 1970s and 1980s, the Glasgow University Media Group (GUMG) claimed to have demonstrated, by means of a series of content analysis studies, that UK news consistently favoured capitalist, middle-class messages, reinforcing the existing political order (1976a; 1976b; 1982).

Television coverage of a series of industrial disputes was accused of bias in favour of employers and against striking workers. Greater attention was deemed to have been afforded, for example, to the negative impacts of strikes on the economy or consumers than the poor pay and working conditions against which workers were protesting. Also, while striking workers were typically depicted in the context of the 'event' imagery of picket lines and protests, employers appeared as part of what were deemed 'factual' sequences, through footage of them wearing suits in offices or being interviewed in news studios.

Employers and government ministers, meanwhile, were deemed to have been given an easier time by interviewers than trade union representatives. For the GUMG, this represented just one example of the exclusion of working-class viewpoints by middle-class journalists who had little connection with or understanding of them (1982). Given this inevitable class bias, as the GUMG saw it, the BBC and ITN's aspirations to impartiality were regarded as an ideological mask – a means of parading subjective class ideology as objective reporting.

Having carried out his own analysis during the same period, however, Martin Harrison (1985) rejects the GUMG's accusations of class bias, arguing that such assertions were themselves biased by the group's pre-existing Marxist understandings of the world. The GUMG's content analysis is deemed to have been selective and its criticisms questionable. While they rejected the claims to impartiality of media providers as ideological, then, the GUMG were happy to claim objectivity for themselves, in privileging their own version of the industrial disputes.

Nick Stevenson (2002), meanwhile, criticises what he deems a confused position on the question of objectivity, whereby news was seemingly attacked by the GUMG for both its lack of objectivity and its quest for objectivity. Absolute neutrality may indeed be unattainable, argues Stevenson, but an aspiration to treat issues in a fair-minded, balanced way and be accountable for one's performance in this respect is surely preferable to the abandonment of any such goals.

A further problem identified by Stevenson (2002) with the GUMG's analysis is their emphasis on the personal middle-class background of journalists as the primary explanation for biased coverage. The logic of such an explanation is that it is impossible for journalists to understand or fairly describe an event or perspective unless their personal backgrounds are identical to that of those involved. This is an essentialist and defeatist premise that offers little in the way of a solution to issues of bias, whether they relate to class, ethnicity or anything else. According to Stevenson, the GUMG's emphasis on the background of journalists neglects the role of the institutional environment, working practices and priorities under which journalists operate.

If Galtung and Ruge underestimated the connection between news values and broader ideology, then the Glasgow Group's approach to ideology might have benefited from some attention to the kinds of operational factors that are at the heart of the operation of news values.

Institutional bias

Other theorists *have* attributed biased or ideological meanings to the ways in which media are owned, controlled and operated. Herman and Chomsky's analysis of the filtering of media by powerful owners, advertisers and interest groups, for example, focuses in particular on the implications for news and 'factual' content (see Chapter 6). According to this view, subordinate or oppositional voices are excluded not because of the class background of journalists, but because the news production system is controlled by, paid for and centred on vested interests.

Sure enough, news is overwhelmingly controlled by large-scale and increasingly concentrated corporate interests. In 2002, two thirds of UK national newspaper sales were controlled by just three corporations, while five companies were responsible for over 70 per cent of the country's regional or local newspaper circulation (Curran and Seaton, 2003).

In turn, news providers themselves are reliant for much of their content on a small number of news agencies or 'wire services' that make money by generating and providing news content to news providers. The majority of international news originates from four of these: Reuters, Associated Press, United Press International and Agence France Presse (Bell, 1991). Meanwhile, Bell (1991) estimates that a further chunk of news copy consists of rewrites of press releases issued by powerful interest or lobby groups, including companies, governments or other Establishment institutions.

The impact of reliance on advertising is also hard to dispute. It isn't only that '"don't bite the hand that feeds you" is written on every newsroom wall', as Bob Franklin (1997: 95) put it, but also that the system of advertising funding has a broader influence on what kinds of news are most profitable. In the newspaper market, for example, the rewards for attracting powerful, high-spending premium consumers arguably creates a bias towards bourgeois and Establishment-friendly versions of news.

According to Franklin (1997), the price advertisers are prepared to pay to reach each affluent reader of a quality specialist newspaper such as *The Financial Times* is 14 times more than the eyeballs of each *Sun* reader are worth. For Curran and Seaton (2003), this explains why an elite minority of consumers are targeted by half of the UK's newspapers, including all of the country's 'quality' publications. Serious, detailed coverage of politics in the press is therefore biased towards elite perspectives and interests, they argue, leaving the majority of the population stuck with the celebrity, sport and lifestyle news that dominates the popular press.

Importantly, the ideological influence of news organizations not only involves the possibility of directly influencing audiences. At times, the latter can be bypassed altogether, with news providers or their owners directly influencing politicians and governments. In the UK, the perceived power of *The Sun* to influence voting behaviour has prompted major party leaders to compete for the support of proprietor Rupert Murdoch. *The Sun*'s decision to abandon its support for the Conservative Party in favour of an endorsement of Tony Blair's Labour party in the 1997 election was preceded by overt courting of Murdoch by Blair, including a visit by Blair to Hayman Island to address Murdoch's annual gathering of executives and senior journalists. Blair spoke to Murdoch on various occasions during his time as Prime Minister, including three phone calls during the fortnight preceding the 2003 US-led invasion of Iraq – a war that all 175 of Murdoch's newspapers around the world endorsed enthusiastically (Greenslade, 2003). In 2009, *The Sun* switched its support back to David Cameron's Conservative Party, following a similar process of courtship to that which took place between News Corporation and Blair over a decade before.

Whether or not one fully subscribes to Marxist approaches to ideology, such a state of affairs surely renders it hard to fully dismiss the notion that news can service powerful interests.

Infotainment and depoliticization

For some commentators, concern revolves less around identification of explicit bias or ideology than the notion that news is becoming increasingly superficial. There has for some decades been concern about the light, entertainment-orientated approach of overtly populist outlets such as the UK's 'red-top' newspapers, but, more recently, concern has focused on the apparent drift of *all* news outlets towards such an agenda. In the UK newspaper sector, for example, 'quality' broadsheets have been accused of responding to declining circulation figures by placing greater and greater emphasis on sports coverage, entertainment news and a range of consumer and lifestyle issues (Barnett, 1998), with *The Times* and *The Independent* even shifting to tabloid (or 'compact' as they prefer) formats, prompting claims of a drastic shift downmarket (Temple, 2006).

It is the populist shift in the emphasis of television news that has generated greatest concern, however (Langer, 1998). The special status afforded by commercial providers in the USA to news as a public service and a subsidized flagship of brand prestige was diluted by the intensification of competition brought about by multichannel television in the 1990s. Increased pressure for news to be profitable in its own right by maximizing viewer appeal prompted a transformation towards so-called *infotainment*. Informing audiences about world events in a thorough, trustworthy, fair-minded manner was no longer sufficient – they also needed to be entertained. With respect to the selection of stories, the emphasis shifted towards those serious stories with the greatest immediate visual, emotional and human interest potential, alongside an increasing proportion of lighter content, such as sport and entertainment. Such priorities, according to Neil Postman and Steve Powers (1992) are geared towards retaining viewer interest:

> the producer of the programme is trying to grab you before you zap away to another news show. Therefore, chances are you'll hear a story such as … royal family happenings, or news of Michael Jackson on tour … And if glitter and glamour won't do the job, gore will (cited in Langer, 1998: 4).

If you think this is an exaggeration, then consider the following comment from a senior UK news executive interviewed by Bob Franklin:

> I know on a minute by minute basis what time people turn off and on during the previous night's news. I'm having that developed into a schematic analysis for the production team to see, so we are more and more focused on the maximization of the audience ratings (cited in Franklin, 1997: 256).

The intensity of this emphasis on audience stimulation is also argued to have affected the construction and presentation of stories, with depth, context, thoroughness and sometimes even accuracy argued to have become casualties. An emphasis on tempo has become paramount, for example, with prerecorded reports as concise and fast-moving as possible and snappy exchanges between presenters and reporters preceding rapid movement on to the next story.

The sense of urgency is further strengthened by a focus, particularly in the case of specialist news channels, on live, breaking news. Bold 'LIVE' captions, rolling onscreen tickers summarizing the latest developments and speculative two-ways with a range of reporters, witnesses or commentators at the scene are intended to captivate audiences, making them feel that they are watching events as they happen – switch off and you may miss something!

Even if few details are known and no new developments have occurred, retaining momentum via unsubstantiated speculation often is preferred to waiting for verified information. Also, priority is given to visual footage of dramatic, spectacular and emotional features of stories, whether in the form of explosions, car chases, fights, injuries or crying relatives. While not entirely excluded, outlining the broader context of what is taking place is often a secondary concern.

More generally, issues of presentation are increasingly important relative to those of substance (Dahlgren, 1995), whether in the form of dramatic music, onscreen captions, elaborate graphic sequences or presenters moving around spaceship-style studios, engaging in friendly banter with one another.

The problem with all this, for critics, is that, much as they may enjoy being entertained by this fast-paced emphasis on personality, entertainment, spectacle and emotion, audiences are unlikely to develop from such infotainment any real or useful understanding of the social and political world. As well as becoming increasingly distracted by trivial matters emanating from lifestyle, celebrity and sports journalism, people's understanding of the serious issues that are touched on is liable to be centred on the immediate emotion and spectacle of incidents rather than the bigger picture of which they are a part. As Peter Dahlgren (1995: 56) has put it, 'these production values of rawness and immediacy ... do not necessarily enhance our understanding: the close-ups on trees may obscure the forest.' Worse still, the *impression* that they are viewing an undistorted, live version of what's happening in the world may prompt viewers, paraphrasing Jerry Mander (1978), to *think* they know more when they know *less*. And an ignorant population, it might be suggested, is unlikely to be well equipped to hold the wealthy and powerful to account.

Conclusion: bad news?

There are some important criticisms we might make of those who bemoan the ideological role of news or the perceived drift towards infotainment. Notions of news and news values as rooted in ideology are subject to the criticisms of broader Marxist approaches to ideology outlined in Chapter 6. Not only do they tend to treat viewers as largely passive dupes, manipulated by dominant meanings, but they also perhaps underestimate the increasing diversity of versions of news on offer to contemporary consumers. The overall differences between the editorial stances of mainstream outlets may not amount to as much as we might hope, but especially if one takes into account the increasing range of columnists who contribute to the online versions of some newspapers, it would be wrong to say that the version of the world we are presented with is entirely monolithic. Meanwhile, a plethora of alternative sources of news and comment exist, from newspapers orientated towards the perspectives of ethnic or sexual minority populations to independent websites and blogs that, between them, cover a substantial range of extreme and moderate positions. More generally, as newsmaking and dissemination technologies have become ever more accessible, the phenomenon of *citizen journalism*, whereby ordinary members of the public contribute to, produce, disseminate or analyse news in a range of ways, now plays a modest but noteworthy role in the range of versions of world events available to us (Allan and Thorsen, 2009; Gillmor, 2006).

Even mainstream media outlets have, at times, brought about change by holding those in power to account – something that sits uneasily with more deterministic models of ideology. *The Washington Post* and *The New York Times*, among other publications, played an important role in the exposure of the huge US political scandal known as Watergate, which involved political conspiracy, criminal activity and a cover-up operation by parts of the CIA, the FBI and the federal government. Ultimately, the Republican president, Richard Nixon, was forced to resign.

On a somewhat smaller scale, UK news providers have been responsible for, among other things, exposing corruption in the Houses of Parliament in the 1994 'cash for questions' scandal, identifying alleged government manipulation of intelligence information in order to justify invading Iraq in 2003 and exposing excessive expenses claims by Members of Parliament in 2009. Those who subscribe to notions of news as ideology may claim, with some justification, that such instances relate to the exposure of selected excesses, while leaving broader systems of power unscathed. Nevertheless, they illustrate that the relations between news providers and other powerful groups can sometimes be far from cosy or amiable.

Though there is some merit in their observations, those who criticize the perceived 'dumbing down' of television news sometimes appear to assume that news either was, could or should ever be an untarnished source of objective, rational information (Langer, 1998). As we have seen, news is always partial and biased, as a result of the circumstances in which it is produced. This includes the version of news often longed for by critics of dumbing down, which tends to represent a particular rationalist, dispassionate and, some would argue, male bourgeois approach to the world (Temple, 2006).

In implicitly promoting this elite, bourgeois form of news, Mick Temple argues, such critics fail to recognize the potential for contemporary news formats to engage members of the population who would otherwise be entirely excluded. Similarly, John Fiske (1991b) argues that if ordinary people are to watch news and think about events, then producers have no choice but to appeal to their tastes and sensibilities, something which means rejecting outdated versions of news as a paternalist form of information. According to this view, popular news amounts not to 'dumbing down' but 'reaching out' (Barnett, 1998). So, rather than dismissing popular news altogether, commentators such as Fiske and Temple call for such providers to balance their emphasis on popular appeal with responsible coverage of matters of importance.

None of this means that the concerns of critics of ideology or infotainment are illusory or insignificant – the news values that govern the selection and construction of stories do result in the overall dominance of a restricted set of understandings of the world and, for better or worse, tend to be supportive of existing structures of power. Likewise, it is hard to dispute that the increasing focus of various news providers on keeping audiences entertained has resulted in a reduction in depth and detail and a shift away from coverage of politics.

It is important that academics continue to analyse and criticize news in these and other respects. Such criticism should demonstrate the ways in which representations are selected and constructed, hold the versions of the world with which we are presented to account and contribute to our ability to distinguish between more and less useful versions of news. As well as being subject to controversy and debate, however, such judgements always will be relative ones for, ultimately, all news is borne of human selection, manufacture and bias.

QUESTIONS AND EXERCISES

1 How do the following terms relate to the process of news construction?

   • Gate keeping.

   • Agenda setting.

   • News values.

   • Selection.

   • Construction.

2 Watch a television news bulletin and assess the stories covered (and the order in which they were covered) in relation to Galtung and Ruge's list of new values. Which news values are particularly important for each story and are there any that appear particularly consistently?

3 a) What role can terms such as 'surgical strike', 'smart bomb' and 'collateral damage' play in the construction of meaning of war stories?

   b) Find an example of a crime story in a newspaper or on a news website. In what ways does the way the story is constructed draw on familiar narrative structures or character types?

4 a) What is Hall's criticism of Galtung and Ruge's approach to news values?

   b) What criticisms can be made of Marxist approaches to news?

   c) Why should the increasing shift of news towards information be the cause of concern? Are such concerns justified?

5 If all news is biased, then is it possible for us to tell the difference between 'good' and 'bad' versions? What criteria could we use?

Suggested further reading

Allan, S. and Thorsen, E. (eds) (2009) *Citizen Journalism: Global perspectives*. New York: Peter Lang.
Collection of chapters focused on different manifestations of 'citizen journalism'.

Cohen, S. and Young, J. (eds) (1973) *The Manufacture of News: Social problems, deviance and the mass media*. London: Constable.
Classic collection of writings on news, including crucial contributions by Galtung and Ruge and Hall.

Franklin, B. (1997) *Newszak and News Media*. London: Arnold.
A critical history of UK print and broadcast news that attacks commercialization and perceived decline in quality.

Glasgow University Media Group (1976a) *Bad News*. London: Routledge & Kegan Paul.
    Famous content analysis of UK news coverage that accused the country's main broad-
    casters of systematic class bias.

Temple, M. (2006) 'Dumbing down is good for you', *British Politics*, 1 (2): 257–73. Also
    available online at: www.palgrave-journals.com/bp/journal/v1/n2/pdf/4200018a.pdf
    A defence of the popularization of news on the basis that contemporary formats are
    more inclusive and less elitist than traditional approaches.

8

Public Service or Personal Entertainment? Controlling Media Orientation

---

Focal points

- Competing views on what media are for and how they should be controlled.
- History and principles of public service broadcasting.
- Arguments about government influence, elitism and questions of quality.
- Debates about censorship of offensive or harmful content, including sex and violence.
- The rise of free market approaches to broadcasting and decline of regulation.

Introduction

Questions such as what media are for and how societies should use them may be seldom considered by most people. Yet, given the extent to which media are integrated into our lives, the answers are of great importance to the kind of society we wish to live in.

With a particular focus on broadcasting, this chapter addresses contrasting perspectives on the purpose of media and the principles that should guide the way they are controlled. We'll look at the contrast between public service models, which endorse government intervention to ensure media are used as a resource for the collective well-being of society, with consumerist approaches, which place emphasis on individual entertainment and corporate profit. We'll also examine a distinct but related set of arguments about the extent to which extreme or controversial forms of media content should be censored in order to prevent harm to society.

As well as closely examining such arguments, the chapter draws on examples to illustrate the ways in which such perspectives have influenced the operation of media. It will become clear that, in recent decades, there has been a significant shift away from public service approaches and towards consumerist, profit-orientated models that focus on commercial freedom and consumer sovereignty.

Public service broadcasting (PSB)

Advocates of *public service broadcasting* (PSB) argue that radio and television should be regarded as crucial resources to be used in a manner that benefits society as a whole. They argue that governments should ensure broadcasting is used for the public good, something they tend to regard as partially or wholly incompatible with the priorities of profitmaking companies.

The approach has its roots in a mixture of moral conservative and *social democratic* ideals. For its conservative supporters, PSB implies controlling media in order to protect the moral fibre of society. For the majority of contemporary advocates, however, the emphasis is on the designation of television and radio as vital collective resources that must be protected from the profit-seeking agendas of powerful business interests and used to enlighten and empower the whole of society. We would not leave our national education system in the unfettered control of the commercial sector, goes this social democratic argument, so neither should we surrender the operation of our most important forms of mass media to such interests (Webster, 2002).

Reith and the BBC

PSB was pioneered in the UK, where, after a brief period of commercial control, the BBC became a public corporation charged with informing, educating and, only lastly, entertaining the public. The personal vision of the corporation's first director general, John Reith, played an important part in the development of an approach to broadcasting orientated to improving the knowledge, taste and moral awareness of audiences and enhancing the collective well-being and cohesion of the nation. The notion

of universality was key – in order to foster national unity and enlightenment, the BBC should have a monopoly on broadcasting and its mix of
programming should be available identically across the nation. Reith was
equally adamant that the BBC must be protected from commercial involvement or competition, which, in his view, would result in an unprincipled
quest to maximize audiences. To have consigned an invention so extraordinary as radio to the pursuit of profit and cheap entertainment 'would
have been a prostitution of its powers and an insult to the character and
intelligence of the people' (1925, cited in Franklin, 1997: 119).

FIGURE 8.1   BBC Broadcasting House, London
© Nick Hawkes

Crucially, Reith sought to challenge and stretch his audience, providing them
with what was beneficial rather than pandering to the easier entertainment
they might have chosen for themselves. He openly acknowledged this, pro-
claiming that, 'it is occasionally indicated to us that we are apparently setting out to give the public what we think they need – and not what they
want, but few know what they want and very few what they need' (1924,
cited in McDonnell, 1991). Reith's opposition to commercial involvement
was supported in 1923 by the Sykes Committee, which recommended that
the then British Broadcasting Company should be funded by a licence fee,

payable annually by every household in possession of a radio. By 1927, on the basis of these conclusions and those of the 1926 Crawford Committee, the BBC had been established by royal charter as a licence fee-funded organization with exclusive rights to the UK's airwaves. In order to protect its independence, the BBC was to be answerable not directly to the state, but to an independent board of governors (now The BBC Trust).

Differing PSB arrangements

Reith's BBC offered a diet of programming more mixed than critics sometimes give it credit for (Franklin, 1997), but, nevertheless, one that placed emphasis on news, high culture, patriotism and Christian morality. Often accused of overt paternalism, this approach partly reflected the imposition of Reith's personal moral principles and his ruthless control over the organization. Yet, many of the broader principles of the BBC served as a model for countries around the world.

Across Western Europe, as well as in countries as far apart as Japan, Canada and Australia, PSB organizations comparable to the BBC emerged, each of which intended to develop radio and, later, television content that was high in quality and beneficial to the national public. Organizational and funding arrangements differed from country to country, however. While in many of the European examples, as well as Japan, a licence fee comparable to the UK's was used, different models were applied elsewhere.

Since 1948, the Australian Broadcasting Commission (now Corporation) has been funded by direct government subsidy. While arguably fairer and easier to administer than a licence fee system, this approach raises concerns as to the level of independence of the broadcaster from the politicians who directly allocate its resources. Meanwhile, the Canadian Broadcasting Corporation, relied from its conception in 1936, on a mixture of direct government subsidy and revenue from the selling of advertising, which prompts additional questions about whether or not it is feasible for effective PSB to coexist with commercial sponsorship.

While in some countries public service broadcasters competed with commercial rivals from an early point, in the UK, Reith was insistent that any involvement of profitmaking interests would undermine the public service remit of the BBC by forcing it to chase audiences. Yet, after a period of extensive debate, the BBC's monopoly was broken in 1955, with the setting up of a commercial form of PSB provided by an amalgam of regional companies under the Independent Television (ITV) network.

As well as forcing the BBC to compete for viewers, this move embraced the notion that broadcasting for the public interest could be provided within an environment subject to commercial pressures. ITV's commercial network was and still is regarded as a public service broadcaster, its affiliates subject to statutory requirements regarding the types of programming they must produce.

Today, the UK also has two further public service broadcasters in the form of Channel 4 and FIVE, both funded by advertising – the latter with fully commercial status and the former a non-profit public corporation.

Developing PSB principles

Despite the variations in approach to PSB in different countries and across time, many of Reith's initial principles have remained constant. In 2004 and 2005, Ofcom, the current UK media and communications regulator, undertook a detailed consultation on the future of PSB, the outcome of which was the identification of four broad social purposes:

- to inform ourselves and others and to increase our understanding of the world, through news, information and analysis of current events and ideas;

- to reflect and strengthen our cultural identity, through high-quality UK national and regional programming;

- to stimulate our interest in and knowledge of arts, science, history and other topics, through content that is accessible, encourages personal development and promotes participation in society; and

- to support a tolerant and inclusive society, through the availability of programmes which reflect the lives of different people and communities within the UK, encourage a better understanding of different cultures and perspectives and, on occasion, bring the nation together for shared experiences (Ofcom, 2004).

Some of the specifics in these elaborations would not have been present in the days of Reith. Yet the clear emphasis on enlightening, educating and informing and the focus on encouragement of national identity and cohesion are consistent themes, even if, in the case of the latter, an emphasis on tolerance, inclusion and diversity has replaced the rather more monolithic Reithian vision of national identity.

These themes also predominate in Michael Tracey's outline of eight principles of PSB, which, among other things, cover the provision of education and information, the nurturing of a national sense of togetherness, provision for minorities, a commitment to quality programming and the liberation of programme makers from commercial or Establishment restraints (1998).

A further theme is the facilitation of public engagement – something that entails a sense of belonging to society and the ability to meaningfully participate in discussions about how it should be run. In this respect, the PSB approach is a model that regards audience members not as isolated, self-centred individuals but as citizens – members of a national public or community with a commitment to one another and a stake in the improvement of society (Murdock, 1992). Sure enough, wherever and whenever it has existed, PSB can perhaps best be summarized by the principle that primary channels of mass media should be used to 'make *us* better than we are' (Tracey, 1998: 19, my emphasis).

Enabling or imposing?

Many of those whose licence fees or taxes are used to pay for public service broadcasters feel resentful of the drain on their money that such institutions appear to represent. Some argue that content is insufficiently distinct from that of commercial competitors, others regard them as out of touch with audiences, while many simply want to be allowed to choose whether or not to pay for their content. 'Why should I pay so much for the BBC', the complaint sometimes goes, 'when I don't even watch most of its programmes?' Justifications for PSB, however, ask us to look beyond the individual, short-term preferences each of us may choose to exercise after a hard day's work and, instead, ask what sorts of services would be most beneficial to all of us in the longer term.

Entertainment and popularity are central to the PSB agenda, not only because collective enjoyment fosters social and cultural bonds but also because of the importance of catering for the whole of society rather than an elite few. Yet public service broadcasters seeks to combine this with loftier goals, such as challenging, enlightening and empowering audiences, making popular content high in quality and quality content popular (Tracey, 1998). This is a tall order, of course and they may not always have been successful in striking such a balance. There are also some broader difficulties with PSB that we should consider.

The limits to independence

The first is the ongoing issue of government influence. In theory, this is a particular concern for broadcasters who are reliant on direct funding from the state and, therefore, have a direct interest in staying on good terms with politicians. Although their funding operates at arms' length from government, however, licence fee-funded organizations are also reliant on government support, which is pivotal for the continuation of their funding arrangements.

The BBC's history is not short of episodes in which its independence has been under question. The first was the general strike in 1926, in which Reith fended off government calls for the corporation to become an instrument of state propaganda (Briggs, 1961). His success in doing so was a significant blow struck for independence, but did not prevent the BBC from coming largely under the control of a government Ministry of Information during World War II (Curran and Seaton, 2003). It has never again been so directly controlled, but the BBC's independence has continued to come under pressure during times of national crisis and war. As recently as 2003, the corporation was the subject of high-profile attacks from senior government ministers and officials for broadcasting a news story suggesting that the government had 'sexed up' the case for invading Iraq. Intense government pressure, alongside a public inquiry regarded by some commentators as an Establishment whitewash, resulted in the resignation of the BBC's director general and the chair of its board of governors.

Questions of quality

While their relationship with governments have always led to tensions, however, the most substantial difficulty for public service broadcasters relates to the fundamental question of who decides what sorts of media content are good or bad for us.

Reith's belief was that the people did not know what was good for them and that it was therefore incumbent on the BBC to decide for them. For all his laudable intentions about making cultural excellence available to all, the approach was a highly undemocratic one (Garnham, 1978). We no longer hear such blunt dismissals of public taste among contemporary proponents of PSB and the range of public service programming on offer is more diverse than in the past. Yet, justifications of PSB continue to rest on an implicit distrust of the choices the public might make if left to themselves in an unfettered commercial marketplace.

This paternalist position is particularly apparent in the constant references made by regulators and public service broadcasters to the importance of maintaining 'quality'. The UK regulator Ofcom, for example, has stated that 'as a society we clearly demand a wider range of high-quality UK content than would be provided by the market' (2005).

Now, at face value, most would accept that quality and excellence are worthy goals. Yet rarely is much elaboration provided on what exactly is meant by quality or by whose standards it is measured. According to David Elstein (1986), quality actually serves as a byword for an elitist agenda that fits in with Establishment values. Media mogul Rupert Murdoch takes a similar view:

> much of what is claimed to be quality television here is no more than the parading of the prejudices and interests [of the British elite] ... producing a TV output which is so often obsessed with class, dominated by anti-commercial attitudes and with a tendency to hark back to the past (2001: 39).

Murdoch's dismissal may be self-serving, but he is not alone in connecting notions of quality to the agendas of elite social class groups. For sociologist Pierre Bourdieu (1984), far from being objective, the concepts of aesthetic quality and good taste reflect and reinforce deep-seated class divisions. Essentially, the bourgeoisie construct a distinction between their own high or pure aesthetic and a diametrically opposed vulgar aesthetic, consisting of what are regarded as the naïve and superficial enjoyments of the working classes. This cultural distinction serves to reinforce class differences because entry into elite social and economic worlds is restricted to those with the requisite *cultural capital* – in other words, those in possession of the appropriate cultural tastes, knowledge and experience. From owning the right pictures to showing knowledge of suitable literature, cultural capital provides a route to social acceptance and, in turn, economic benefits, such as easier access to elite forms of education or employment.

Proponents of PSB may argue, with some justification, that their versions of quality are less restricted than those associated with Bourdieu's high aesthetic and that, in attempting to distribute it to the masses, they are seeking to challenge rather than reinforce class distinctions. Yet Bourdieu's broader emphasis on the culturally constructed nature of taste serves as an important reminder that notions of quality will always reflect the particular cultural context, or habitus as he would call it, of those who invoke them. To put it much more simply, quality is, to some degree, subjective – one person's quality may be another person's dross. In empowering particular elite individuals or organizations to produce or ensure quality programming, then, we may be endorsing the imposition on society of a very particular set of aesthetic and social priorities.

Yet, perhaps, if it is acknowledged and justified, this position is not so untenable as it may seem. After all, do any of us, of whatever class background, feel that our everyday viewing choices are necessarily the most beneficial for us or society? We may strongly defend the importance of our right to make them, but this ought not to be taken to mean that we would like our personal choices, and the kinds of market demand they create, to be the sole determinants of our collective cultural future. It goes without saying that the public service agenda is born of a particular set of ideals with its roots in particular sections of society. Yet the pursuit of such ideals by encouraging particular kinds of programming may still be powerfully justified, not because the tastes of one class group are inherently superior, but because certain kinds of content may have greater collective benefit than others.

Perhaps in future, we might, as John Mepham (1990) has suggested, define quality not as inherent aesthetic purity, but something determined by the social usefulness of different forms of media. Arguments will rage about what is useful and what is not, argues Mepham, which is precisely how things should be in an inclusive, accountable PSB system. It may not always have been effective at doing so, but PSB should serve and be accountable to the public – offering the population a permanent stake in ongoing debates about which kinds of programming are valuable and which are not.

Censorship: preventing harm and offence

Supporters of PSB endorse what is sometimes termed 'positive' media regulation – that is, they believe broadcasting systems should be set up and controlled in a way that encourages the production of desirable types of content. A distinct, but equally important, set of arguments emphasizes the need for 'negative' forms of regulation, or *censorship*, to prevent or limit content deemed problematic or harmful to society.

Pro-censorship arguments are somewhat distinct from contemporary arguments in favour of PSB, so it should not be assumed that all those who support the former also support the latter. On the contrary, some of the strongest critics of PSB nevertheless support censorship of sex and violence, while supporters of PSB sometimes feel uncomfortable about censorship. There is a clear connection between the arguments in favour of PSB and censorship, however, in that both entail the belief that media should be subject to regulation in the best interests of society.

Avoiding majority (and minority) offence

Arguments in favour of censorship sometimes draw on ideas developed by Patrick Devlin (1965), who argued that, in order to maintain an orderly and functional society, it is necessary to nurture and protect a moral consensus. If deviant moral behaviour, such as homosexuality, for example, were permitted or encouraged, then it might proliferate, causing the *fragmentation* of the shared bonds of moral consensus and the breakdown of society: 'If men and women try to create a society in which there is no fundamental agreement about good and evil, they will fail', he said, and 'if, having based it on common agreement, the agreement goes, the society will disintegrate' (Devlin, 1965: 10).

For Devlin, in order to prevent such disintegration, society has the right to restrict the freedom of individuals to do as they please. If the majority find a particular form of behaviour offensive, then, in the interests of social cohesion, such an act should be restricted. While Devlin's primary concern was with individual behaviour, his arguments have profound implications for media depictions of opinions, behaviour or ways of life offensive to the majority. In short, they suggest that such expressions should be censored.

Devlin's emphasis was on the importance of moral consensus itself rather than the inherent rightness or wrongness of any particular behaviour, but other conservatives took a more absolutist approach, campaigning for censorship on the grounds that certain forms of media content are, quite simply, immoral and wrong.

In the early 1960s, attempts were made to ban the paperback publication of D. H. Lawrence's *Lady Chatterley's Lover* on the grounds that its sexual content, explicit language and depiction of adultery were obscene and depraved. While bans of the book were implemented in some countries, a landmark trial ended in the UK with a verdict of not guilty, the jury deciding that the literary merit of the work justified its publication. Despite this pivotal victory for liberalism, calls for the censorship of content deemed immoral and religiously offensive persisted.

In the UK, Mary Whitehouse famously launched a 'Clean Up TV' campaign, calling for action to curb the increasingly explicit depiction of sex. She also used a dormant blasphemy law to successfully prosecute *Gay News* for having published a James Kirkup poem that fantasized about sexual contact with a recently deceased Jesus Christ. In 1979, Monty Python's *Life of Brian*, which offered a satirical parallel to the story of Jesus, was the subject of protests and local bans in the UK, the USA and elsewhere, having been accused of blasphemy.

More recently, the BBC's decision to screen the satirical musical, *Jerry Springer: The Opera* in 2006 prompted extensive protests led by evangelical Christian groups, who argued that its satirical depiction of Jesus and the Devil as Springer guests was blasphemous. By this point, however, such groups probably did not speak for most of the UK population, making their campaigns incompatible with Devlin's argument about protection of the morals of the majority. As with campaigns from some European Muslim groups against the publication of Salman Rushdie's *The Satanic Verses* in 1989 and of newspaper cartoons depicting the prophet Mohammad in 2006, they were perhaps more compatible with the notion of censorship to prevent offence to religious groups who formed a minority within the countries in question.

Pornography

Importantly, pro-censorship arguments are not confined to those with conservative agendas. Campaigns to censor pornography, for example, bring together an unlikely alliance of conservative defenders of religious values and left-wing feminists concerned about female exploitation.

The conservative case centres on the argument that porn undermines family values and heterosexual monogamy, threatening traditional understandings of sex as a dignified expression of love within marriage and inducing social consequences, such as rising divorce rates, teenage pregnancies and sexual diseases. The campaign group Mediawatch-UK put it in the following way:

> We believe that pornography, because of its casual, immoral and responsibility-free approach to sexuality, contributes significantly to the social problems of sexual dysfunction, the continually rising rates of sexually transmitted infections, the increasing rate of marital breakdown and the annually rising sexual crime rate (2005).

The final point here, on sexual crime, is perhaps the only connection between Mediawatch-UK's case and that of radical feminists such as Andrea Dworkin (1981) and Catharine MacKinnon (1988), who were involved in an attempt to ban pornography in Minneapolis and Indianapolis on the basis that it violated women's civil rights.

Far from threatening existing values, for Dworkin and MacKinnon, pornography is entirely consistent with a patriarchal society, which for centuries has treated women as sexual objects. In porn, it is argued, women's sexuality is controlled and violated by men: by the male-controlled porn industry which makes money out of subjecting women to humiliating, degrading and sometimes violent sexual acts; by the men who consume women's sexuality by watching porn and by the male actors depicted in pornographic texts. For Dworkin, therefore, there is little substantive difference between porn and prostitution, both of which involve men selling women's bodies to other men. Rape, too, is deemed consistent with the status porn establishes of women as sexual commodities, except, here they are stolen instead of paid for. At one with Robin Morgan's (1980: 128) often cited assertion that 'pornography is the theory, rape is the practice', Dworkin is clear that the two legitimize one another:

> Pornography as a genre says that the stealing and buying and selling of women are not acts of force of abuse because women want to be raped and prostituted because that is the nature of women and the nature of female sexuality (1995: 240).

Violence

Media violence has been another focal point for censorship campaigns. Certainly, there can be little doubt as to the quantity of violence consumed by media audiences. Referring to the USA, George Gerbner argues that:

> The average viewer of prime-time television drama ... sees in a typical week an average of 21 criminals arrayed against an army of 41 public and private law enforcers ... An average of 150 acts of violence and about 15 murders entertain them and their children every week, and that does not count cartoons and the news (2002).

The notion that such onscreen violence may be harmful is frequently supported by media campaigns focused on its increasing availability to vulnerable individuals and its alleged connection with high-profile murders. In the UK, the presence of a *Child's Play 3* video in the house of one of the teenagers who in 1993 killed toddler Jamie Bulger prompted calls for the film and others like it to be banned, while, in 1999, US news media partially blamed the content of computer game *Doom 2* and the music and imagery of Marilyn Manson for the Columbine school shootings carried out in 1999 by Dylan Klebold and Eric Harris.

Such media campaigns sometimes have directly resulted in the tightening of restrictions by governments. In 2008, the consumption of 'extreme pornography' was banned in the UK, following the murder of Jane Longhurst by a man who was a heavy consumer of online materials deemed to fall within this category.

Often drawing on experimental and survey-based studies from behavioural psychology (see Chapter 5), campaigners argue that vulnerable individuals such as children may be liable to directly imitate media violence or to respond to stressful situations in an aggressive manner (Berkowitz, 1984). Others argue that, over a longer period of time, violence may be rendered normal by our repeated exposure to it, either desensitizing us to its negative impacts (Drabman and Thomas, 1974) or leading to an excessively fearful understanding of the world (Gerbner, 2002).

Even if it doesn't prompt imitative behaviour or increased aggression, onscreen violence may seriously frighten, disturb or upset audience members and this, in itself, may be seen as a significant social harm.

Preventing harm or inhibiting freedom?

Pro-censorship arguments offer valuable reminders of the potential for media content to upset, offend or cause specific forms of harm. The question of whether, and in what circumstances, regulators should restrict or remove offending content is a complex and controversial one, however.

Devlin's approach seems difficult to justify in the context of contemporary multicultural societies. While many recognize the value of social cohesion, the banning of otherwise harmless forms of minority behaviour and expression as a means of achieving such bonding seems unrealistic and counter productive. The nineteenth-century ideas of John Stuart Mill – against whom Devlin pitched parts of his argument – arguably have retained greater application.

Specifically warning against the tyranny of the majority, Mill argued that individual freedom of behaviour and expression ought to be a key foundation of enlightened societies. Majority opinion at any moment in time, he argued, is potentially fallible and must be allowed to be tested against different approaches in order for societies to progress:

> The peculiar evil of silencing the expression of an opinion is that it is robbing the human race ... If the opinion is right, they are deprived of the opportunity of exchanging error for truth: if wrong, they lose what is almost as great a benefit, the clearer perception and livelier impression of truth, produced by its collision with error (Mill, 1975: 24).

Society should only have the right to restrict individual freedom, according to Mill, if clear harm is caused to others. The law should not seek to protect society or its members from the offence or hurt feelings that minority practices may cause, then, and neither, except in the case of those 'incapable of self-government' (principally children), should it try to protect individuals from themselves by forcing them to behave in a way that society deems good for them. Beyond this, however, Mill's 'harm principle' leaves plenty of scope for discussion. After all, many of the arguments in favour of censorship assert that, in one way or another, harm is in danger of being caused. The problem is that many of these claims are controversial.

In the case of accusations about the harmful effects of exposure to media violence, evidence is inconsistent and questionable. Speculation about the causal impact of media in relation to isolated murder cases can offer no sustainable basis for censorship, however shocking the headlines. When it comes to broader evidence, many studies appear to show the potential for some sort of effect on audiences, though others are less clear. Moreover, the experimental and survey-based approaches of the studies in question have been subject to extensive criticism, making it difficult to know how much credence to give their findings (see Chapter 5). Meanwhile, most commentators agree that, even if media violence does have the potential to result in an increase in viewer aggression, it is only liable to lead to seriously harmful consequences in the case of a handful of individuals with an existing propensity to violence attributable to other factors. In light of this, it seems reasonable to ask if the attentions of policymakers might be better focused on the range of unusual factors at work in the lives of these extraordinary individuals rather than on the impacts on essentially non-violent people of media content viewed by millions of them every day (Gauntlett, 1998).

The degree of harm caused by pornography is also a subject of contention. Although many sex offenders have a history of pornography use, it is far from clear that it contributed to their criminal behaviour. Overall levels of sex crime in particular countries, meanwhile, do not seem to be correlated with levels of pornography use (Segal, 1992).

It remains possible that pornography may contribute to a broader media portrayal of gender that promotes a version of femininity focused on objectification and the achievement of sexual attractiveness to men (see Chapter 11). Yet, recognition of this more general problem renders the singling out of pornography rather unconvincing. We might find them less edifying, but are we quite sure that the explicit portrayals of sex in porn are actually any more harmful in terms of their representation of femininity than, for example, portrayals in fashion and beauty magazines, romantic fiction or some Hollywood blockbusters?

One of the factors emphasized by those feminists who do single out porn is that it is specifically demeaning or harmful to the actresses involved in its production. Yet, if women choose to earn their money in this way (and if they are forced, this already would be illegal), then an argument suggesting that they should be prevented from making such a choice is an uncomfortable one. As well as conflicting with Mill's assertions about protecting people from themselves, it carries the danger, according to other feminists, of stigmatizing those who work in the sex industry:

> We are exhorted to save our sisters ... but of course most sex workers are not looking for feminist salvation. On the contrary they complain bitterly about the stigmatization of women who work in the sex industry by anti-pornography feminists (Segal, 1992: 9).

It is also important to remember that, despite an undoubted overall bias towards the selling of female bodies to heterosexual male audiences, *men's* bodies feature in porn, too, and there is a substantial porn audience among heterosexual females and among homosexuals and bisexuals of both genders.

Arguably, then, there is sufficient doubt about the arguments and evidence presented by those who regard violence and pornography as the cause of specific social harms that the restrictions on freedom that heavy censorship would impose are hard to justify. That does not mean such forms of expression should be uncritically celebrated, nor does it mean censorship should be entirely abandoned.

It is of great importance that, as societies, we continue to try and understand the consequences of media use and are prepared to cautiously intervene in those cases where it can be agreed significant harm is likely be caused. The most obvious example, perhaps, is the managing of the extent to which and ways in which children consume different forms of media content. While the criteria they should use are debatable, the use of legally enforceable classification systems is a measure regarded as valuable by many parents. Like the development of optional password systems and child-friendly filters for digital television and the Internet, classification helps parents to make their own decisions as to the suitability of content for their children.

There are also opportunities to vary levels of restriction and control according to the public accessibility of content. Richard Collins and Cristina Murroni (1996) propose that the more private a channel of communication is, the less it should be subject to censorship. Therefore, an e-mail exchange between members of a small group of friends normally should, with the exception of serious intimidation or threats of violence, be free from censorship. In contrast, some restrictions may be justified in the case of free-to-air television, the audience for which consists of a large cross-section of the population. In between these extremes, Collins and Murroni place forms of media that are consumed only after a clear and conscious decision on the part of an adult viewer to select and/or purchase them. Orientation towards a 'volunteer audience' means that such channels of communication – including subscription-based television channels, websites or specialist magazines – require less stringent controls because there is less chance of their accidentally being stumbled on by those liable to find them offensive or upsetting.

Commercial competition and consumer choice

So far, this chapter has focused on the merits and problems with the arguments of those who – sometimes from substantially differing points of view – believe that governments should seek to achieve benefits for society by exerting controls over media. Our discussion now turns to those who believe it is *wrong* for governments to interfere with media in the interests of social goals.

Opposed especially to the PSB approach, this position draws on a *neo-liberal* political ideology. Influenced by the eighteenth-century economic theory of Adam Smith, the primary concern of this form of liberalism is not with individual political or moral freedom, though these can feature in the approach, but with *market* freedom – the freedom to buy, sell and make money.

Smith's doctrine called for a free market, or, 'laissez-faire' (leave to do) economic system in which government interventions are reduced to a minimum, allowing businesses to compete freely in a quest to maximize profits without barriers such as trade tariffs, state subsidies or regulations. Instead of trying to manipulate markets in order to achieve particular financial or social outcomes, governments should loosen their grip and allow economic and social outcomes to be determined by the 'invisible hand' of the market (Smith, 1904).

The success or failure of products, services or ideas, it is argued, should be determined primarily by the laws of supply and demand, not by government meddling. If there is a need for something scarce, then the market will provide it as a result of the profitability of doing so. If there is too much of something or if it ceases to be useful, then it will also cease to be profitable and the market will shift to provide something else.

After a decline in the influence of laissez-faire economics during the mid-twentieth century, so-called neo-liberal approaches became dominant during and after the 1980s, with the relaxation of regulations on businesses, reductions in taxation and government spending and the selling off state-owned utilities to the private sector.

Neo-liberal approaches

When it comes to media, neo-liberals believe that it is wrong for governments to decide what broadcasting should be for or to artificially engineer things in an effort to achieve such social purposes. Instead, they argue, commercial organizations should be free to provide media products and services in whatever way they see fit, their success or failure decided not by government-imposed priorities, but by supply, demand and market competition. The invisible hand of the market, it is argued, will most effectively provide whatever products and services are required, because consumer demand makes provision profitable. Furthermore, free competition between companies will force each to improve the standard of the products that they are offering, to innovate new ideas and to reduce costs and, hence, prices.

In contrast, the guaranteed income streams provided by government subsidies, licence fees and restricted market places are deemed to promote, not quality, but complacency and stagnation. Rather than being forced to consume a diet of media content viewed as being good for them by members of the elite social classes, consumers in a free market system would be trusted to determine their own preferences.

Calling for the deregulation of the UK broadcasting market, dominated at the time by the BBC and its commercial rival ITV, media mogul Rupert Murdoch summed up the neo-liberal approach to broadcasting in a lecture at the end of the 1980s entitled 'Freedom in broadcasting':

> Competition lets consumers decide what they want to buy: monopoly
> or duopoly forces them to take whatever the seller puts on offer.
> Competition forces suppliers to innovate products, lest they lose busi-
> ness to rivals offering better; monopoly permits a seller to force out-
> dated goods onto captive consumers. Competition keeps prices low and
> quality high; monopoly does the opposite. Why should television be
> exempt from these laws of supply and demand? (R. Murdoch, 2001: 38)

Murdoch went on to attack the notion of PSB itself, arguing that 'special
favours' afforded to so-called public service broadcasters result in a service
valued by those who run it but of little relevance to the public it supposedly
serves. Redefining the notion of a public service broadcaster as 'anybody
who ... provides a service which the public wants at a price it can afford'
(2001: 39), Murdoch asserts that it is competitive commercial companies
in an open marketplace with minimal restrictions and controls that can
deliver such services most effectively.

Murdoch's wholesale rejection of PSB, except in the sense of 'providing a
service the public wants', goes to the root of the argument. It is the satisfaction and enjoyment of individual consumers that should be the primary
purpose of broadcasting according to this view. For Murdoch, the profitability of providing such satisfaction acts as guarantor that the market will
deliver it. Rather than focusing on the long-term needs of society as a whole,
the neo-liberal approach casts us all, first and foremost, as individual consumers and prioritizes the need to satisfy each of us in this role.

In the very same Edinburgh International Television Festival lecture slot
in 2009, Murdoch's son, James – by then chairman and chief executive of
News Corporation Europe and Asia – made a very similar argument, attacking the 'authoritarianism' and 'lack of trust' that, he argued, characterize
government attempts to regulate media, and asserted that an unconstrained
commercial system is the only way to maximize creativity, create a plurality
of independent media voices and provide choice for consumers (J. Murdoch,
2009).

US broadcasting: a free market model

In the USA, a long-established embrace of the free market, together with the
specific protection afforded to freedom of the press in the first amendment
to the country's constitution, have contributed to a history of broadcasting
centred on commerce and profit.

From its earliest days, the US radio system was dominated by a competitive
marketplace and commercial sponsorship. Some regulation was deemed necessary in order to protect limited bandwidth. The Federal Radio Commission

(later the Federal Communications Commission, or, FCC) was set up in 1927 to allocate broadcasting licences and it was even established that licensees should serve 'public convenience, interest and necessity', but, unlike countries that had fully embraced PSB, the industry was largely left to decide for itself what this meant (Baker and Dessart, 1998).

Meanwhile, competition for listeners was assured by the number of licences awarded in each area. While regulators elsewhere were acting to restrict competition, the FCC's most notable early interventions in the market were designed to protect it by avoiding the establishment of monopolies. Meanwhile, the audiences whose attention broadcasting companies coveted acted as the means of attaining their primary goal, which to attract commercial sponsors.

The US system did allow some space for PSB, or 'public broadcasting' as it is known there. In the early years, local educational radio and television stations were run by colleges, universities and charitable organizations such as the Ford Foundation. A more coordinated public system, complete with modest state funding, was developed in the 1960s, with the creation of the Corporation for Public Broadcasting, which was responsible for distributing government money to public stations, and eventually the Public Broadcasting Service (PBS), which acted as a connecting organization for a plethora of local broadcasters (Baker and Dessart, 1998). PBS enjoyed moderate successes, notably in children's educational programming and, most famously, perhaps, with the globally successful *Sesame Street*. Ultimately, however, the paucity of government funding has resulted in a reliance on donations, viewer contributions and, increasingly, advertising, as well as an inability to seriously compete with overwhelmingly powerful commercial networks.

Isolated attempts were also made to impose public service regulation on the content of commercial stations, the most notable of which was the Fairness Doctrine, which, in 1949, imposed on all FCC licensees a requirement to broadcast programmes on matters of public importance and to offset any particular viewpoints covered with opposing perspectives. A principle was established that broadcasters had a responsibility to provide balanced coverage of matters of politics and controversy.

A toaster with pictures: the decline of regulation

From the 1980s onwards, much of the regulation that did exist in the US system has been relaxed, in a climate increasingly dominated by neo-liberal voices, some of whom argued that, rather than being regarded as a unique societal resource, broadcasting should be treated no differently from any other commercial goods or services. 'TV', said Mark Fowler, chairman of the FCC from 1981 to 1987, 'is a toaster with pictures' (cited in Baker and Dessart, 1998: 27).

Against the background of the onset of multichannel cable television, Fowler oversaw the relaxation of a variety of rules, including the withdrawal of the Fairness Doctrine in 1987. The neo-liberal political climate that Fowler represented, combined with the development of satellite, cable and the Internet, was to have an even more dramatic impact on those countries which, unlike the USA, had broadcasting histories dominated by powerful public service broadcasters.

Multichannel television offered the perfect partner for neo-liberal voices because, by bringing spectrum scarcity to an end, it created the technical possibility for precisely the kind of open, competitive marketplace they envisaged. Viewers could be offered such extensive choice that they would no longer need governments to intervene in the marketplace to ensure that certain kinds of programming would be made available or that others would not. If viewers felt offended by content on one channel, then a free market multichannel television system would provide plenty of alternatives more suited to them. Likewise, if they felt insufficiently challenged or informed by soaps and game shows, then they would be able to watch news, complex dramas and documentaries on different channels. Their demand for such products would mean that a market unfettered by technological or government limitations would supply them. Instead of a small number of heavily regulated channels that are expected to cater for the needs of everyone, then, we would each choose from a plethora of specialist commercial channels. The relationship between multichannel television and the neo-liberal revival has resulted in a substantial decline in the status of public service broadcasters across the world (Tracey, 1998). In the UK, a multitude of cable, satellite and, now, digital channels awarded licences since the 1990s have been able to operate free from the public service obligations expected of the country's terrestrial broadcasters.

Commercially funded public service broadcasters such as ITV have found themselves subject to intense competition from opponents who, unlike themselves, are subject only to light touch, minimum regulations. Such competition has created massive pressure to reduce costs and chase audiences, something increasingly incompatible, according to those running such services, with public service obligations. The provision of satellite, cable and, subsequently, digital television services and set-top boxes, meanwhile, has, to a significant degree, been entrusted to commercial organizations, giving them considerable gatekeeping influence (Franklin, 1997), although the BBC eventually became involved in the provision of a non-subscription basic digital television service called 'Freeview'.

The future funding of core public service broadcasters also is in doubt. The ability to easily enable or block access to different forms of content via a set-top box creates the technical possibility of funding organizations such as the BBC or CBC by voluntary viewer subscription instead of a universal licence fee or government subsidy. Instead of being forced to pay for their country's main public service broadcaster whether they watch its output or not, consumers would only pay if they chose to subscribe – bringing an end to the principle of universality so important to Reith. The broadcasters would have to orientate themselves towards an appropriate market and compete for subscribers rather than receiving their funding automatically. The influential Peacock Report in 1986 had recommended such an arrangement for the BBC once the appropriate technology became available, though, so far, UK governments have resisted such recommendations. The corporation retains high profile within the UK and around the world and has pioneered developments in on-demand Internet television. Further reviews into the viability of alternative sources of funding are ongoing, however, and the licence fee may be on borrowed time.

Censorship has also been in relative decline in many countries since the second half of the twentieth century, although, as we shall see, the thirst for controls on media in respect of moral decency remains strong in some quarters. In part, the decline of censorship has reflected a relentless pushing at the boundaries of acceptability by artists, broadcasters and others and a concurrent decline, in some countries at least, in the influence of pro-censorship moral conservatives. The relaxation of negative regulation also reflects the way in which competitive market environments can encourage the challenging of boundaries relating to violence and sex, in order to excite viewers and stay one step ahead of the competition.

Technological developments have emboldened anti-censorship arguments further by strengthening the case that those offended by content can simply change channel and by enabling potentially offensive or harmful content to be permitted on restricted subscription-only channels. Meanwhile, as outlined in Chapter 3, the convergence of media and blurring of public and private communication brought about by the Internet has rendered acceptable limits more difficult to establish and enforce.

Censorship persists in various places, however. Despite general relaxations in the levels of sex, violence and bad language permitted, the UK passed laws in 2006 against the 'glorification' of terrorism and 'incitement to religious hatred', both of which were labelled by opponents as direct attacks on freedom of expression. Counter-intuitively, meanwhile, the otherwise 'laissez-faire' US media environment continues to have relatively strict negative regulations on broadcasters relating to decency. Programming that is deemed 'obscene' is banned outright, while 'indecent' or 'profane' content is only permitted during the hours when children are less likely to be watching (FCC, 2008). The attempt by the FCC to fine Viacom for the much reported Janet Jackson Super Bowl 'wardrobe malfunction' (see Chapter 3) may have been unsuccessful, but it demonstrated a continuing zeal to intervene when it comes to sexual decency in a country dominated by a mixture of neo-liberal economic thinking and conservative moral values. This illustrates a more general tendency for those on the right of the political spectrum to argue in favour of the free market when it comes to the matter of public service broadcasting but support intervention when it comes to the censorship of violence and, particularly, sex.

Conclusion: a rosy commercial future?

Despite the continuing significance of censorship and PSB, deregulation seems liable to become more concentrated in the coming years. The competitive commercial environment called for by Murdoch has, to a significant extent, been unleashed in many of the countries that had originally embraced restricted public service approaches to broadcasting. And if the funding and structure of public service broadcasters is eventually reformed consistent with free market principles, it is hard to envisage arrangements such as the BBC licence fee ever being reimplemented. So, should PSB be defended or should we celebrate the increasing marketization of media?

Competition and markets, alongside the development of multichannel media, undoubtedly have brought advantages in terms of viewer choice. No longer do people have to accept the particular cultural agenda of one or two national broadcasters or, indeed, of regulatory bodies. Rather, they are indeed free to select their own cultural path from the range of content made available by competing commercial providers. The choices that individuals make in this respect are also liable to influence the future scheduling decisions of broadcasters. It would be unrealistic, then, to deny that competition has placed greater pressure on all broadcasters – including those with public service obligations – to ensure they remain in touch with viewers. It is also becoming clear that, in the new media environment, markets increasingly do cater for many specialist minority groups, some of whom report a preference for such commercial services (see Chapter 10).

There are substantial problems with the free market approach to media, however. Rather than replacing powerful public broadcasters with an open marketplace comprising a plethora of competing independent companies, deregulation tends to reinforce trends towards the domination of mass communications by a small number of transnational corporations (McChesney, 1999). Intensified competition for advertising revenue, meanwhile, has prompted a ruthless emphasis on audience maximization, as well as an increasing bias towards those types of content that are most compatible with *consumer culture*. Although viewers enjoy greater choice, then, options remain limited to what a small number of media organizations choose to put on offer (Murdock, 1992). And while specialization and innovation undoubtedly account for elements of the commercial portfolio, a substantial amount of commercial programming, across a variety of channels, continues to consist of repeated, standardized formulas pitched at broad, mainstream audiences and centred on the minimization of costs and risks. As Graham Murdock puts it, 'more does not always mean different' (1992: 36).

'So what?', free marketers may say, 'the consumer gets what the consumer wants.' Leaving aside whether or not such a claim is valid, the key question, perhaps, is, do we want the future of our communications system to be quite so enslaved to the immediate and sometimes lazy decisions we all make with our television remote controls when flicking from one channel to another? Do we want such instant choices to guide the future or would we prefer to have the opportunity to collectively improve the broader, longer-term priorities and principles through which media are operated? Ultimately, are we content to be temporarily amused individual consumers or should we be striving for a media system that we believe is truly good for us – one which improves and empowers us and addresses us as active, engaged members of society?

QUESTIONS AND EXERCISES

1   Compile a list of arguments for and against the funding of the BBC by means of a compulsory licence fee payable by all households with a television. Bear in mind the possible alternatives to the licence fee in your answer.

2   a)   Try to produce a definition of quality that could be used to judge television programmes.
    b)   Is it feasible for regulators to fairly judge the quality of broadcasting output?

3   a)   In what circumstances, if any, is the censorship of media content beneficial to society?
    b)   What is the difference between moral conservative arguments in favour of the censorship of pornography and those of feminist campaigners such as Dworkin and MacKinnon? Is either set of arguments convincing?

4   a)   Is Rupert Murdoch right to say that commercial competition provides consumer choice, creates innovation and drives up quality?
    b)   In light of such claims, how might PSB be defended?

5   What are media for? What should their role in society be?

Suggested further reading

Baker, W. and Dessart, G. (1998) *Down the Tube: An inside account of the failure of US television*. New York: Basic Books.
Critical account of the history of the commercial television system in the US.

Dworkin, A. (1981) *Pornography: Men possessing women*. London: Women's Press.
Feminist attack on pornography as a manifestation of the objectification and exploitation of women by men.

Mill, J. S. (1975; 1859) 'On liberty', in J. S. Mill and R. Wollheim, *Three Essays: 'On liberty', 'Representative government', 'The subjection of women'*. Oxford: Oxford University Press.
Classic liberal defence of freedom of expression.

Murdoch, J. (2009) 'The absence of trust', MacTaggart Lecture, 2009 Edinburgh International Television Festival. Available online at: http://image.guardian.co.uk/ sys-files/Media/documents/2009/08/28/ JamesMurdochMacTaggartLecture.pdf
An attack on UK media regulation and the BBC by the chief executive of News Corporation Europe and Asia and son of Rupert Murdoch.

Tracey, M. (1998) *The Decline and Fall of Public Service Broadcasting*. Oxford: Oxford University Press.
Outlines the principles of PSB and provides a critical account of its decline around the world.

9

Decline of the National Public: Commercialization, Fragmentation and Globalization

Focal points

- Understandings of media as potential facilitators for a participatory public sphere.
- The role of media in the construction of national identity and culture.
- Arguments that commercialized media distort and discourage public engagement.
- Fragmented and globalized digital media and the decline of national cultural cohesion.
- Criticisms of the public sphere and attempts to nurture national identity.

Introduction

What role do contemporary media play in the ability and enthusiasm of people to identify with and participate in their society? Do television, magazines or the Internet enable and encourage us to engage with the culture and politics of our nation or do they facilitate a mass 'opting out' into a fragmented and globalized world of consumption?

Building on some of the arguments discussed in previous chapters, the forthcoming pages address the complex relationship between media, national culture and democracy. We'll begin by focusing on the theme of citizenship and the role of media in facilitating what is known as the *public sphere*, with particular attention being paid to the influential work of Jürgen Habermas. The chapter goes on to discuss the ways in which media facilitate and construct national community and the implications of this for belonging and engagement.

The second half of the chapter focuses on the impact of recent changes in the world of media on the distinctiveness and cohesion of national societies and, in turn, political and cultural participation. This will involve a consideration of the implications of an increasingly interactive, fragmented and globalized media environment.

Media and the public sphere

Habermas' public sphere

Discussions about the role of media as facilitator for citizenship and the public sphere often revolve around some of the early work of Jürgen Habermas – a contemporary German theorist who emerged from the Frankfurt School. Habermas' argues that the project of human emancipation is dependent on the ability of publics to participate in ongoing rational communication about matters of significance to their society and its future. According to his idealistic vision, societies should collectively progress and improve on the basis of public agreement reached as a result of inclusive rational discussion, free from the corrupting influences of money and power.

Writing in the 1960s, Habermas (1992) discusses, as a model for his vision, the development of the eighteenth- and early nineteenth-century bourgeois public sphere in Europe. The public sphere, he argues, consisted of a space for the development of shared culture and ideas, located between the realm of 'public authority' (government) and the private realm of 'civil society', which encapsulated commercial relations and the domestic sphere. Private individuals would come together into a shared space and public opinion would be developed through discussion of ideas, values and events. These ongoing discussions would feed into government and the commercial sector, guiding their direction and holding them to account.

The primary physical setting for this eighteenth-century public sphere, argued Habermas, consisted of coffee houses within major European cities, and its participants were the educated, bourgeois clientele of such establishments. Equally important to the process, however, was the development of a critical, politically orientated newspaper industry, which fed into, represented and responded to public discussion and opinion.

While he accepts that this eighteenth-century culture of elite gentlemen was far from inclusive, Habermas insists that this ought not to obscure the broader possibilities highlighted by what took place. It offered a model for the notion that private individuals might come together to form a rational, participatory public sphere and that the private interests of individuals and commerce would be balanced with those of the greater good.

Habermas argues that, during the heyday of the coffee house era, a productive equilibrium was achieved between the state, business, family and, of course, the public sphere itself. As capitalism expanded, however, public culture is deemed to have found itself increasingly squeezed by an expanding state and a drastic growth in the power and reach of industry and commerce.

Referred to as the *system*, these 'steering mechanisms' of society, including administration and the market, were dominated by instrumentalism and, specifically, an emphasis on their own reproduction and expansion. The gradual *saturation* of the system's influence in the realm of everyday culture, or the *lifeworld*, is argued to have resulted in the proliferation throughout that sphere of an instrumentalist, pragmatic logic and the ever greater distortion of the once open, independent, free and critical public sphere (Habermas, 1987). The open, rational public culture on which Habermas focused so much attention, then, was choked by the increasing domination of all aspects of society by hierarchical, instrumentalist ways of working and thinking.

In the course of the rest of this chapter, we'll focus on how these abstract elements of Habermas' account of the decline of the public sphere relate to the practicalities of media within contemporary societies.

Media and public engagement

Many have taken up the public sphere ideal sketched out in Habermas' early work as a vision for societies to strive for, often focusing on the role of media in such a project. They envisage a situation in which voting and elections constitute merely the tip of the iceberg as far as public engagement is concerned, with far greater importance attributed to the nurturing of an informal, open culture of everyday microcultural interaction, where values, ideas and opinions are constantly shared, exchanged and debated. The developing outcomes of such public interactions would then feed back into governing bodies in a substantive and ongoing manner.

Such theorists are united in their belief that media and communications have a substantial role to play in the development and/or survival of such a public culture. Let's examine why.

Stimulating and informing debate

The first role of media in the facilitation of the public sphere is the provision of a detailed and reliable appraisal of events, ideas and discussions of public interest – not least those relating to the activities of governments and other powerful institutions. In other words, news, documentaries and other forms of media should act as trustworthy stimulators of public debate and reliable providers of the background knowledge necessary to participate in an informed manner. One can hardly engage in meaningful, rational discussion without being strongly acquainted with the subject matter and a range of existing viewpoints and forms of evidence. As we have seen, it is not conceivable for media to be entirely neutral, 'factual' or unbiased, but for proponents of the public sphere this does not mean we ought to regard all versions of the world as equally valid or useful. An effective, empowered public sphere, it is argued, requires journalism to be trustworthy, rational, reliable, honest and thorough, as well as accessible to the whole population.

Representing public opinion

An effective public sphere would also require that the developing outcomes of micro-debates across society are relayed back via media to everyone else, both to facilitate the further development of discussion and to enable influence on powerful institutions, such as commercial corporations and government. In the ongoing provision of information and outlining of opinion, then, media must be highly responsive, reflecting the range of developments in public culture and opinion rather than imposing an elite agenda. A circular process of stimulating and relaying should take place, continually feeding and being fed by society's ongoing conversation with itself.

Acting as an inclusive discussion forum

As well as relaying public culture and opinion back into media through the intermediary of journalists, writers, actors and others, media should act as forums for the direct expression of ideas, opinions and information by members of the population themselves. Media should set themselves up as virtual spaces, then, in which members of society directly interact and engage with one another. Letters pages, phone-in shows and comment facilities on news websites all constitute examples of this, though, in practice, they are often rather limited ones.

Nurturing public belonging and community

For many commentators, the public sphere also implies participation in a broader public culture and the nurturing of a sense of cohesiveness, common identity and belonging. The political functions of the public sphere, it is argued, could not be fulfilled unless people feel that they have a stake in society and their engagement is worthwhile.

For Nicholas Garnham (1992: 369), this implies the need to nurture some sort of common set of values: 'it is impossible to conceive of a viable democratic polity without at the same time conceiving of at least some common normative dimension.' Such an emphasis on the generation of community draws on the use of the notion of *fraternity* by French philosopher Jean-Jacques Rousseau to refer to the importance of developing a cohesive national brotherhood characterized by strong bonds of attachment and mutual obligation and responsibility.

Consistent with Rousseau, the sense of belonging and community evoked by many advocates of the public sphere also tends to centre on the nation. After all, Habermas' account of the bourgeois public sphere is, as Nick Stevenson (2002: 61) puts it, 'explicitly connected to the nation state' rather than anything more local or international. Interestingly, in his later work Habermas questions the need for political engagement to be to rooted in normative cohesion or community and rejects the automatic centring of the public sphere on the nation state itself (1996; 2001). For many of those influenced by his early work, however, the facilitation by media of national identity and community comprises a key component of connecting private individuals with a culture of public participation (Garnham, 1992; Scannell, 1989). And it so happens that media and national identity do have a long-standing relationship with one another – the former often being credited with a key role in the development of the latter.

Nation as 'imagined community'

The notions of national belonging, community and pride relates to cultural convention rather than natural affinity. 'Nationalism is not the awakening of nations to self-consciousness; it invents nations where they do not exist,' argues Ernest Gellner (1983: 169). There is little doubt about the pivotal role of communications technologies here. From the mass publishing of books and newspapers to the development of the telegraph and eventually the telephone, communication created greater links and commonalities between localities, the distinctiveness and separation of each becoming gradually less significant than the larger entities of which they were a part.

For Benedict Anderson (1991), the combination of mass printing technology and the early stages of European capitalism enabled the mass distribution of books across national territories, creating large-scale, geographically distributed reading publics. The gradual standardization of print languages across national markets contributed to a concurrent homogenization of everyday language from locality to locality. Equally important, common printed materials generated shared cultural agendas and experiences, making it possible for people across each nation to read and engage with the same piece of literature. The development of newspapers amplified this by providing a time symmetry to the shared experience of the nation, whole countries engaging with the same sets of controversies and events at the same time.

Media were partly responsible, then, for the development of a sense among disparate people that they had something in common or, even, that they belonged to one another. Anderson (1991: 6) terms this media-induced sense of sameness *'imagined community'*. 'It is imagined', he argues, 'because the members of even the smallest nation will never know most of their fellow members, meet them, or even hear of them, yet in the minds of each lives the image of their communion.'

If the distribution of print media was heavily responsible for the construction of national identity prior to the twentieth century, then the responsibility was taken up by radio and then television in the years that followed. In most geographically small or medium-sized countries, the most prominent broadcasters reached the whole nation simultaneously and, even in larger places such as the USA, independent local or state broadcasters soon were rivalled by national networks that replicated content on channels throughout the country. The combination of spectrum scarcity and regulation ensured that only a limited number of channels and programmes could be made available each day – something that ensured listening and viewing often involved the collective engagement of substantial proportions of the national population with a shared set of cultural experiences. Especially in countries such as the UK, where prominent content was often broadcast simultaneously to the whole country, it became possible for the entire nation to sit down 'together', digesting the same stories, ideas or music at the same time. This had profound implications for citizens' everyday mutual awareness of one another and the distinct national culture that they formed.

As we saw in Chapter 8 the conscious fostering of national identity has also been a central element of public service broadcasting since the early days of Reith's BBC. While much has changed since the 1920s, media theorists continue to emphasize the importance of PSB in bringing national publics together – something that is often regarded as a prerequisite for more political forms of engagement.

Arguing that, 'broadcasting has brought into being a culture in common to whole populations and a shared public life of a quite new kind', Paddy Scannell (1989: 138) draws particular attention to the construction by television of a shared sense of time – in the form of both everyday shared activities and of a collective annual calendar, so that the population is brought together at regular intervals to experience and celebrate key symbolic events, from – in the example of the UK – the FA Cup Final to the state opening of Parliament, the events of Armistice Day and the Queen's Christmas message. One-off events, of course, can be equally important – none more so, in the case of UK audiences, than the wall-to-wall coverage within the country of Princess Diana's funeral.

Importantly, Scannell argues that the continued nurturing of shared public culture – which he explicitly connects to broader public participation and citizenship – is dependent on maintaining common media experiences across the population. For Scannell, this requires the continued promotion of a limited number of national mixed programming channels for everyone:

> equal access for all to a wide and varied range of common informational, entertainment and cultural programmes ... must be thought of as an important citizenship right in mass democratic societies. It is ... perhaps the only means at present – whereby common knowledges and pleasures in a shared public life are maintained as a social good for the whole population (1990: 26).

For Michael Billig (1995), meanwhile, as well as bringing members of populations together, news media provide regular reminders to audiences about their national identity. Overt expressions of national sentiment, for example, can often be found within coverage of national sports teams, immigration and wars. Yet Billig argues that, under the surface of such overt expressions there lie a multitude of mundane and barely noticeable everyday reminders of nation.

Illustrating the point with discourse analysis of UK daily newspapers, he demonstrates that, regardless of the political or market position of the publication, nation was evoked as a means of framing the most everyday and ordinary of stories: 'Britain's best cartoons', 'Worst places in Britain to be without a job', 'Britain basked in 79 degree temperatures yesterday' are among numerous unexceptional examples. The use of 'we', 'us' and 'our' as universal, unspoken code for 'nation' was even more prevalent, whether in headlines, captions or article text, as in 'Europe taking *our* money' or 'Time *we* changed Government.' 'We' could, in theory, refer to all manner of collectivities, but no one needs telling that, in these contexts, it refers to the nation. It is this barely noticeable 'banal nationalism', argues Billig, that makes more overt expressions possible.

In a number of different ways, then, media have played a pivotal role in constructing the sense of belonging, sameness and togetherness that tends to characterize nations. Media have provided shared national spaces that enable the imagining of broader publics, have provided shared experiences and agendas to connect people and have explicitly and repeatedly flagged our allegiance via references to and representations of the national 'us'. Particularly in the twentieth century, perhaps, media tended to operate in what we could call a *centripetal* manner, drawing geographically and sometimes culturally disparate people into shared spaces and, to an extent at least, binding them together.

For theorists such as Garnham (1992), meanwhile, the facilitation of such public cohesion forms an important component of the development of inclusive forms of *political* engagement and citizenship, such as those envisaged by Habermas in his original account of the public sphere. As we shall see, however, both Habermas and many of those influenced by his work accept that, as a result of a variety of factors, the bourgeois public sphere declined alongside the continued rise of capitalism and commercial mass media. Contemporary conditions meanwhile are deemed far from ideal for the generation of a contemporary public sphere. In Habermas' original account, the role of media in this failure relates to the inability of a commercialized communications system to facilitate democratic participation. For others, the recent dilution and fragmentation of broader national community as a result of processes of *digitalization* is also highly significant.

Decline of the public sphere

Despite the importance of media as a facilitator of shared national experience and identity during the twentieth century, the public sphere had already failed by this point, according to Habermas. The increasing domination of society by markets, the state and *instrumental reason* were deemed to have undermined his vision of a genuinely free, critical and inclusive space characterized by informed and rational public discussion. As part of this, he identifies a number of specific failures of media. The theme that unites these is commercialization – something which coheres with his emphasis, in common with earlier Frankfurt School theorists, on the rise of instrumentalism.

From facilitators to shapers

The range of small-scale newspapers and pamphlets in operation during the eighteenth and early nineteenth centuries was regarded by Habermas as suited to the task of facilitating public discussions by both feeding and absorbing a range of ideas, observations and viewpoints.

Subsequently, he argues, the expansion and intensification of capitalism precipitated a concentration of media power. As greater and greater control of the press – and subsequently of broadcasting and other media – fell into the hands of a small number of commercially motivated organizations, the impact of media was deemed to have shifted from facilitator to shaper: 'Whereas previously the press was able to limit itself to the transmission and amplification of the rational–critical debate of private people assembled in a public, now conversely this debate gets shaped by the mass media to begin with' (1992: 188). And this influence was deemed to have been used by corporate media to promote whatever set of political arrangements would best facilitate the consolidation of their profit and power. Rather than empowering the people by holding dominant institutions to account, media themselves became synonymous with the powerful – colonized by the system, as Habermas would put it.

As we have seen in previous chapters, the concentration of media control and ownership has been considerably accentuated since Habermas first broached the subject, with horizontally and vertically integrated transnationals exerting massive control across newspapers, television, film, publishing, Internet services and so on. Such extensive concentrations of control over the flows of information and discourse appear to centralize power rather than assist in its devolution to the public.

Commercially driven content

A further consequence of the colonization of media by commercialism is, according to Habermas, an ever more concentrated emphasis on profitability in relation to the kinds of content made available to the public. In an argument with which readers will be becoming familiar, it is suggested that the communication of culture and discourse becomes merely the means to attract audiences and advertising revenue.

Following in the footsteps of earlier Frankfurt School theorists such as Adorno and Horkheimer, Habermas blames this profit orientation for an emphasis on immediately stimulating but superficial forms of culture. His interest, though, is specifically in the implications of this for the public sphere. An emphasis on trivia, sensation, emotion and personalization, he argues, means that media distract the public from any interest in participating in important public sphere discussions and ensure that any debate which does take place is liable to be superficial, misinformed and centred on simplistic emotional responses rather than sophisticated critical reasoning.

In particular, Habermas laments the corrosive impact of a consumerist emphasis across all forms of media content, arguing that audiences are lulled into believing that their contribution to society lies in short-term decisions about the purchase of goods rather than collective participation in democracy: 'private enterprises evoke in their customers the idea that in their consumption decisions they act in their capacity as citizens' (1992: 162). For Graham Murdock, too, the empowerment offered by this consumerist vision is a superficial one:

> The consumer marketplace offers an array of competing products, but it doesn't confer the right to participate in deciding the rules that govern either market transactions or the distribution of wealth and income that allows people to enter the market in the first place. It provides choice at a price, but without empowerment (1992: 19).

Addressed in relation to news in Chapter 7, the theme of media 'dumbing down' often is associated with theorists interested in the relationship between media and the public sphere. Michael Tracey (1998: 264), for example, castigates 'the corrosive influence of the main currents of popular culture', which he blames for 'the trivialization of public discourse, an evangelism of the *ephemeral*, the celebration of the insignificant and the marginalization of the important'. Tracey connects this trend not just to deregulation in general but also to the decline of public service broadcasting, which typically has placed particular emphasis on facilitating public knowledge and participation via reliable, in-depth coverage of matters of public controversy and interest.

The circulation of culture, ideas and opinion, then, is argued to have become a largely one-way process, dominated by a media-driven agenda of superficial distractions, consumerism and self-serving current affairs coverage. Rather than enabling public culture to shape those in power, it might be argued that media, the state and other powerful institutions are involved in an ongoing dialogue with one another, with the population reduced to the role of onlookers.

For some theorists, however, the problems do not end there. Recent deregulation, alongside the digitalization of media, is argued to be threatening to dilute the broader national public culture that had been facilitated by the mass media of previous centuries and to undermine social cohesion and belonging. Habermas himself became increasingly convinced that cultural unity was not essential for the regeneration of the public sphere, but, for others, the erosion of belonging to a society threatens to remove a crucial basis for participation and citizen engagement in that society. Either way, the apparent decline of national cohesion is a profoundly significant development.

We'll examine challenges to national public culture on two fronts: first, via fragmentation from within and, second, via increasing contact with global culture.

Digital dilution of the nation

Fragmentation

The construction and facilitation of national identity by media in the twentieth century was reliant, as Scannell observes, on the common engagement of the national population with a limited range of content. Media bound society together, then, because a combination of spectrum scarcity and regulation meant that substantial sections of the population would have no choice but to watch or read the same thing. The daily agendas and conversational topics of whole societies were strongly influenced by a small number of programme schedulers for universally targeted, mixed content channels. In the UK prior to the 1990s, for example, it was not unusual for individual programmes to be viewed simultaneously by the majority of the national audience. Such was the homogeneity of the broadcast experience that people could be confident of their ability to converse with peers, colleagues or even relatives across the country about the previous evening's viewing.

Digitalization and deregulation, however, seem liable to substantially decrease the amount of media experiences that national populations share with one another in the future. By enabling the simultaneous transmission of numerous discrete signals, digital technology, alongside relaxations of government restrictions on the awarding of licences, has enabled a rapid shift towards a multichannel age where television viewers select from tens, or even hundreds, of different channels. Rather than trying to offer something for everyone, as the broadcasters of the analogue age had done, digital channels are increasingly focused on attracting advertisers by delivering particular blends of programming orientated towards specialist audience groups. Dedicated channels for sport, film, comedy, drama, music, current affairs and nature, as well as for all manner of specialist population groups, are a key feature of the emerging digital future. For champions of national shared culture, such as Scannell, such division of the national audience into different demographic or taste groups threatens the notion of a unified national public:

> Generic programming fragments the general public that is still constituted in today's four national UK television channels into particular taste publics whom advertisers are increasingly keen to target. In so doing it destroys the principle of equality of access for all to entertainment, information and cultural resources in a common public domain (1990: 26).

As well as offering an increasing range of specialist channels, digitalization also is providing greater options to consumers with respect to the time that programmes are viewed. In addition to the growing number of '+1' channels, which offer the opportunity to view programmes later than scheduled, personal video recording technologies (PVRs) such as Sky Plus and TIVO enable viewers to pause and rewind live television, as well as to manually or automatically record programmes onto a hard drive for later viewing. Adherence to predefined programme schedules is further loosened, meanwhile, as broadcasters offer viewers the opportunity to download or stream programmes via the Internet at a time of their choosing. This personalization of viewing schedules suggests a further dissipation of the common media experiences that predominated in the past.

If, at various points in their past, media have had a *centripetal* social impact, by binding members of society together, then, many commentators suggest, the new media environment is more likely to have a *centrifugal* impact, facilitating social and cultural fragmentation (see Figure 9.1).

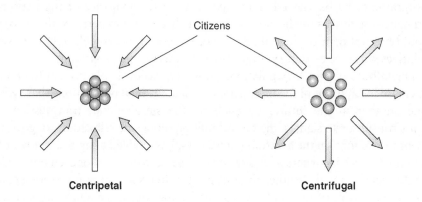

Centripetal   **Centrifugal**

FIGURE 9.1   Illustration of centripetal/centrifugal media impact

Tracey connects the pluralization of media with a 'retribalization' of society and with the demise of concern with shared culture or discussions over matters of common importance. 'Difference and diversity', he argues, 'may be socially formed, but they are helped along the way by new systems of communication, developed in the past two decades, which are profoundly individualistic and definitely not collective, public, shared or coherent' (1998: 263). When offered an increased range of choices as to what media to consume and when, then, it is argued that people tend to gratefully accept the opportunity to opt out of the broader national public sphere altogether in order to pursue specialist or individual interests and identities.

Globalization

At the same time as generating potential for the internal fragmentation of national public culture, contemporary media form an important component of processes of globalization, whereby national boundaries are increasingly bypassed by international flows of culture. Media are far from the only factor here, with the global expansion of capitalism as perhaps the primary driver – improved communication facilities and more efficient transport of goods enabling businesses to operate globally.

Meanwhile, the cheaper, faster movement of people has enabled substantial contact between cultures, contributing to internal diversity as well as intimate connections between minority groups and their country of origin (see Chapter 10). Related to such developments, however, the specific transfer from country to country of sounds, images and ideas has made a substantial contribution to transnational commonalities and connections.

Arjun Appadurai (1996) conceptualizes the relationship between media, communication and other elements in the process of globalization via five interrelated and overlapping global 'scapes'.

Financescapes refers to the globalized worlds of commerce and *ethnoscapes* to a world of people increasingly characterized by transnational movement, whether in the form of tourism or migration. *Technoscapes* provides Appadurai with a way of referring to the development and global distribution of technologies, including those that facilitate more efficient transnational communication. *Ideoscapes* constitute the world of political ideas, images and ideologies which, to an extent are also argued to have spread globally, despite a lingering focus on the nation state here. The element which most directly concerns us here is his notion of *mediascapes*, which refers to the transnational media worlds with which we all engage. These are enabled by the global spread of the means to produce and receive media, as well as the increasingly rapid transnational flows of content itself.

Consumers based around the world, then, can be expected to have consumed many of the same films, television programmes and music recordings as one another, to say nothing of the global paraphernalia and celebrity culture associated with them. Global chains of influence, meanwhile, also prompt the spread of successful narrative structures, programme formats and genres. Satellite and Internet technologies have even enabled collective global news experiences, whereby people across the world engage simultaneously with the same event. The death of Michael Jackson in 2009 provides an excellent example – millions upon millions of people around the world engaged, in real time, with the same sets of sounds and images, whether via radio, television or the Internet. The latter technology perhaps promises the biggest impact of all, offering users potential access to seemingly infinite amounts of imagery, sounds, music, commerce and ideas from anywhere in the world.

We ought not to assume that an increase in transnational connections and similarities of experience necessarily equates to the development of a monolithic global mass culture, as envisaged in the cultural imperialism theories discussed in Chapter 6. There is no shortage of global mass cultural products, from Hollywood blockbusters to high-profile popular musicians, and it also seems reasonable to refer to the spread via such mass images of a more general culture centred on consumption. As well as being received differently by different national or regional populations, however, mass cultural goods account for only a proportion of the global mediascapes envisaged by Appadurai. Universal transnational super-products, such as Coca-Cola and Kylie Minogue, are accompanied by a range of smaller-scale and more specialist forms of expression that also have a global reach. Rather than global homogenization, what is occurring may be more akin to a combination of fragmentation and globalization, resulting in the expansion across national borders of distinct, specialist cultures as well as more standardized forms of expression. We should remember that, as ULF Hannerz has put it, 'What is personal, primary, and small-scale, is not necessarily narrowly confined in space, and what spans continents need not be large scale in any other way' (1996: 98).

Neither should it be assumed that national consciousness is automatically consigned to the past by such processes. While the increase in global flows is undoubted, a significant degree of national distinctiveness continues to pervade the primary media channels and broader cultural identities of most countries. This is particularly so in the case of news agendas, which continue to be dominated by domestic stories and by national angles on international events (see Chapter 7). Meanwhile, well over a decade since Billig's work, newspapers continue to regularly remind us of our national affiliation in their references to the collective 'us'.

It is also clear, however, that, in their combination, fragmentation and globalization imply a weakening of people's everyday participation in broader national public cultures. I may be constantly reminded of my Britishness to the extent that it is ingrained in my consciousness, but it seems likely that the imagined sameness envisaged by Anderson is liable to recede at least a little as my everyday engagements with media and culture become more distinct from those of many other Britons and more similar than before to those of certain groups of non-Britons. Like millions of others, I may find myself increasingly opting out of the shared national public sphere and taking up instead the opportunity to follow my own more particular cultural path. And if cultural allegiance gradually erodes, it seems reasonable to ask, whether my interest in participating in national political culture is liable to recede with it.

The Internet: interactive but fragmented

As we have seen, Habermas placed the blame for the decline of the public sphere on the expansion of instrumental reason, including the commercialization of media. Yet, the affordances of dominant mass media technologies such as analogue radio and television also are deemed by many theorists to have played their part. Such media have facilitated linear mass communication from the few to the many and, while this may have been effective in the generation of national consciousness, it does not fit well with the notion of directly facilitating the exchange of culture and ideas by ordinary members of society. The hierarchical impact of concentrations of media power, then, was probably exacerbated by the one-directional bias of technologies (Mander, 1978). Occasional examples of audience involvement, such as programmes involving phone-ins or participating studio audiences, may have some significance and potential (Livingstone and Lunt, 1994), but they tend to provide the exception that proves the rule.

Emphasis on the perceived hierarchical nature of twentieth-century broadcast technologies has prompted some to ask if the development and diffusion of the Internet, which offers far greater potential for interactivity, might signal a revival of the public sphere. The capacity of the Internet to facilitate mass communication, alongside the interactive potential for millions of users to both consume and produce content, precipitated optimistic predictions about the re-engagement of ordinary people and their seizing back of power and influence from the Establishment. John Hartley (2009), for example, perceives a shift in the social role of television, from a broadcasting age where populations were represented in particular ways by a centralized media Establishment, to an age of online democratized productivity, where everyone can contribute to the creation of content and citizens increasingly speak for themselves. For Al Gore, meanwhile, an apparent switch away from the linear, hierarchical flows of traditional forms of television suggests that the Internet may herald a new era of interactive public discussion and citizenship:

> In the world of television, the massive flows of information are largely in only one direction, which makes it virtually impossible for individuals to take part in what passes for a national conversation. Individuals receive, but they cannot send. They hear, but they do not speak. The 'well-informed citizenry' is in danger of becoming the 'well-amused audience ....' Fortunately, the Internet has the potential to revitalize the role played by the people in our constitutional framework ... It is the most interactive medium in history and the one with the greatest potential for connecting individuals to one another and to a universe of knowledge. It's a platform for pursuing the truth, and the decentralized creation and distribution of ideas (2007).

Sure enough, the Internet does enable an unprecedented combination of scale and interactivity. It provides a seemingly limitless array of information, conjecture and culture for us to engage with and this engagement entails numerous possibilities for us to choose what we engage with and to produce as well as consume content. According to Maria Bakardjieva (2005: 127), such interactivity offers the potential for people to experience political and media institutions as something within 'attainable reach' of their everyday lifeworld something they have the power to interact with and influence.

Perhaps the Internet is more suited than its predecessors, then, to a situation in which society truly talks to itself rather than being talked at by the powerful few? From resistant citizen journalists blogging inside war-torn or illiberal countries to global anti-capitalist movements, there are plenty of examples of situations in which particular interest groups or individuals have effectively utilized the potential of the Internet to publicize or mobilize support for their perspective. Millions more interact with one another in relation to matters of everyday culture or politics via websites, blogs or discussion groups.

Important though such examples may be, we should be cautious about proclamations that the Internet will bring about a fundamental shift in power relations or a resurgence of democracy. From the companies that sell us our computers, software and broadband connections to those which offer the most popular Internet content and services, the Net has, despite its decentralized structure, become a highly effective means for large-scale corporations to maintain and develop their dominance (see Chapter 2). Sitting alongside new 'dot com' giants such as Google in this respect are many of the companies that dominated the 'old' media environment who have moved rapidly and effectively to establish online market share.

Crucial though it may be as a socio-cultural development and an object of study, the majority of the content created and published by ordinary users will only ever be engaged with by tiny audiences. Despite notable exceptions, such as high-profile user-generated sites of the likes of Wikipedia and those occasional user-generated YouTube videos or blogs that generate significant interest among the public as a whole, the most widely viewed and influential Web content tends to be attributable to powerful organizations of one kind or another. After all, it is only they who have the initial presence and means of promotion to consistently attract such attention.

For Howard Rheingold (2000), this apparent replication of existing power relations on a new medium is not surprising and optimistic proclamations about the revival of the public sphere may only serve to play into the hands of those seeking to exploit the commercial potential of the Internet.

Not content merely to dispel what he sees as optimistic myths, Rheingold, alongside David Lyon (1998) and others, suggests that the interactivity of the Internet may subject those who generate and/or publish content to Establishment surveillance and control. From the content of our e-mails to the websites we visit, the items we purchase, the music we download and the images we publish on social networking sites, everything we do on the Internet can be tracked and recorded. 'The spider spins the web in order to entangle and entrap the unsuspecting fly,' suggests Lyon, who goes on to argue that 'without disputing whether inherently democratising possibilities lie latent in the Internet, it is worth exploring the capacity of the "Web" to capture and control, to target and to trap, to manage and to manipulate' (1998: 33). We may be able to say more, then, but comparatively few people are likely to hear us and what we say may be monitored by controlling interests.

A further difficulty with optimistic proclamations of an online public sphere revival is that, at the same time as introducing greater interactivity into everyday media use, the vastness and diversity of the Internet seems liable to have a fragmentary effect even more concentrated than that of digital broadcasting. Rather than encouraging people to share content with or engage with diverse groups of others as part of broad publics, the ability to choose exactly what or who to engage with seems more likely to result in pursuit of particular interests and association with narrower groupings. This has two implications in relation to discussions of the public sphere. First, it is easy for Internet users to avoid any contact with matters of public or societal importance, such as current affairs and political controversies. Rather than encourage political interest, knowledge or participation among those for whom such subjects had little previous appeal, the Internet maximizes the ease with which people can opt out of the broader public sphere in favour of their existing interests.

Second, those who do use the Internet to learn about or engage in political discussions may not always do so via diverse forums orientated towards broad cross-sections of society. Many may, instead, seek out content and other users that cohere with their existing perspectives. An increasingly fragmented political climate may emerge, whereby people converse with those of a like mind and avoid those of a different persuasion. Rather than testing and developing their ideas and explanations against a range of others across society, then, conservatives, liberals, environmentalists and Marxists, as well as different sexual, ethnic and other minorities, may each converse only with others like themselves, preaching to the converted rather than broadening their horizons and thereby exacerbating fragmentation (Hill and Hughes, 1998). Combined with the increasing specialization of other media forms, this may result in a situation where, instead of having a single public sphere, we find ourselves faced with a range of distinct and separate 'public sphericules' (Gitlin, 1998).

Conclusion: national public – good riddance?

The discussions above suggest that, despite certain interactive possibilities, the notion of a national public may end up being further diluted by a new media environment that appears liable to encourage cultural fragmentation, disengagement and increasing flows of culture across national boundaries. It is equally clear, meanwhile, that the increasingly commercialized nature of the media environment seems less than ideal for the facilitation of democratic participation along the lines envisaged in Habermas' account of the bourgeois public sphere. Yet if, for one reason or another, the public sphere does look a distant prospect, should we lament this or celebrate it? For some critics, the notion of the public sphere has always been a problematic one.

The ideal of fully inclusive, equal and informed participation may sound laudable, such critics argue, but, in practice, the rationalist version of public culture called for by Habermas privileges a very particular elite set of cultural ideas while excluding other forms of culture and expression. A particular target for criticism is the eighteenth- and early nineteenth-century bourgeois public sphere on which Habermas bases so much of his vision, which consisted exclusively of the perspectives, viewpoints and priorities of wealthy and powerful white males. 'Was it ever open to the scrutiny and participation, let alone under the control, of the majority?' asks Kevin Robins, 'If so, where were the workers, the women, the lesbians, the gay men, the African Americans' (cited in Morley, 2000: 144).

Now Habermas may acknowledge these limitations of the bourgeois public sphere, but this does not prevent him, according to critics, from retaining significant elements of its elitist character in his own approach to the question. Some argue, for example, that the scientific reason which informs his ideal of rational critical discussion is itself derived from particular kinds of bourgeois, white and masculine ways of looking at the world which privilege certain types of argument and debate as legitimate, while excluding others (Morley, 2000). Notably, there is no place in Habermas' rationalist vision for emotion, affectivity and subjectivity, all of which are dismissed as commercialized distortions orientated towards the realm of the personal rather than that of the public. Likewise, champions of the public sphere who are critical of 'dumbing down' have tended to be particularly dismissive of content such as soap operas, game shows, popular news formats and celebrity culture, which tend to place emphasis on emotion, identification and empathy and also to be disproportionately popular among women and the working class.

It is suggested, then, that, while making proclamations of inclusivity and participation, some public sphere advocates end up systematically excluding subordinate forms of expression. This is argued to be particularly so in the case of those theorists who advocate the nurturing of cohesive national culture and identity as a base for political participation in the public sphere. That is because it is hard to envisage the defining and reinforcing of collective parameters, priorities, values or goals without the drawing of boundaries and the exclusion or marginalization of those who fail to fit in, whether in relation to class, gender, sexuality or ethnicity. Likewise, it has to be accepted that attempts via public service media to provide unitary space for engagement with shared or national culture are unlikely to be able to avoid marginalizing certain voices or identities. As Morley put it:

> By the very way (and to the extent that) a programme signals to members of some groups that it is designed for them and functions as an effective invitation to their participation in social life, it will necessarily signal to members of other groups that it is not for them and, indeed, that they are not among the invitees to its particular forum of sociability (2000: 111)

Some advocates of the public sphere are more flexible than others in relation to the issues outlined above. Some, for example, recognize the valuable contribution of a range of different 'rational' and 'arational' forms of expression towards public culture and debate (Dahlgren, 1995). Others reject what they regard as the exclusionary project of national cultural cohesion, focusing instead on the possibility of a looser, more dynamic and diverse set of different spheres of culture and discussion (Downing and Husband, 2005). Habermas, himself, meanwhile, has sought to move away from the notion of the public sphere as a national configuration and from the assumption that it must rest on any sort of deep cultural sameness. In light of trends towards fragmentation and globalization, he calls for the development of postnational public spheres, discussing a pan-European sphere as a potential example (2001).

Habermas' vision of a pan-European public sphere is unconvincing, however, and it remains questionable whether his ideals of popular participation and engagement can truly be separated from the existence of at least some degree of cultural connection and common ground between the different segments of society. Will people across the cultural spectrum really be minded to participate regularly and substantively in politically orientated discourse concerning the future of a broader society they feel little or no investment in? Dahlgren (1995) is surely right to emphasize that there remains the need for at least some sort of 'common domain' that connects together the myriad of groups and individuals that make up societies and addresses them in their common identity as citizens.

QUESTIONS AND EXERCISES

1 What might be the role of media in the development of the public sphere? To date, how successful have they been in this respect?

2 a) What does Anderson mean by 'imagined community'? In what ways have media contributed to the construction of national imagined community?

   b) Conduct your own analysis of the content of a daily newspaper. Identify as many references to nation as you can, including implicit references to the national 'we' or 'us'.

   c) Is the nurturing of common national identity and culture an essential prerequisite for the encouragement of political engagement in the public sphere?

3 a) What does it mean to suggest that media have shifted from being a largely centripetal force to a predominantly centrifugal one?

   b) In what ways have recent developments in media contributed to processes of fragmentation and globalization?

4 Is use of the Internet likely to enhance democracy and the public sphere or contribute towards their decline. Consider as many factors as you can in your answer.

5 a) Despite its inclusivist intentions, in what ways has the notion of the public sphere been argued to be an elitist one that excludes and marginalizes subordinate groups?

   b) Can there ever be any such thing as a fully inclusive national public?

Suggested further reading

Billig, M. (1995) *Banal Nationalism*. London: Sage: Chapter 5.
   Analysis of the ways in which national identity is regularly 'flagged' in daily newspapers.

Butsch, R. (ed.) (2007) *Media and Public Spheres*. Houndmills, Basingstoke: Palgrave Macmillan.
   Collection of chapters focused on the relationship between media and a range of large- and small-scale publics.

Morley, D. (2000) *Home Territories: Media, mobility and identity*. Abingdon: Routledge: Chapter 5.
   Discussion of the links between media, the public sphere and exclusivist constructions of national identity.

Rheingold, H. (2000) *The Virtual Community: Homesteading on the electronic frontier* (revised edn). Cambridge, MA: MIT Press: Chapter 10.
Offers a critique of suggestions that the Internet will automatically bring about a resurgence of democracy and the public sphere.

Scannell, P. (1989) 'Public service broadcasting and modern life', *Media, Culture and Society*, 11 (2): 135–66.
A defence of the role of public service broadcasting as a means of generating national togetherness.

PART THREE

MEDIA, IDENTITY AND CULTURE

10

Media, Ethnicity and Diaspora

Focal points

- The connections between nationalism and racial exclusion.
- Stereotypical media representations of ethnic minorities.
- Arguments about the promotion of 'positive' images of ethnic minorities.
- The concept of 'new ethnicities' and representations of 'diaspora'.
- The increasing use of specialist media by ethnic minority groups.

Introduction

What is the role of media in the construction of ethnic identities and the development of race relations? Can media contribute to an atmosphere of mutual understanding and inclusion with respect to different ethnic groups or are they more likely to exclude, foster misunderstanding and divide? Long-term and more recent patterns of migration have resulted in a situation where many countries have considerable ethnic diversity within their populations. Alongside the effects of war and natural disaster, the increasing globalization of markets suggests that movements of people may be liable to increase.

This chapter's exploration of the relationship between media and ethnic identities within contemporary societies begins with a focus on the relationship between media constructions of nation and exclusionary or racist forms of discourse – something that has implications for our discussions of the national public sphere in Chapter 9. We'll then focus more specifically on the question of representations of ethnic minority groups in media, engaging with debates about stereotyping and assessing different approaches to the improvement of the situation.

Finally, we examine the use of media by different ethnic groups, focusing particularly on specialist and transnational media consumption. Here, we'll focus on the implications of such specialist media use for the facilitation of global ethnic communities and the relations between such groups and the broader nations in which they reside.

Racism and exclusion

The notion of racial difference is now widely accepted to be a cultural construct, based not on essential biological differences but on a particular history of human behaviour, thought and discourse. It is this historically specific set of interactions and representations that established that, while some of the characteristics differentiating humans tend to be ignored, others, such as skin colour, form the foundation for collective racial types regarded as naturally distinct.

Important in the development of such understandings were negative Western representations of the perceived character of non-white people during the days of slavery and colonialism. Whether through literature, music, drama, journalism or cartoon, racial exploitation was justified by representing those on the receiving end as irrational, animalistic, lazy, uncivilized, childlike and, depending on the context, either dependent slaves or savage natives (Pieterse, 1992).Thomas Carlyle (1849), for example, wrote of 'a merry hearted, grinning, dancing, singing, affectionate kind of creature with a great deal of melody and amenability in his composition', while Rudyard Kipling (1899) suggested that white men carried the noble burden of passifying 'fluttered folk and wild ... sullen peoples, half devil and half child'.

As well as establishing specific negative perceptions that were to permeate culture for years to come, such discourse contributed to the more underlying understanding of human beings as divided into internally homogenous and externally distinct 'races', the relative superiority or inferiority of which were rooted in their fundamental essence.

More recent forms of white racist discourse – developed in the context of the migration of populations from former colonies to Western countries – have drifted away from notions of natural or biological racial inferiority and towards the notion of essential differences of culture. Ethnic communities, it is argued, have naturally different and incompatible collective values, priorities, allegiances and ways of living. This is deemed to make the co-presence of different groups within the same territory a threat to each of their identities and a cause of natural hostility and conflict. Consistent with such emphasis on territory, Martin Barker (1981) emphasizes that this 'new racism' is intricately interwoven with constructions of national identity.

Political reactions to the migration of blacks, south Asians and others to the UK from the mid-twentieth century onwards provide a case in point. Anti-immigration rhetoric centred on the perceived encroachment of essentially different 'others' on to British territory and the resulting threat to (white) British cultural identity (Solomos, 1993). Conflict was seen as being an inevitable result. Calling for the repatriation of immigrants, Enoch Powell famously suggested in 1968 that whites were becoming strangers in their own country and that a bloody conflict was in danger of breaking out. A decade later, Margaret Thatcher lamented the potential 'swamping' of the 'British character' and, more recently, the 'flooding' of British culture by a mixture of asylum seekers and economic migrants has been alluded to by various UK politicians and national newspapers (Malik, 2002). The importance of a cohesive national identity, then, is often used to justify the exclusion of those considered to be 'outsiders'.

Such connections between constructions of national culture and exclusionary, racist discourse have led some theorists to criticize all forms of nationalism within media. The sense of shared experience and belonging necessary for meaningful nationalist expression is deemed to entail an inevitable boundary between insiders and outsiders. Identities, after all, are relational, which means every 'us' is reliant for its meaning and significance on its differentiation from one or more 'thems' (Woodward, 1997). In Powell's formulation, the 'us' consisted of a particular white British identity, given meaning by its essential difference from the culture of immigrants. For example, 'it is ... truly when he looks into the eyes of Asia that the Englishman comes face to face with those who would dispute with him the possession of his native land' (cited in Baker et al., 1996: 4). While the strength of Powell's rhetoric has become less acceptable, representations of Britishness have continued to be dominated by a particular form of whiteness, consistent with Paul Gilroy's (1987) memorable assertion that 'There Ain't no Black in the Union Jack'.

As well as implying strong criticism of media themselves, such arguments raise difficult questions for those who argue that statutory regulators or public service broadcasters should seek to develop content that represents or fosters a cohesive national public culture (see Chapters 8 and 9). Such objectives tend to be inclusive and democratic in their motivation, but is it possible to encourage a clear and meaningful sense of a national 'us' without also generating a marginalized 'them'? If national identity, by definition, tends to exclude, then can there ever be any black in the Union Jack or is it the Union Jack that is the problem?

Depressingly for those who advocate the use of public service broadcasting to promote inclusive forms of national cohesion, broadcasters such as the BBC are often rejected in favour of more specialist commercial alternatives by ethnic minority viewers, many of whom continue to feel excluded from the national cultural agenda of the former (Morley, 2000; Ofcom, 2007b; Sreberny-Mohammadi and Ross, 1995).

Representation

The unhappiness of ethnic minorities in this respect brings us on to some long-running discussions about representations of marginalized groups in the mainstream media outlets of the countries in which they reside. Such debates concern, first, the extent to which ethnic minorities are represented *at all* within such media and, second, the ways in which they are depicted.

Under-representation

Media on both sides of the Atlantic have a history of under-representing ethnic minorities. Drawing on a range of studies, David Croteau and William Hoynes (2000) demonstrate that, until the 1990s, the proportion of African American characters on US television was significantly lower than the proportion of blacks within the country's population. The situation is deemed gradually to have improved, partly thanks to the development of a range of newer cable channels, but other minorities, including South Americans and Asians, continue to be under-represented. Ethnic minority media presence in the UK, meanwhile, was low prior to the 1980s, when a period of racial unrest prompted a concerted attempt to adopt a more inclusive approach.

Despite substantial improvements in the decades that followed, Annabelle Sreberny was minded to conclude in 1999 that, 'If you flick through the national channels for ten minutes, everything is white, white, white' (1999: 27, cited in Morley, 2000). This sentiment was apparently confirmed in 2001 by the then director general of the BBC, Greg Dyke, who described his own corporation as 'hideously white'. Importantly, Dyke's criticism was directed as much at under-representation within the staff, particularly the higher management, of the BBC as at the corporation's output.

If representation is examined from a more general institutional and industry point of view, it is clear that the situation has improved significantly, though there remains a degree of under-representation in key decisionmaking roles. Ofcom (2007a) reported, for example, that, while they accounted for 9.3 per cent of the employees of UK broadcasters – which is slightly higher than their proportion of the UK population (7.9 per cent), ethnic minorities only filled 6.6 per cent of senior management and board positions.

Stereotypical representations

Even more importantly, perhaps, the roles in which ethnic minorities have been depicted in media texts have tended to be *stereotypical*, constructing a narrow and generalized version of the lives and identities of such populations. If they are repeated often enough, stereotypes, according to Michael Pickering, are liable to 'render uniform everyone associated with a particular feature' (2001: 4). If people who are gay are repeatedly and exclusively depicted as feminine and theatrical, for example, then audiences may gain the impression that *all* gay men have such characteristics or even that they are defining traits of homosexuality. Importantly, while media stereotypes of powerful groups undoubtedly exist, it is subordinate and minority groups who tend to be affected the most, both in terms of the pervasiveness of the stereotypes and the depth of their impact. 'Stereotyping reduces, essentializes, naturalizes and fixes "difference",' argues Stuart Hall and 'tends to occur when there are gross inequalities of power' (1997: 257–8).

Stereotypical depictions of ethnic minorities have been a constant feature of the history of media content. Among the stereotypes that developed during the years of slavery and colonialism were the devoted and childlike 'Uncle Tom', the lazy, ignorant 'Coon', the larger than life 'Mammy', the 'happy go lucky' entertainer and, of course, the dangerous, animalistic native, all of which presenting blacks as irrational and inferior.

Although the most overt expressions of white superiority gradually receded, for much of the twentieth century, depictions of blacks and other minority groups were restricted to a limited number of often repeated character types. For some decades, African American film actors found that they had little choice but to play stereotypical slaves, housekeepers or violent criminals in a white-dominated media industry. The situation is parodied beautifully in the 1987 film *Hollywood Shuffle*, which includes a satirical advert for a 'Black Acting School' in which white instructors teach aspiring black actors how to play slaves, rapists and gang leaders and chastise students for failing to authentically walk or talk 'black'.

One of the most prominent African American representations in early television, meanwhile, was an adaptation of the radio comedy show *Amos and Andy*, whose presentation of the exploits of two uneducated black characters drew heavily on slavery-related stereotypes of ignorance and buffoonery (Corea, 1995). While the television version at least involved black actors, the original radio version had featured white comedians, in keeping with the broader minstrel tradition in which white entertainers mimicked African Americans.

The civil rights movement of the 1960s and 1970s had a significant impact on media and the variety of roles in which African Americans were depicted slowly expanded. By the 1990s, it was common to see blacks as policemen, doctors, newsreaders or even respectable sitcom families. Meanwhile, in more recent years, black Hollywood actors such as Denzel Washington, Will Smith, Hallé Berry, Wesley Snipes and Morgan Freeman have begun regularly to be cast in a range of starring Hollywood roles, including the latter as the President of the United States in disaster block-buster *Deep Impact* in 1998. The impact on media representations of the election of a real black president in 2008 is a matter of great interest.

Despite improvements, many prominent representations of African Americans remain stereotypical. In the case of the music industry, for example, opportunities for black artists are largely restricted to R&B and hip hop music and mainstream representations of these genres have become increasingly dominated by stereotypes of urban gang culture and, specifi-cally, a blend of male criminality, violence and heterosexual aggression on the one hand and passive, sexualized and commodified female groupies on the other (Perry, 2003; Rose, 2008). A far cry from the grass roots empow-erment associated with some earlier and/or more underground forms of hip hop, such images account for a significant proportion of the representa-tions of black culture seen in the United States and across the globe.

The gradual improvement in the range of representations of African Americans across other media forms, meanwhile, has not been replicated in the case of other minority groups, with the representation of South Americans remaining limited, for example.

In the UK, immigrant communities have also found themselves subject to media stereotyping. Depictions of Afro-Caribbeans and South Asians have centred consistently on criminality, violence and trouble, with images of angry young non-white men dominating *moral panics* in the news about muggings in the 1970s (Hall et al., 1978) and about urban riots, gang cul-ture, shootings and stabbings in the decades that followed (Alexander, 2000; Malik, 2002). The resonance of such news images with the stereo-types that dominate commercial hip hop has rendered the latter hard to dislodge, despite a substantial expansion in the overall range of representa-tions on television over time.

Black people also are often represented as athletes and other sportspeo-ple, though more rarely as coaches or sports presenters – something that has potentially counter-stereotypical elements, but may sometimes rein-force stereotypes of black aggression and physical power, as against thought, intelligence and responsibility, for example.

Representations of South Asians, meanwhile, sometimes reference a con-venience store owner stereotype, something which can include hints of dishonesty and corner cutting. South Asian representations also have also focused on themes such as religious conservatism, strict parenting, a refusal to 'integrate' with British culture and arranged marriages, with South Asian women often depicted as quiet, passive and subordinated victims of the latter. Such stereotypical depictions are increasingly challenged by a range of less conventional depictions, but progress in this respect remains partial.

Reporting of international events often has a significant impact on representations of ethnic minorities. Since the events of September 11th 2001, images of Muslims have become increasingly centred on religious extremism and terrorism, in both fiction and non-fiction, in many non-Muslim countries. More generally, the operation of news values ensures that reporting of Africa, the Middle East and South Asia in Western media is sparse and tends to be dominated by high amplitude negative stories about conflict, famine, corruption or extremism. Alongside romanticized depictions of traditional culture within tourist-orientated representations, such extreme and negative images perhaps tap into a broader form of orientalism – a fear of and fascination with the exotic, irrational 'other' (Said, 1978). This international element reinforces stereotypes of black, Arab or Asian minorities in white-dominated countries, as well as the populations of their countries of origin.

The reproduction of subordination

The impact of the under-representation and stereotyping of ethnic minorities is impossible to gauge in precise terms, but theorists are largely agreed that it has significant implications for race relations. First, such representations may adversely affect the way in which minority populations are viewed and treated by the dominant majority. Generalized and prejudiced expectations of black, Asian or South American people in Europe or North America may be reinforced, for example, and this may contribute to hostility or discrimination. As a result, minority populations may experience a consolidation of barriers to their achievement of employment or promotion, they may be more frequently stopped and searched by the police or be more likely to be refused tenancy.

Second, stereotypes may have an impact on the self-esteem, ambition and attitude to society of members of the stereotyped group themselves. If all or most of the people who look and sound like you and your peers in the media display particular characteristics, then, it is argued, this may increase the chances that you come to associate yourself in some way with such characteristics, whether you positively aspire to them or not. The absence of a range of representations and, in particular, of successful role models may compound existing socio-economic deprivation and everyday discrimination, further reducing hope or ambition.

A further possibility is that the experience of media stereotyping and other forms of discrimination by ethnic minority populations may prompt an active rejection of the values and goals of a society that has apparently rejected them. The more they feel stigmatized and oppressed, the more they may be pushed into developing separate, oppositional values, identities or 'survival strategies' (Hall et al., 1978).

Because the interplay between representations and broader relations of power is a circular one, any concentration in majority prejudice or minority disaffection brought about by media stereotypes may feed back into future representations. There is a danger, then, of a self-perpetuating cycle, whereby the cultural and material subordination of minority groups is reinforced by their representation in a white, bourgeois-controlled media and, in turn, the stereotypical depictions are themselves reinforced by the concentrated cultural and material subordination of minority groups (see Figure 10.1). In a broader sense, restricted or stereotypical media representations can be seen as one element of process in which the divisions between different ethnic groups are consolidated and hegemonic power relations are reinforced (Hall, 1997; Pickering, 2001).

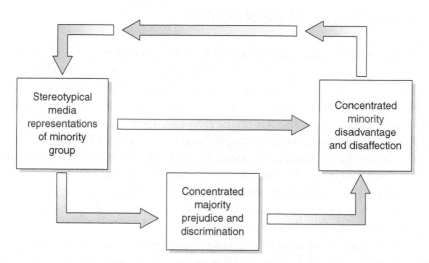

FIGURE 10.1   Simplified cycle of subordination

Promoting 'positive' images

While most agree that stereotypes can be damaging, there has been much debate as to the most effective way to address the problem. During the

1970s and 1980s, various attempts were made to promote 'positive' images of ethnic minorities, which, in one way or another, sought to reverse stereotypes (Hall, 1997). Yet these attempts differed in terms of which 'negative' images they tried to change and what exactly counted as positive.

Reversing stereotypes of passivity

With respect to African Americans, some 1970s practitioners felt that priority should be given to reversing of stereotypes of passivity, ignorance and deference that stemmed from the days of slavery. A range of representations of black Americans emerged that sought to substitute subservience and ignorance with strength, assertiveness, rebelliousness and superiority over whites. In particular, a series of so-called 'blaxploitation' films, targeted primarily at black audiences, featured funk or soul soundtracks, storylines centred on the ghetto and an emphasis on strong, black lead characters. Negative white characterization was also sometimes a feature, whether in relation to corruption, criminality or merely as the object of humour.

Focusing on the most well-known film of the genre, *Shaft* (1971), which features the exploits of a strong, cocky, sexually successful police detective, Stuart Hall (1997) argues that this sort of stereotype reversal may lead to its own problems. Consistent with the counter-stereotypical agenda, John Shaft occupies a position of authority and respect, as well as being the film's hero. Meanwhile, his maverick, rule-breaking character – who has been compared with James Bond and Dirty Harry – is anything but passive or subservient towards his white colleagues and superiors, and also retains a clear attachment to his roots in the ghetto and fellow blacks. The lyrics to the introductory theme music sum it up: 'He doesn't take orders from anybody, black or white, but he'd risk his neck for his brother man' (Hayes, 1971). Yet, as Hall explains, *Shaft*, like many of the other films in its 'blaxploitation' genre, ended up reinforcing a different set of black stereotypes, playing on the familiar theme of black male sexual prowess – 'He's a black private dick who's a sex machine with all the chicks', according to the introductory music – and depicting a ghetto full of stereotypical black pimps, drug dealers and gangsters. One set of stereotypes, then, was replaced with another:

> To reverse the stereotype is not necessarily to overturn or subvert it. Escaping the grip of one stereotypical extreme (blacks are poor, childish, subservient ...) may simply mean being trapped in its stereotypical 'other' (blacks as motivated by money, love bossing white people around, perpetrate violence and crime ... indulge in drugs, crime and promiscuous sex) (Hall, 1997: 272).

Successful, well-adjusted, integrated

Whereas blaxploitation films replaced subservience with black defiance and solidarity, a more common approach since the 1980s has been the development of images of ethnic minorities as successful and upstanding members of society. In the UK, a concerted drive towards the inclusion of 'positive' ethnic minority representations in the media, which began in the 1980s, has borne some noticeable results, to the extent that it is now unremarkable to see black or Asian presenters of news broadcasts, documentaries, children's programmes and other respected forms of output. Similarly, ethnic minority actors often are now cast as professionals, such as doctors, teachers and police.

Here, the promotion of 'positive' images implies replacing stereotypes of separatism and criminality with the depictions of ethnic minorities as integrated members of society who hold positions of influence and responsibility, are at ease with their place in the world and have mainstream aspirations.

A particularly important example of this approach is *The Cosby Show* – a US sitcom featuring an all black cast – that achieved extensive success among ethnically diverse audiences, both domestically and around the world. The show features the Huxtables, a harmonious and amiable middle-class nuclear family, who, with the exception of their ethnicity, are comparable to other mainstream sitcom families. Both husband and wife are successful professionals and caring parents, while their children are intelligent and well-adjusted. By achieving such popularity for a programme depicting so successful a black family, Bill Cosby, the writer and star of the show, had, according to Michael Dyson, 'permitted Americans to view black folk as human beings' (1993: 82). Yet, despite this, Dyson is not alone in criticizing the series.

The issue is with whether or not, in its uncompromising emphasis on upper middle-class normality, *The Cosby Show* adequately represents what life is actually like for African Americans. They may be 'positive', but the levels of affluence and harmony depicted are far removed from the low socio-economic positions of the majority of blacks in the USA. This prompts Mark Miller (1988) to suggest that, rather than easing the country's racial problems, the show reinforces the myth of the American Dream, acting as a reassuring mask that hides the inequalities which prevent most blacks from achieving the social position of the Huxtables (cited in Corea, 1995). While recognizing the achievements of the show, Dyson questions its failure to address issues of inequality and racism, suggesting that, in elevating a particular middle-class version of black identity towards social acceptance, Cosby may even have reinforced the marginalization of the rest of black society.

Such criticism seems harsh when levelled at a single programme. After all, diversity may be valuable in itself and *The Cosby Show* certainly contrasted with many other representations of African Americans at the time. It also demonstrated that not *every* programme about black people had to be about poverty, crime or, indeed, race. The perspective of the critics is worthy of greater consideration, however, when it comes to broader attempts to promote integrated, successful and financially comfortable representations of ethnic minorities across media output. Unless pursued with great care, such a body of socially acceptable representations may risk either not ringing true for audiences or obscuring the poverty and disadvantage suffered by many ethnic minorities. Furthermore, if pursued too stringently, the promotion of characteristics deemed 'positive' by mainstream society may be argued to privilege an assimilationist vision of race relations and to implicitly label as 'negative' anything that looks or sounds more ethnically distinctive. As Dyson put it, 'being concerned about issues that transcend race and therefore display our humanity is fine, but that does not mean we should buy into a vacuous, bland universality that stigmatizes diversity, punishes difference and destroys dissimilarities' (1993: 87).

There are two key points to take away from such debates. First, there is a range of different versions of what constitutes a 'positive' or 'negative' image and it is far from easy to arbitrate between them (Malik, 2002). To some, Shaft is positive because he is proudly and defiantly black, while to others he reinforces negative stereotypes of black promiscuity, separatism and violence. Likewise, some regard clean-cut, middle-class conformist television personalities as positive while others regard the promotion of such images as part of a project whose emphasis on the merits of integration risks stigmatizing ethnic distinctiveness.

Second, whether or not it is a worthwhile enterprise, it is important to understand that the promotion of 'positive images' may not always intersect with the promotion of a faithful overall picture of the lives of ethnic minorities. After all, even the most problematic stereotypes often have some sort of highly selective relationship with reality. No one would seriously suggest, after all, that South Asian people *never* own convenience stores, or that *no* black people have *ever* been involved in criminal behaviour. The problem with stereotypes – including those relating to South Asian convenience store owners and black criminality – is that they select, exaggerate and disproportionately emphasise certain character types while systematically excluding a whole range of others. Unfortunately, the same may be true of at least some attempts to promote 'positive' images (Pickering, 2001; Barker, 1981).

The burden of representation

A further problem with the 'positive' images approach is that it has encouraged the development of a *burden of representation* on ethnic minorities in the media and the arts who, as a result of being isolated within predominantly white media institutions, have found themselves being expected to stand for their entire ethnic group (Mercer, 1990). Unlike whites – whose ethnicity tends to be rendered invisible in Western countries by their majority status – the attitudes and behaviour of ethnic minorities in the media tend to be taken as representative of *all* those of their skin colour, origin or religion.

Attempts to promote positive images can reinforce the pressure on writers, directors, artists and actors to ensure that a socially acceptable impression is conveyed. As a consequence, limits are placed on feasible character types and storylines. Crucially, the operation of the burden of representation rests on broader assumptions that ethnic minorities are sufficiently monolithic that they can be represented by a handful of media characters or personalities. Contemporary representations may (sometimes) be 'positive' in one sense or another, but audiences still tend to be encouraged to think of ethnic minority identities in *essentialist* terms – that is, black people are regarded as all essentially similar and collectively different from South Asian people and so on. It is for this reason that Sarita Malik suggests that attempts to replace negative images with positive ones 'do little to displace the assumptions on which the original stereotypes are based' (2002: 29).

The problem is linked to that of *tokenism*, which refers to the tendency to have a single token black or ethnic minority character, presenter or guest in order to give the impression of being inclusive. Isolated in a cast of whites, the ethnic difference of minority characters can stand out strongly, further encouraging audiences to associate their actions and storylines with their ethnicity rather than more complex individual traits or contexts.

Tokenism of a different kind can be found in recent approaches to the reporting of racial issues in news and current affairs programming. In a well-intentioned attempt to refer to ethnic minority experiences and perspectives, journalists consistently refer, in the singular, to 'the black community' or 'the Muslim community', reinforcing the impression of undifferentiated blocks of people who have an identical experience and a unified viewpoint. This is further reinforced by equally common references to 'spokespeople' or 'community representatives' for such groups. Such references may help ensure the inclusion of views that previously were entirely excluded, but, in the process, it further reinforces the view of ethnic minorities as essentially different, abnormal or *other*. Imagine the derision news in Western Europe or North America might face if it were to refer to 'representatives of white opinion'.

New ethnicities and diaspora

New ethnicities

Partly in response to the problems described above, many theorists have shifted away from essentialist approaches in favour of an emphasis on the diversity and complexity of ethnic and racial identities. Associated with the work of Hall (1992), the notion of *new ethnicities* highlights the culturally constructed and malleable nature of ethnic identities.

If we regard ethnicity as a product of ongoing processes of human thought and representation rather than nature, then it follows that, rather than being a fixed state of *being*, ethnic identities are always developing, changing or *becoming*. They may retain certain stable or shared elements, but are constantly open to development, influence and diversification according to changing social circumstances – not least, experiences of migration. The process of becoming involves ongoing encounters with new cultural influences as well as long-standing negotiations with intersecting aspects of identity, such as social class, gender, sexuality, locality, career and even strongly held leisure-related affiliations. The fluidity of ethnic identities, then, makes them subject to internal differentiation and external overlap.

Hall's approach focused attention on visible developments in the identi-ties of second- and third-generation members of minority groups in coun-tries such as the UK. The affiliation of these younger generations to their ethnic roots was increasingly becoming intertwined with the experience of growing up in urban, media-saturated Western environments. Rather than being simply 'Muslim', 'Chinese' or 'black', they were becoming distinctly and visibly 'black and British' in addition to more specific attachments to neighbourhood, age group, cultural interests and peer groups.

These complex emerging identities have been illustrated by some theorists with reference to the hybrid forms of popular culture they have given rise to. The development and consumption by British Indian youth of Bhangra and post-Bhangra forms of music, for example, entailed a fusion of selected elements of traditional Indian music with Western urban dance rhythms and sequences (Huq, 2006). The hybrid nature of Bhangra, along with a range of local variants of hip hop and other 'mixed' cultural forms, serves to illustrate the richly complex ethnic identities of those who created and consumed them and, specifically, the reconciling of heritage with everyday multiracial local contexts (Back, 1996; Gidley, 2007).

The notion of new ethnicities encapsulates these cultural developments by young people as part of a more general emphasis on the complexity and fluidity of *all* ethnic identities. It implies a rejection of positive image campaigns and tokenistic approaches to questions of media representation that reinforce the notion of ethnic identities as monolithic. If British Indian consists of countless different combinations of local, generational, age, gender, class, caste and peer-group identities, then to speak of the representation of British Indians by a single spokesperson, character or personality looks simplistic in the extreme. This, though, should not be taken to mean that ethnicity is insignificant or that it does not continue to engender crucial shared experiences, affiliations and collective differences. In order to capture the continuing importance of shared ethnic experience in the context of historical patterns of migration, many theorists have turned to the notion of diaspora.

Diaspora

Originating from biological references to the scattering of seeds, the sociological use of the term *diaspora* refers to the dispersal around the globe of people who share a common point of origin. Diaspora encompasses both migrants themselves and their descendants who grow up within the destination or 'host' country. At the same time as allowing for the development of internal differences within each diasporic population – not least in terms of age, generation and contrasting destination country experiences – diaspora also draws attention to enduring affinities with and attachments to the transnational diasporic community and, in particular, the country or continent of origin – usually referred to as the 'mother country'.

For Paul Gilroy (1993), diaspora encompasses not just a mutual connection to shared *roots* in the mother country or continent, but the shared experience of migration itself – the sense of common *routes* across the globe. In the case of those of African origin, we can envisage a triangle of historical migration routes across what Gilroy terms *The Black Atlantic*, consisting predominantly of forced movement between Africa, the Caribbean and USA during the days of slavery and then voluntary migration from both the Caribbean and Africa itself to countries in Europe after the World War II. In the case of populations associated with the Indian subcontinent, migration routes from the second half of the twentieth century onwards have taken populations to Western Europe, North America and the Middle East, among other destinations. There are numerous other examples of diasporic groupings, the transnational migration routes of which were formed in different ways, for different reasons and at different times.

No concept is perfect, but the notion of diaspora offers a way of thinking about ethnicity that enables exploration of fluidities and differences within particular groups at the same time as recognizing the sense of identification which often either loosely or strongly binds members together.

Representing diaspora

In contrast to attempts to encourage specifically positive images, a range of ethnic minority film makers in the UK have sought to generate more complex sets of representations that seek to be faithful to some of the shared realities of life for ethnic minorities at the same time as exploring a range of complexities and differences. So-called '*diaspora films*' often centre on the ways in which a range of characters negotiate their own path between cultural traditions associated with their ethnic heritage and elements of life within the society they live in.

The aim has been to contest stereotypes and essentialist notions of ethnicity by presenting the trials, tribulations and conflicts of complex, rounded characters. Such films, whose depictions have involved the courting of controversy from some sections of the ethnic minority groups concerned, include *My Beautiful Laundrette* (1985), *East is East* (1999), *Brick Lane* (2008) and two films directed by Gurinder Chadha which we'll examine very briefly: *Bhaji on the Beach* (1993) and *Bend It Like Beckham* (2002).

Bhaji on the Beach offers a glimpse into the varied and complex lives of a multigenerational group of South Asian women during a day out to the quintessentially English seaside town of Blackpool. The film's title, soundtrack and central storylines point to the negotiations of the characters between South Asian diasporic traditions and life in Britain, covering both intergenerational and gender differences relating to teenage sexuality, domestic violence, marriage separation, multiracial relationships, non-marital pregnancy and the shared experience of white racism.

The themes of generational conflict and of negotiating between different cultures are taken up a decade later in Chadha's lighter, more mainstream-orientated *Bend It Like Beckham*. The plot centres on the love for football of teenage Sikh girl, Jess (Jesminder), and the tensions this creates with her parents. Both Jess and her older sister, Pinky, break their parents' rules, but while Pinky's hyper-feminine identity and premarital sex eventually are channelled into a traditional marriage, Jess' ambitions are orientated towards a professional football career and her romantic designs on her white coach – something that creates further tensions. A range of representations of young male Asian identity are also encountered along the way, including Jess' gay friend, Tony, and a range of more peripheral laddish characters.

The varied and complex representations found in diaspora films have been built on by other forms of media centred on ethnic minority life, including comedy. The UK series *Goodness Gracious Me* presents a satirical interpretation of a range of distinctively British Asian character types, referencing both diasporic heritage and negotiations with British life. Various facets of both young and old Asian identities are mocked from a knowing, insider's point of view, as are aspects of established British culture, including its treatment of Asians. In one sketch, for example, the obsession of white British people with going to Indian restaurants is satirized by a group of Asian characters 'going for an English' (including belching, patronizing the waiter and ordering the 'blandest thing on the menu') after a night out drinking. The show is of particular interest, according to Malik (2002: 103), because it goes 'inside the stereotype', tackling it head on and even at times colluding with it, but with a crucial knowing wink.

None of these forms of representation is beyond critique. Even in their desire to counter monolithic views of ethnicity with a complex diversity of depictions, directors of diaspora films have sometimes ended up reinforcing certain familiar stereotypes (Hussain, 2005). Certainly, images such as the repressive Asian husband and backward-looking Asian parents and traditions seem to have been reinforced in texts that, at times, present an overly crude dichotomy between established diasporic traditions and a younger generation keener to embrace modern Britain.

A further difficulty is that – with the possible exception of *Bend It Like Beckham* – the emphasis on ethnic minority lives and identities tends to result in diaspora films being pigeonholed as specialist ethnic minority texts. Even in the case of *Goodness Gracious Me*, which gained a substantial mainstream audience, the distinct and deliberate 'Asianness' of the programme rendered it, too, vulnerable to pigeonholing. Despite its range of satirical characters, it may ultimately have been viewed by many as an Asian spectacle – an amusing and entertaining portrait of the curious ways of the 'other'. Nevertheless, complex representations such as these have played a role in a gradual, if stuttering, trend towards a greater range of representations and, as part of this, more complex characterizations that refuse to fit into simple 'positive' or 'negative', 'integrated' or 'non-integrated' pigeonholes.

Audience segregation

As the range and complexity of media representations of people from different ethnic groups gradually increases, so does another trend. As part of a broader proliferation in the range of media available to audiences, there has been a growth in the use by ethnic minorities of specialist media. Connected with developments in media technologies and deregulation, this trend reflects an ongoing disillusionment among many minority groups with the ways in which they are represented elsewhere (Gillespie, 1995; Sreberny-Mohammadi and Ross, 1995).

It also relates, though, to the obvious appeal of an increasing number of media outlets that offer the prospect of reinforcing connections with the transnational diaspora and country of origin. Myria Georgiou explains that, for dispersed populations, 'the construction of shared imagination, images and sounds have always been key elements of sustaining community' (2002: 3).

Newspapers, video and global Bollywood

The use of specialist media by ethnic minority groups is not entirely a phenomenon of the digital age. Specialist newspapers have long formed an important part of diasporic communications networks and continue to do so today, with local retailers within areas with high concentrations of particular groupings often stocking a range of such publications. Many of these are based within and orientated specifically towards such localized populations, while others are distributed globally. For example, in the case of newspapers serving the Tamil diaspora, *Puthinam* is orientated particularly towards Tamils based in London, while *Eelamurazu* is distributed across the diaspora throughout Europe and Canada (Antony, 2009). Specialist local radio can also play an important role. Georgiou, for example, emphasizes the significance of Greek London Radio as a source of community participation for members of the Greek diaspora located within the city (2001).

During the 1980s and 1990s, video became a significant facilitator of diasporic identities. In her study of the use of media use by Punjabi young people and their families in the London suburb of Southall, Marie Gillespie (1995) demonstrates the importance of video as a means of engaging with forms of media content associated with the diaspora and unavailable on UK television. Such was the demand in Southall for the films of Bollywood, for example, that dedicated networks of specialist video hire stores had emerged. Gillespie explains that the viewing of such films, alongside a range of other specialist videos, was sometimes driven by parents, who would use them as a means of bringing the family together, discussing matters of morality and encouraging their children to engage with Hindi or Punjabi language and their broader diasporic cultural roots. However, she also emphasizes the independent enthusiasm for Bollywood and associated fashion, celebrities and magazines of many young people, particularly girls.

Defying theories that suggest the globalization of media is a one-way process, Bollywood has become a massively lucrative enterprise, the success of which partly rests on the large-scale export of films to communities associated with the Indian diaspora (often referred to as non-resident Indians, or, NRIs). Indeed, Bollywood – along with its associated fashion, music and celebrity industries – has become increasingly orientated towards the potential of its export market, producing increasing numbers of films, including the London-based *Dilwale Dulhania Le Jayange* (1995), which feature NRI settings, characters and experiences, including generational tensions. This orientation, alongside the gradual pushing of boundaries of taste and decency has ensured that this NRI market includes younger as well as older generations, cementing its place in the shared cultural imagining of the transnational Indian diaspora.

Digital specialization

Recent transformations in media technology have substantially expanded the range of possibilities for specialist intra-diaspora communication. Digital television services offer the potential to avoid mainstream mixed channels altogether in favour of more specialist alternatives that are defined partially or wholly by their ethnic orientation. Viacom's Black Entertainment Television network, for example, covers a blend of music, film, religious broadcasts and news targeted towards the US's African American population and, in 2008, it began to broadcast in the UK, too. Meanwhile the Zee TV network broadcasts a mixture of drama, comedy, news, documentaries and films to South Asian audiences in the UK, Europe and the USA. While such content is often enjoyed within the domestic sphere, Georgiou shows in relation to research on Greek Cypriots in London, that transnational television stations also play an important role when enjoyed publicly in spaces such as minority community centres (2001).

The popularity of such specialist television services is as clear as is the disillusionment of many ethnic minority populations with established broadcasters within their country of residence. Research by UK media regulator Ofcom (2007b) confirms that minorities are less likely than whites to watch content produced by the country's dominant public service broadcasters and their comparatively high take-up of digital services often relates to a desire for specialist content. In response to this situation, the BBC recently has developed specialist ethnic minority radio services in the form of Radio 1 Extra, which is orientated towards a range of black music genres, and BBC Asian Network, which covers music, culture and discussion orientated towards British Asian youth. Given the historical emphasis of the corporation on attempting to unite the nation by means of universal programming, the development of separate services for minorities represents a considerable departure.

Online diaspora

Also of significance are the increasing possibilities of the Internet with respect to the reinforcement and development of transnational diasporic communities. Research by Ofcom (2007b) indicates that Internet take-up by ethnic minority groups is higher than that of the UK's population as a whole and that adults from India and Pakistan spend more hours online than any other grouping. Qualitative research, meanwhile, suggests that the maintenance of diasporic cultural connections constitutes a significant component of the use of the Internet by minorities. According to Georgiou, the Internet allows communities that are disenfranchised by the mainstream national media to 'gain access and the right to speak in a transnational public' (2002: 2).

In her study of diaspora groups within Europe, Georgiou (2002) highlights extensive use of public Internet resources, including information and news websites and interactive community forums where individuals could directly participate in the exchange of ideas. The New Vision site, for example, offered a support service for Ethiopian refugees and constituted a source of information as well as a hub for political mobilization and a facilitator of shared identity and social networks. Typically hyperlinked together with networks of similarly orientated sites, the use of such resources can facilitate what we might conceive of as highly specialist and ethnically distinct transnational imagined communities or public spheres (Dayan, 1998). Similarly, Internet use by a range of ethnic minority respondents in a Canadian study by Maria Bakardjieva (2005) was dominated by engagement with news websites and online radio stations orientated towards their mother countries. One respondent even used the information from such sites to produce a radio programme orientated towards members of the Ethiopian population of his host city, while others participated regularly in diaspora-orientated online forums. According to Bakardjieva, such facilities enabled ethnic minorities in Canada to keep their country and culture of origin 'within attainable and restorable reach' (2005: 125). The increasing ease with which multimedia content can be downloaded or streamed from the Internet, meanwhile, raises the prospect that such transnational connections may intensify as a result of the direct consumption of mother country television, radio and film content.

In addition to its role in the facilitation of public communication between members of diaspora groups, the Internet facilitates the maintenance and development of disorganized sets of personal ties via more private forms of communication. In both Georgiou and Bakardjieva's studies, extended family and friendship networks were maintained across thousands of miles by means of e-mail or instant messenger conversations and the exchange of photographs and other electronic artefacts. Social networking sites such as MySpace, Facebook and Twitter may provide even more effective and flexible means of reinforcing personal social networks across the diaspora by combining elements of both private and public communication (boyd, 2008).

Conclusion: empowerment or ghettoization?

In many respects, the increasing availability of specialist local and transnational forms of media to ethnic minority groups may be regarded as a positive note on which to end the chapter. Populations long under-represented, stereotyped and saddled with the burden of representation are able to engage with extensive amounts of public culture, discussion and ideas orientated specifically towards people of their ethnicity as well as to maintain regular personal contact with friends and relatives, both locally and across the global diaspora. Many members of diasporic populations are connected intensively to broader networks of representation, interaction and ideas with which they feel able to identify and, as a consequence, their sense of belonging to distinct transnational imagined communities seems likely to be reinforced, with all the social and political benefits that may bring.

For John Downing and Charles Husband (2005), the development of specialist ethnic minority media forms a key component in the positive affirmation of difference and self-determination by ethnic minority groups and refuses Establishment pressure to abandon specificity and be assimilated into the culture of host countries. Governments should support the further development of such media, it is argued, in the hope of expanding ethnic minority opportunities for expression and developing a new, disparate and multi-ethnic form of public sphere.

Although laudable in its rejection of *assimilation*, Downing and Husband's optimism about increasingly separate media for different ethnic groups may be a little complacent about such developments. If different ethnic groups increasingly participate in separate or parallel spheres of communication, might there not be a danger that the resulting reduction in communication and common experiences *between* groups could lead to an increase rather than a decrease in mutual prejudice and discrimination? As well as letting mainstream media off the hook in terms of the need to improve the service they offer to ethnic minorities, increased segregation within a separate media sphere may mean that the physical ghettoization of minorities within particular neighbourhoods is complemented by a similarly restrictive media ghettoization. Strong internal connections and communications may carry great benefits, but the cost of this may be an even more concentrated exclusion of minority groups from the societies in which they reside.

The situation may not be quite as simple as this, however. Particularly in the case of younger generations of ethnic minority populations, studies have tended to show that specialist minority media form only part of individual portfolios of media tastes and interests that tend to encapsulate a range of genres and influences. Gillespie's (1995) study of Punjabi youth, for example, demonstrates that, in addition to their viewing of Hindi films and other overtly diasporic media, respondents enjoyed a range of youth-orientated elements of UK and international popular culture, including soap operas such as *Neighbours*, the plots and characters of which were intricately drawn into the everyday contexts of their own lives and identities. It should also be remembered that, if ethnic minority groups increasingly are rejecting broad mixed-content media in favour of specialist alternatives, then they are far from alone in doing so. As the digital revolution embeds itself more deeply, audiences of all backgrounds are liable to become more fragmented depending on a whole variety of demographic features and cultural preferences.

It remains important that the obvious interest of many ethnic minority populations in specialist ethnic or diasporic media does not result in their being sectioned off and excluded from the rest of the developing range of media available. This makes it paramount that progress is accelerated regarding the need to include a diversity of representations and forms of culture across all types of media. In particular, public service broadcasters such as the BBC, must ensure that they continue to prioritize the needs of ethnic minority audiences across the range of services they offer and not just on segregated or specialist services. Perhaps, in combination with the proliferation of diaspora media, such a drive towards wider inclusivity might offer a balance between affirmations of distinctiveness and the erosion of essentialism and prejudice.

QUESTION AND EXERCISES

1 In what ways are discourses of racism connected with those of nationalism?

2 a) Why is there so much concern about the media stereotyping of ethnic minorities? What is the connection between stereotypes and power?

   b) To what extent do representations of ethnic minorities continue to be restricted in contemporary media? Consider a range of examples in your answer.

3 a) As approaches to the development of more 'positive' representations, what is the difference between *Shaft* and *The Cosby Show*? Which approach is preferable do you think?

(Continued)

(Continued)

b) What is meant by the 'burden of representation' and how does this connect to attempts to promote positive images?

4 a) What is meant by the terms *new ethnicities* and *diaspora*?

b) Carry out a detailed analysis of *East is East, Bhaji on the Beach, Bend It Like Beckham* or *Brick Lane* with respect to the ways in which ethnicity and diaspora are represented. What are the strengths and weaknesses of the film you have chosen in this respect?

5 Is the increasing availability and use of specialist transnational media orientated towards ethnic minority groups a positive or a negative thing do you think?

Suggested further reading

Dyson, M. (1993) *Reflecting Black African-American Cultural Criticism*. Minneapolis, MN: University of Minnesota Press.
  Detailed discussion of a range of expressions of black American culture, including critical analysis of *The Cosby Show*.

Georgiou, M. (2006) *Diaspora, Identity and the Media*. Cresskill, NJ: Hampton Press.
  Explores the role of a range of media in the facilitation of global diasporic networks and identities.

Gillespie, M. (1995) *Television, Ethnicity and Cultural Change*. London: Routledge.
  Study of the role of different forms of television in the interplay of tradition and change in the lives of South Asian youth in London.

Hall, S. (1997) 'The spectacle of the other', in S. Hall (ed.), *Representation: Cultural representations and signifying practices*. London: Sage.
  Includes critical analysis of attempts to challenge stereotypical depictions by reversing them, as in films such as *Shaft*.

Malik, S. (2002) *Representing Black Britain: Black and Asian images on television*. London: Sage.
  Wide-ranging critical discussion of representations of ethnic minority groups on British television.

11

Media, Gender and Sexuality

Focal points

- Feminist criticism of media representations of gender.
- Changing representations of femininity – from domestic goddess to glamorous career woman.
- Studies of 'active' female media users and cultural producers.
- Understandings of media representations of masculinity.
- Arguments about the marginalization of non-straight sexualities in media.

Introduction

Questions about the relationship between mass communications, gender and sexuality have formed the basis for countless books, articles and dissertations. As in the case of ethnicity, discussions about the nature and possible impact of media representations have long been at the centre of such writings. We'll focus on such matters early in this chapter, outlining the contributions of a range of critical feminist studies on the depiction of women in popular media forms. We'll then look at contrasting approaches that question what they regard as an overly dismissive approach to forms of culture and representation enjoyed by millions of women. This leads us to a switch of focus, towards audience studies orientated towards the way women use, enjoy and make sense of commonly derided media forms such as romance novels, soaps and magazines. We'll then discuss a growing body of work on masculinity and media before engaging with questions about the representation of non-heterosexual behaviours and identities in media.

Running through the chapter is the underlying notion that gender categories are culturally constructed. Our understandings and experiences of male, female, masculinity and femininity are, like our conceptions of black, white and Asian, products of a history of human discourse. Drawing on the work of Michel Foucault (1990), Judith Butler (1990) argues that gender should be understood as a series of performances based on prevailing understandings of what it is to be male and female. Gender, then, can be thought of as something that we *do* rather than something that we *are*.

Crucially, at the heart of these performances of male and female is an equally constructed set of understandings of sexuality that centre on the predominance of heterosexual, opposite sex desire. Dominant constructions of masculinity and femininity, then, revolve around discourses of difference from and desire for the opposite sex. The marginalization of same sex desires and identities forms an integral part of this. Meanwhile, rather than being arbitrary or equal constructions, feminists argue that prevailing notions of masculinity and femininity form part of a patriarchal system that legitimates male power and female subordination.

Constructions of femininity

Female marginalization

Although women figure prominently within media content as a whole, their role often is secondary to that of men. The number of blockbuster films with a female in the lead role – as opposed to one in which she functions as 'companion' and/or 'love interest' for a male star – remains low despite gradual improvements, a situation replicated across a range of other dramatic genres.

In the prestigious media sphere of news and current affairs, meanwhile, the Global Media Monitoring Project concluded that 'the world we see in the news is a world in which women are virtually invisible' (2005: 17). The study, which consisted of content analysis of news content across the world, found that women depicted within news are outnumbered by men on a scale of five to one and that there was not a single major news topic in which women outnumbered men. When it came to the 'experts' interviewed as part of news items, a massive 83 per cent were male. The situation was slightly better when it came to the gender of media reporters themselves, 37 per cent of whom were female, though forms of news regarded as 'harder' or more 'serious', such as politics and government, remained male-dominated.

Women also tend to be under-represented within key decisionmaking roles in media institutions. According to Ofcom (2007a), the proportion of UK broadcasting industry employees who were female was 44.9 per cent in 2007, but the proportion of senior management roles taken by women was lower, at 35.1 per cent, and, within the boardroom, the figure was 18.8 per cent.

Despite the importance of this continuing marginalization of women in management and media content, much of what has been written about gender representation has focused on an analysis of the particular roles in which women are represented. Often coming from an explicitly feminist perspective, such analysis has attacked media for reinforcing a *patriarchal* system in which women are subject to systematic male domination across society.

The male gaze

The most famous critique of the depiction of women in media is perhaps a short article by Laura Mulvey on 1970s cinema. Drawing on developments of Sigmund Freud's theory of psychoanalysis, Mulvey (1975: 6) argues that cinema reflects 'the unconscious of patriarchal society' and reinforces the subjugation of women to heterosexual male control and desire. Cinema, she argues is centred on *scopophilia* – a Freudian term for childhood voyeurism or the pleasure of 'taking other people as objects, subjecting them to a controlling and curious gaze' (1975: 8). In its stark separation of a darkened, anonymous auditorium from the world that unfolds onscreen, cinema functions as a voyeuristic medium, she argues, encouraging us to take pleasure from looking on an objectified private milieu.

Crucially, this process is gendered, so it is females in films who are set up as the object of scopophilia and males who bear the controlling and sexually objectifying gaze. This is ensured by the emphasis on visual sexual appeal in the construction and presentation of female characters:

> In their traditional exhibitionist role women are simultaneously looked at and displayed, with their appearance coded for strong visual and erotic impact so that they can be said to connote to-be-looked-at-ness … She holds the look, plays to and signifies male desire (1975: 9).

This role, as visual object, operates partly within the fictional world of the film, but its ultimate orientation is towards the *male gaze* of the cinema audience. Sometimes the audience gaze is mediated through the orientation of male characters in the film, while in other sequences this mediating role is bypassed and the female display is addressed directly to the camera.

The gender imbalance is exacerbated by another aspect to the operation of scopophilia in cinema. This relates to *narcissism*, or, the gaining of pleasure by gazing at one's own image. In outlining the 'mirror stage' of child development, Jacques Lacan (2001) argues that the child enjoys in the mirror not a reproduction of himself, but something distinct, superior and closer to perfection – an external, idealized image against which the self develops.

For Mulvey, cinema replicates the role of this superior mirror image, constructing idealized onscreen images of human subjectivity for audiences to identify with and aspire to.

This narcissistic element is also deemed to be strongly orientated towards the male audience. While female characters are optimized in their function as sexual objects for the male gaze, the cinematic depiction of males is as subjects of audience identification and aspiration: 'a male star's glamorous characteristics are thus not those of the erotic object of the gaze, but those of the more perfect, more complete, more powerful ideal ego conceived in the original moment of recognition in front of the mirror' (Mulvey, 1975: 11). The male cinema goer, then, projects his identity on to the active, powerful male star, colluding in his possession and objectification of women.

In summary, Mulvey argues that cinema is systematically patriarchal: men are active, independent and in control of their destiny, while the role of women is to satisfy the male gaze and, ultimately, to be possessed.

Patriarchal romance and domesticity

Mulvey's notion of the male gaze and her broader emphasis on the media subjugation of women have proved enormously influential, forming part of a broader critique of gender representations. While critical feminist analyses of pornography, such as those focused on in Chapter 7, apply the notion of female objectification to the most explicit media depictions of female sexuality (Dworkin, 1981; MacKinnon, 1988), other theorists have focused on more everyday, mainstream media depictions, which presented women as subordinate to and dependent on men, particularly within the domestic roles of wife and mother.

A study by Erving Goffman (1979) identifies a series of themes pervading the representation of men and women in magazine advertisements. When heterosexual couples were presented together, men were either taller or higher up than women and the implied power difference was reinforced by an admiring gaze from the latter. Also, women were frequently represented in submissive postures – lying down, bending their knees, canting their heads or smiling deferentially.

Another common trait was 'licenced withdrawal', where women appeared to be distracted – avoiding eye contact, withdrawing their attention, day-dreaming or fiddling with objects. In relation to this trait, Goffman notes that, while men's use of objects tended to be functional and definite – grasping the shaving foam purposefully, using the toothbrush in the most efficient manner – women frequently were shown caressing objects in a distracted, emotional or sexual way.

Overall, Goffman concludes that men are presented in adverts as independent, purposeful and clear thinking, while women appear subordinate, dependent, emotional and absent-minded.

The depiction of women in magazine representations, meanwhile, has been focused on by a range of feminist commentators, who have regarded such depictions as part of a broader patriarchal system of male dominance. A semiological study of teenage girl's magazine *Jackie* by Angela McRobbie in the 1970s illustrates a relentless emphasis on heterosexual romance. Picture stories with titles such as 'As Long as I've Got You' depicted cliché-ridden tales of love between 'dewy eyed women' and 'granite jawed heroes', for example (McRobbie, 2000: 81). Getting and keeping a man was presented as the primary concern of the girls – a goal whose achievement involved reconciling this natural female desire for romantic attachment with an equally natural promiscuous tendency in males.

Other dominant codes throughout the magazine reinforced this emphasis on getting and keeping a man. Pop music coverage was focused on the romantic potential of male stars, while a relentless emphasis on fashion and beauty is deemed by McRobbie to have been similarly 'predicated upon the romantic possibilities it precipitates' (2000: 101). In a nod toward Mulvey, McRobbie emphasizes that the Jackie girl 'is intended to be looked at' (2000: 76), something requiring close attention to images of beautiful models and articles on clothes and make-up.

The emphasis on women as dependent on men forms one of a litany of complaints against media representations of gender raised by Gaye Tuchman (1978), who argues that representations in news, television and adverts, among others, were responsible for the 'symbolic annihilation of women'. Reviewing a range of quantitative studies, she argues that women were disproportionately represented within the home, reinforcing their association with cooking and childrearing, as well as their financial dependence on men. Occasional appearances at work, meanwhile, were restricted to subordinate roles, such as nursing and clerical work, and women within such roles, she claimed, were often condemned or trivialized (1978: 8). Such conventions predominated, she argues, even within female-orientated media, such as soap operas, women's sections of newspapers and women's magazines. While more prone to respond to progressive social change than television, the latter ultimately are deemed to have retained a clear emphasis on marriage, motherhood and domesticity (1978: 24).

Post-feminist independence?

Representations of women have changed considerably since the 1970s. In particular, the emphasis on domesticity, deference and traditional romance identified by Tuchman and others has been partially replaced by more independent, assertive versions of femininity – something that can sometimes include a proud and explicit quest for sex. Targeted at financially independent career women, magazines such as *Cosmopolitan* and *Glamour* have for some time constructed an image of women who, on the face of it, go out and get what they want – something expressed in their careers, disposable income and ability to have sexual relationships on their own terms (see Figure 4.1, page 64). Such magazines even sometimes feature objectifying pictures of naked men (Gauntlett, 2008).

Sometimes referred to as 'post-feminist', this more confident, independent female also appears frequently in advertising. Chanel's campaign for its Allure perfume range in the early 2000s, for example, played on connotations of independence by featuring images of assertive and successful women set against captions such as 'sculptor, London' and 'women's rights activist, Somalia'. Chanel's campaign took inspiration, perhaps, from Virginia Slims' long-running attempts to associate its cigarette brand with women's liberation in the United States (see Chapter 6).

Such championing of female independence also extends to cinema and television. One of the most talked about recent examples, on both the small and big screen, is the globally successful *Sex and the City*. The show centres on the sexual exploits and dilemmas of a group of professional thirty-something women – a PR consultant, an attorney, an art dealer and a newspaper sex columnist. The four have different attitudes to sex: Charlotte longs for the perfect marriage, while Samantha is unremittingly promiscuous and Miranda proudly independent – but all have a range of brief sexual encounters, periods of being single and longer-term relationships.

As well as celebrating their differences, the show explicitly highlights the independence and assertiveness of the women – they consume autonomously, engage in relationships on their own terms and sometimes manipulate and exploit men. Their all-female friendship group, meanwhile, is presented as the one consistent and dependable thing in their lives.

The enduring gaze

In comparison with earlier representations, the presence and popularity of images of single, financially and sexually autonomous women should not be underestimated. It both illustrates and contributes to changing social attitudes about what it is to be female and what role women should play in society. Yet not everything has changed. She may be a professional success story rather than a domestic goddess and she may be sexually assertive rather than romantically deferential, but two elements identified by earlier theorists remain: the need to look good and the need to get male attention. And the two are inextricably linked, of course, by Mulvey's notion of the male gaze. It is partly for this reason that McRobbie (2008) argues that such images constitute a post-feminist masquerade: they emphasize particular versions of female independence, while simultaneously reinforcing elements of *patriarchy*.

If anything, the shift towards the confident city girl representation has concentrated the emphasis on looking good and doing so by consuming. According to Ellen McCracken (1992), rather than being coincidental, this emphasis relates to a mutual dependency between media and the cosmetic and fashion industries. McCracken's influential study of women's magazines illustrates the way in which the editorial agenda of such publications fits seamlessly with the need to sell advertising space to fashion and cosmetics companies. Such magazines link together the two themes of looking attractive and consuming fashion and beauty products with a third one: (hetero)sexual attention and relationships.

Assertiveness and independence are regularly emphasized and encouraged, but still the life of the *Cosmo* woman revolves around a more familiar goal – getting male attention. Even the pose of the model or celebrity on the cover of women's fashion and beauty magazines implies an out-of-shot male presence, argues McCracken (1992), her confidence, status and beauty associated with being looked on, admired and gazed at by the opposite sex. This cover image of perfect femininity and heterosexual success is deemed to act as a 'window to the future self' of the reader, who can strive towards it by taking heed of the fashion and relationship advice in the magazine and consuming the clothes, shoes and make-up promoted by its advertisers.

Similar themes can be identified in *Sex and the City*. The main characters are united by an emphasis on using their considerable wealth to indulge in extensive consumption, most of which is orientated towards clothing and accessories and, hence, the priority of looking attractive. It is no surprise that, like fashion and beauty magazines, the franchise has made substantial amounts of money from clothes, cosmetics and other product placements. Even more overriding, however, is that the identities and aspirations of all four women revolve around their relationships with men. The relationship patterns undoubtedly contrast in some respects with previously dominant images – particularly in the case of the proudly promiscuous Samantha – but, as the series progresses, the non-attached lifestyles of the girls are subject to greater and greater questioning, while the more traditional theme of 'looking for Mr Right', as Rosalind Gill puts it, looms ever larger (2007: 242).

Amid all her short-term liaisons, the story of the show's central character, Carrie, is dominated throughout the six series by an on-off relationship with one man – 'Mr Big'. The show's much vaunted climax involves 'Big' travelling to Paris to tell Carrie what she has always wanted to hear since their first encounter – that he loves her. The 2008 film adaptation goes one step further, with Carrie marrying Big and, therefore, leaving behind the single life that had defined the show. By the end of the series, all four of the women are in long-term, loving heterosexual relationships and, of these, Samantha's is the only one not to survive to the end of the first film. As a consequence, Gill argues that *Sex and the City* 'works to re-establish and re-affirm precisely the boundaries it appears to threaten' (2007: 246).

The increasingly dominant glamorous career woman representation exemplified by *Sex and the City* is also vulnerable to criticism in terms of what it excludes. Consistent with the vast majority of representations in the fashion and beauty industry, Carrie, Samantha, Charlotte and Miranda are white, slim, glamorous, straight, wealthy and upper middle-class. The show's version of beauty and empowerment almost entirely excludes larger, darker-skinned and working-class women – something made all the more stark in the movie offshoot, where Carrie's employment of a PA barely connects to the rest of the plot and comes across as a thinly veiled attempt to tick all three boxes in a single character. The dominant white, bourgeois image of femininity, both onscreen and in print, is also unremittingly heterosexual, with representations of homosexuality restricted to quickly forgotten moments of curiosity and, of course, stereotypical depictions of gossipy, fashion-obsessed gay male friends.

Not all 'progressive' mainstream representations of women in recent decades have entirely fitted into the wealthy, consumerist (hetero)sex-orientated stereotype, however. Various police series, including *Cagney and Lacey*, *Juliet Bravo* and *Prime Suspect*, have featured strong female lead characters and focused primarily on career-related exploits rather than consumption or sex, as have a number of hospital dramas.

Meanwhile, although their most frequent depiction of women continues to centre on some variant of the love interest and/or sex object role, blockbuster movies increasingly feature females as active, powerful lead characters in their own right. Ripley in the *Alien* films is infinitely tougher, cleverer and more determined than all her comrades of either gender and not primarily coded as a sex object. Likewise, Sarah Connor develops into a physically and mentally strong female lead throughout the first two *Terminator* films and a spin-off series, without overt recourse to objectification. Interestingly, both the depictions in *Alien* and *Terminator* focus on another traditional feminine theme – that of motherhood – but, in this respect, the action-filled roles of Ripley and Connor are about as far as one could get from the passive domestic goddess. In various other cases where females have been portrayed in tough central roles, however, equal emphasis has tended to be placed on their feminine sex appeal, as in *Lara Croft: Tomb Raider*, *Charlie's Angels*,

FIGURE 11.1 Wondermark comic!
Courtesy of wondermark.com, © 2009 David Malki, www.wondermark.com/521

Wanted and *Buffy the Vampire Slayer*, or on their status as a companion for the male hero, as in *The Matrix* or *Die Another Day*.

There are also representations of women who come across as more unambiguously objectifying. Principle among these are depictions within lads' magazines, such as *FHM*, *Loaded*, *Nuts* and *Maxim*. Nothing, perhaps, could illustrate the continuing importance of Mulvey's observations about the male gaze more effectively than the presence of close-up images of glamorous women on the covers of both women's and men's magazines. In lads' magazines, the images are overtly sexualized, focusing explicitly on semi-naked bodies and aroused poses. Such publications have made much of their ability to persuade female pop stars, television presenters, actresses and others to pose for them and a lad mag photo shoot has become a potentially valuable career move for female personalities seeking to climb the celebrity ladder. Women can be successful, intelligent and independent, it seems, but only if they don't lose sight of their primary role as sexual object. For Gill, this observation applies to images of women across media – in news, television programmes, film and, particularly, advertising, where:

> in the boardroom and in the bedroom, in the kitchen and in the car, wife and mother or executive or pre-teenager, women are being presented as alluring sexual beings (2007: 81).

Elitist critics?

Despite the apparent persistence of representations of women that might be deemed problematic, some feminists have been cautious of making criticisms of such depictions, questioning what they regard as the overly dismissive approach to media and popular culture of some of their peers. Since the early 1980s, concern has been expressed that the uncompromising criticism of writers such as Gaye Tuchman might be having the effect of denigrating lifestyles and media genres that have been central to the everyday lives of large numbers of ordinary women. There are three elements to this concern.

First, in implying that the representations they were critical of were 'negative' and that they distorted femininity, some critics are argued to have ignored the elements of congruence between such 'negative' images and the everyday experiences of millions of women (Pickering, 2001). Calls for the replacement of 'negative' representations with 'positive' ones suffered, as did similar arguments in relation to ethnicity (see Chapter 10), from difficulties with respect to what exactly was 'positive', who got to decide and what the relationship was between being 'positive' and representing women's lives in a faithful manner. In general, the approach of the early feminist critics equated positive with assertive, independent, powerful, rational and career-minded representations. This meant that images of domesticity, marriage and attachment to the family were in danger of being dismissed as negative or inauthentic forms of female experience.

Second, some feminist critics appeared to fall into a somewhat elitist dismissal of certain kinds of cultural texts. In particular, the targeting of criticism at media genres associated with female audiences – from women's magazines to romance genres – was deemed to have established a wedge between such feminist critics and many of the women they claimed to speak for. Given that such media were highly popular with female audiences, there seemed to be an implication that such audiences were ignorant, duped or suffering from false consciousness.

Some of the feminist criticism is deemed to have adopted a tone comparable to more general attacks on mass culture and ideology, such as those of the Frankfurt School and contemporary critics of 'dumbing down'. Often made by male academics, these broader criticisms have also tended to target those types of media most popular among women – popular music, consumer magazines, daytime talk shows, soap opera and celebrity news to name a few. Among other things, such genres are sometimes derided for an emphasis on the personal, the emotional and the private or domestic sphere – all of which are traditionally associated with femininity. Such criticism, it is argued, yearns for a version of quality that satisfies a dispassionate, masculine, public agenda, while attacking feminine tastes and priorities. By themselves attacking 'feminine' genres – albeit for different reasons – early feminist media critics are deemed to have reinforced this broader denigration of female perspectives, tastes and pleasures (Modleski, 1982). Joke Hermes outlines her concern about this approach as follows:

> The feminist media critic is prophet and exorcist, even while being, as many claim, an 'ordinary woman' too. Feminists ... speak on behalf of others who are, implicitly thought to be unable to see for themselves how bad such media texts as women's magazines are. They need to be enlightened; they need good feminist texts in order to be saved from their false consciousnesses and to live a life free of false depictions ... of where a woman might find happiness (1995: 1).

This brings us to a third problem. Like many other deconstructions of ideology in media content, feminist critics have tended to assume that gendered meanings are predetermined and that audiences are liable to be passively influenced by them. In Mulvey's critique of cinema, for example, it is assumed that the gaze of the audience is always positioned as male so that even female audience members are forced into this perspective by the ways in which films are coded. Greater consideration of audience dynamics surely would illustrate that this assumption is too rigid and that, despite the tendency towards patriarchal coding, there are various opportunities for women to gain visual or erotic pleasure, either via a heterosexual gaze focused on male characters or a lesbian female-to-female gaze (Gauntlett, 2008). Determining that a representation is definitively either patriarchal or counter-hegemonic, then, may take insufficient account of the way the texts in question are used by audiences. A range of studies of female audiences since the 1980s have sought to address this inadequacy.

Empowering possibilities

Reading the romance

One of the first studies to focus in detail on female audiences was Janice Radway's analysis of the world of romantic fiction. Popular with female audiences, this literary genre had been subject to extensive criticism from some feminists. Such critics attacked the apparently standardized, patriarchal and heterosexist narratives of the stories, which invariably would involve a lost, unfulfilled woman finding salvation and fulfilment in the arms of a tough, assertive male lover. Janice Radway (1987) does not fully reject such criticism, but she asserts that, in order to fully understand the significance of romantic fiction, we must examine how it is used by audiences. Focused on detailed qualitative interviews with members of a group of avid readers, Radway's study foregrounds the role that novels played within everyday lives dominated by domestic and maternal responsibilities.

Radway learned that one of the most important motivations for reading was that the *act* of reading *itself* enabled women to claim time and space within the home. It was 'a way of temporarily refusing the demands associated with their social role as wives and mothers' and even 'a declaration of independence' (1987: 9). Yet, rather than being isolating, reading also connected them to a broader imagined community of romance readers, as well as to their local reading group.

Turning to their engagement with the content itself, Radway emphasizes the sophisticated and highly informed choices made by women regarding which authors and plot types fitted best with their particular preferences. Their preferred endings, as they themselves understood it, tended to involve not only the submission of the heroine to the masculine sexuality of the male but also his submission to her desire for more feminine forms of love. Radway argues that such plots provided emotional replenishment for women who were constantly called upon to support and care for others, because they offered a fantasy of being nurtured and supported as well as being sexually fulfilled. Neither this nor the other themes focused on by Radway are deemed to make the act of reading counter-patriarchal – after all, dependence on the male still seems to be reinforced in the plots and the women's escapist use of them. Yet, Radway insists that the women enacted a small-scale appropriation of the texts, interpreting the plots in ways that resolved unsatisfactory elements of their everyday contexts.

Subversive pleasures?

Radway's study is widely regarded as a pioneering contribution to the study of female audiences. Yet she is criticized by Ien Ang (1996) for having still ended up being too detached from the women in her study, interpreting the political significance of their accounts from an 'outside' feminist position rather than seeking to understand their enjoyment of media on its own terms. Ang's own best-known work (1985) also focuses on audience responses to a popular and often derided product – the US soap opera *Dallas*, which, among other things, was the subject of accusations that it formed part of the swamping of the globe with superficial US mass culture. Ang rejects such 'ivory tower' accusations and resists presenting use of the text as a form of compensation for downtrodden audiences. Instead, she emphasizes the fundamental importance of the everyday emotional pleasures associated with 'loving *Dallas*' – pleasures connected with the show's emotional realism, which, rather than acting as an 'escape', became intricately interwoven with everyday life and identity. Ang also demonstrates the ways in which lovers of the show used a range of different defensive discursive strategies to reconcile the pleasures they gained from their viewing with dominant criticisms of it as a form of mass culture.

Other theorists have placed greater emphasis on the potential for women to generate progressive or subversive meanings from soap opera. Christine Geraghty argues, for example, that through their emphasis on strong, influential female characters and perspectives, soaps allow audiences to engage with discourses about 'the way in which relationships ... between men and women could be differently organized on women's terms' (1991: 117). Similarly, John Fiske (1987) outlines a range of features deemed to offer the potential for counter-patriarchal readings. The ongoing multinarrative structure of soaps, for example, is deemed antithetical to one-dimensional patriarchal narratives that have a beginning, a middle and a happy ending of heterosexual love.

In place of this masculine final climax model, soap narratives are ongoing, so that romantic arrangements are never complete and always subject to disruption and threat. The narratives often depict everyday difficulties faced by women, sometimes offering the space for audiences to interpret infidelity as an understandable response or a subversive expression of independence. Soaps are argued to be less overtly centred on feminine spectacle than some other genres, allowing a focus on sexuality as 'a positive source of pleasure in a relationship, or a means of her empowerment in a patriarchal world' (1987: 187). Fiske recognizes, however, that soaps also offer possibilities for patriarchal readings, pointing out, for example, that, in some cases, female infidelity may be understood via stereotypes of sluttishness.

Although they place emphasis on differential readings and uses, studies such as those of Radway, Fiske and Geraghty remain focused on the issue of the generation of meaning and the significance of text as the basis for this. In contrast, a study of women's magazine readers by Joke Hermes (1995) avoided textual analysis, focusing exclusively on the role of reading itself within the everyday lives of readers. Indeed, a key finding of the study was that readers themselves didn't always attach much importance to content or take it particularly seriously. Most found some features useful either in practical or emotional terms and selectively integrated these into their lives. But Hermes' interviews were dominated by discussion of the compatibility of the act of magazine reading itself with everyday routines. As a media format, they were easy to pick up and put down as well as being ideal for 'relaxation' – a term that might, in different cases, imply taking time out from work, worries or other people. Magazine reading is interpreted as providing sets of active experiences, then, that are only partially related to the detail of the representations on the pages of the publications.

Focusing more closely on readers' engagements with the specific content of magazines, a reader study by David Gauntlett (2008) identified a pick 'n' mix approach with respect to which sections people read and which they drew into their own lives. Some regarded the images and advice in magazines as providing goals and means for self-improvement, some enjoyed criticizing the kinds of identity depicted, while others regarded the magazines as an escapist pleasure of little relevance to their own lives. Readers also displayed a range of views about the potential impact of the magazines and some were sharply critical of the versions of femininity and masculinity they presented.

Without fully rejecting feminist criticisms of magazine content, Gauntlett emphasizes that they offer a more contradictory set of ideas than they are sometimes given credit for and that readers draw on and respond to these in a variety of ways.

From consumers to producers

Attention has been focused by some scholars on the activities of women who have challenged dominant gender relations, not only as active audiences but as producers of their own media texts. With respect to popular music and youth culture, for example, the 1990s Riot Grrrl scene centred on countering male domination within the music industry through a focus on all-female bands who angrily repudiated traditional gender roles, flaunting an aggressive and uncompromising sexuality through music, imagery and on-stage performance.

While successful bands such as Bikini Kill, Hole and L7 attracted much of the attention, the scene also was characterized by a punk-inspired DIY ethic, in which, as well as being encouraged to pick up guitars or organize events, participants produced a substantial grassroots network of printed and online *fanzines*. Content was focused partly on bands and events, but also on articles, illustrations, poetry and lyrics about gender, sexuality and female empowerment (Leonard, 1998; Schilt and Zobl, 2008). Although the movement gradually shifted out of the public eye, Kristen Schilt and Elke Zobl argue that the network of DIY communication it gave rise to continues to thrive underground in the form of websites, blogs and online forums (2008).

Studies of the fans of popular media fiction have also looked at productive activities that challenge traditional gender roles. Constance Penley (1991), for example, focuses on the female-dominated phenomenon of 'fan fiction', whereby individuals produce and distribute their own stories based on the setting or characters of existing fiction. Such fan-produced stories – usually distributed to other readers via online discussion forums – are diverse, but Penley's focus is on 'slash', a subgenre focused on the development of romantic and sexual storylines. Typically, such stories subvert the largely patriarchal and heterosexual orientation of the original fiction by exploring homosexual encounters between male characters. As well as contesting dominant understandings of mainstream fictions such as *Star Trek* and, more recently, *Harry Potter*, such interpretations present an understanding of sexuality as flexible and unfixed, something that contrasts with narratives of heterosexuality and the discourse of male dominance and female subordination to which they are connected.

Despite their significance, Riot Grrrl and Slash are both relatively small in scale, relative to the mass circulation of popular media products. Yet, in recent years, millions of ordinary young women, alongside their male counterparts, have begun to regularly distribute their own media via social networking sites such as MySpace, Bebo and Facebook. Central to the use of such sites are representations of oneself and one's friends via photographs and, according to Amy Dobson (2008), these now form an important component of the ways in which young people both contribute to and learn about constructions of male and female. Focusing on images of young women on MySpace, Dobson argues there is much within the content of such images that appears subversive of dominant versions of femininity. Women may still be the subject of visual attention, but, rather than seeking to approximate perfect constructions of feminine beauty, they tend to emphasize assertive, humorous and laddish poses and activities, including:

> images in which girls are making 'silly' or caricatured faces; wide open mouths and protruding tongues; poses which would typically signify a 'masculine' body (miming rear-entry penetration, squatting, legs wide apart, limbs akimbo and occupying space); and displays of drunkenness and rowdy behaviour (Dobson, 2008: 6).

Dobson acknowledges an undoubted sexual element to many of the images, some of which might even be interpreted as partial simulations of pornography. Yet she shows how their emphasis on what she regards as an active, humorous and grotesque bodily representation, contrasts markedly with feminine ideals emanating from the fashion and beauty industries.

Remaining critical

Studies of the activities of female audiences and producers, then, have been important in illustrating the limitations of feminist criticism of popular media texts. Yet, critical textual analysis ought not to be abandoned in favour of a complacent celebration of audience pleasure and/or empowerment.

Ang's endorsement of viewing pleasures, for example, may have been politically convenient in avoiding criticism of ordinary consumers, but, on its own, such an approach might risk letting media producers off the hook with respect to the ways they construct gender. Similarly, although Hermes' emphasis on the validity of magazine reading as an active and partially empowering activity is illuminating, the strength of her dismissal of more critical and text-based approaches is open to question. Williamson's accusation that feminist audience studies were in danger of endorsing a 'pointless populism' (cited in Gill, 2007: 16) is overly harsh, but the warning therein that feminist approaches to media must be careful not to lose their critical edge is pertinent.

The testimonies of female audience members illuminate a range of complex details about their diverse engagements and sometimes critical negotiations with media texts, reminding us that that the societal role and impact of media texts ought never to be taken for granted. Such details, though, do not preclude the possibility that consistent themes in media representations might have a broader pervasive influence. If there are limits to the range of understandings of femininity that are readily accessible within the content of a given advert, magazine, film or television programme, and if these limits are consistent with dominant existing understandings, then it does not seem unreasonable to identify the text as having the potential to reinforce such understandings. This does not mean all texts do this or that we should gloss over complex ways in which audiences engage with them. It does suggest, however, that the constructions of gender available within media content may be restricted and that they merit critical analysis.

Media and masculinities

Partly as a result of the crucial contribution of feminism to the establishment of the study of gender and media, a good deal of what has been written on the subject is centred on women – something reflected in the structure of this chapter, too. Yet, the ways in which masculinity is constructed in media, alongside the role of men as media producers and audiences, is every bit as important to discussions about gender, sexuality and identity. Over the past two decades, increasing academic attention has been devoted to this.

Masculinity or masculinities?

As Lauva Mulvey observes, the cinematic male lead is typically a dominant, powerful and sexually successful focus for male-centred audience identification.

Despite important elements of diversity, the last four decades of popular film have been dominated by representations of active, powerful male characters who use their prowess – whether physical or otherwise – to overcome the forces stacked against them and, often, win the love of the film's lead female.

For John Fiske (1987), another key element of media representations of masculinity is a practical orientation towards the successful achievement of goals. Thus, the narrative structure of male-orientated television series, he says, tends to consist of a one-dimensional plot progression towards a climax of achievement induced by masculine performance of some kind. Most obviously, male power is emphasized, for Fiske, through both physical imagery of muscular bodies triumphing in fist fights and via male control of trucks, fast cars and guns. The focus for Fiske's analysis was 1980s' series such as *The A-Team*, *Knight Rider* and *Magnum* and most commentators would agree that there has been a degree of diversification of narrative structures and themes since that time. Nevertheless, it isn't too difficult to find an emphasis on masculine purpose and toughness in contemporary action series (*24*, *Prison Break*), blockbuster movies (*Casino Royale*, *Die Hard 4*, *The Dark Knight*) and, of course, countless computer and video games. Even when they are not portrayed in physically tough roles, men regularly are represented as active, goal-orientated and competitive and as occupying positions of power, authority and responsibility.

Yet, masculinity in media is not quite as one-dimensional as it may first appear. Even the most extreme patriarchal versions of onscreen masculinity may entail ambiguities with respect to their social significance. The visual construction of extreme physical male prowess, for example, may lend itself in some cases to use as sexual objectification for the female or the homosexual male gaze. The clear and quite deliberate emphasis on the body of Daniel Craig walking out of the sea in swimming shorts in the marketing for *Casino Royale* represents just one example of this. The significance of representations of spectacular male physical power to heterosexual male audiences is also ambiguous.

For Fiske, rather than reinforcing everyday male experience, such images are more likely to act as unrealistic fantasies that compensate for the lack of independence, control or power characterizing most men's lives, particularly in the contemporary workplace (1987). The ongoing decline of traditional male jobs in manufacturing industries has arguably exacerbated the separation between most ordinary men and the physical exploits of their screen heroes, while the diversification of relationships and families, the growth of female employment and changes in attitudes towards gender have also contributed to ambiguities in the status of masculinity.

Sometimes the changing reality of everyday masculinities is itself the subject of media representations. At the beginning of the 1990s, there was much media reference to the 'new man', presented as comfortable with gender equality and concerned about his appearance and style. This was reflected in the growth of male-orientated style publications, such as *The Face* and *ID* magazine, and in a rapidly expanding portfolio of advertisements for men's cosmetic and fashion products. Women's fashion and beauty magazines placed emphasis on the desirability for women of this more image-conscious, sensitive male.

Another source for the 'softening' of male images was the phenomenon of the boy band, which re-emerged in the 1990s in the form of groups such as *Take That*. Orientated particularly towards young female and gay male audiences, the boy band combined some traditional elements of masculinity with style-conscious, highly sensitive, vulnerable and slightly built 'boy next door' features. Meanwhile, as Gauntlett points out, popular sitcoms such as *Friends* frequently depicted men who combined certain traditional masculine qualities with 'characteristics of sensitivity and gentleness, and male-bonding' (2008: 65).

Lads' mags and contradictory representations

Yet, far from moving seamlessly from a regime of aggressive, powerful stereotypes to one dominated by sensitive caring representations the development of masculinities is full of apparent conflicts and contradictions. While Bob (now Raewyn) Connell (2000) argues that there is always at any one moment in time a hegemonic version of masculinity that is more influential than a range of others, Rosalind Gill (2007) suggests that the identification of such a single dominant type is difficult, given the increasing range of competing and overlapping versions of what it is to be male. The development of 'lads' magazines' in the 1990s and 2000s provides an illuminating illustration. Centred on sex, drinking, cars, sport, gadgets and 'male' popular culture, such publications presented themselves as a reassertion of authentic masculinity in the face of the figure of the sensitive 'new man', who was derided as feminine and/or homosexual. The narrative throughout the magazines, according to a study by Peter Jackson, Nick Stevenson and Kate Brooks (2001), is on the pragmatic use of women for sex and the avoidance of compromising one's masculinity by being trapped in permanent relationships. Women, then, are a source of pleasure but also a threat to men's natural love for adventure, drinking and having a laugh with their mates.

Underneath the hysterical hypermasculine exterior of babes, beer, cars, sport and laughs, however, are elements to the 'new lad' that sit less easily with traditional masculine confidence. Fashion and personal grooming are a constant feature and, as with women's magazines, this connects with an array of cosmetic and clothing advertisements. The stereotypical carefree male, with little concern for his appearance, may not be particularly profitable, making an emphasis on the need to look good a valuable modification from a commercial point of view. Furthermore, beneath their confident, cocky headlines, advice columns focus on health problems and relationship guidance, suggesting at least a degree of self-consciousness and insecurity. For Jackson et al., (2001) it is only through adopting their hypermasculine veneer that lad's magazines can get away with the inclusion of such features.

While Jackson et al.'s account remains critical of lads' magazines overall, Gauntlett (2008) is more sympathetic, pointing to the range of possible meanings and uses of such texts for male readers and to constant indications in the content of male weakness and confusion. He also argues that the exaggeration and irony in the hypermasculine façade of the magazines reflects a playful set of performances informed by an underlying acceptance of gender equality. For example:

> The FHM writer, and their projected reader, do actually know that women are as good as men, or better; the put downs of women ... are knowingly ridiculous, based on the assumptions that it's silly to be sexist ... and that we are usually just as rubbish as women (Gauntlett, 2008: 177).

Based on both textual and audience research, Gauntlett's argument is compelling in its recognition of the complexity of the representations within what initially appear to be one-dimensional texts. Nevertheless, his account comes across as a little complacent. He successfully demonstrates that non-patriarchal readings of the publications are possible, but it is far from clear that most readers are liable to interpret the magazines through the prism of liberal views such as his own. Meanwhile, an ironic tone does not negate the possibility of reinforcing broader and more serious assumptions about gender and may even act as a device that helps to protect crude gender constructions from criticism (Jackson et al., 2001).

Beyond heterosexuality

One problem with lads' magazines that is acknowledged by Gauntlett is their tendency to overtly exclude non-heterosexual identities from the version of masculinity they construct. And though their approach may be unusually stark, they are far from alone in contributing to the marginalization of gay and bisexual men. Likewise, we already have seen that homosexual desires and identities tend to be excluded from dominant media representations of femininity. Opposite sex attraction, encounters and relationships lie at the core of the way in which media discourses construct masculinity and femininity and the marginalization of non-heterosexuals forms an integral part of this heterosexual matrix or hegemony (Butler, 1993).

Alluding to Tuchman's earlier attack on media representations of women, Larry Gross (1995: 63) argues that homosexuals have been 'symbolically annihilated' or rendered invisible by mass media, adding that 'when they do appear, they do so in order to play a supportive role for the natural order' (1995: 63). In other words, media representations of minority sexualities have tended to reinforce as much as challenge the prevailing heterosexual hegemony. That is because sexual minorities have tended, like ethnic minorities, to be pigeonholed within a limited number of stereotyped roles and narratives. Historically, many of the lesbians to make an appearance in mainstream media, for example, were butch, aggressive, dysfunctional or unhappy characters (Arthurs, 2004). Meanwhile, Marguerite Moritz (2004) identifies an ongoing tendency for fictional narratives involving lesbians to restore heterosexual order, sometimes by positioning lesbians as troubled, dysfunctional or nasty characters who ultimately either are punished (by being killed off or imprisoned, for example) or restored to happiness by means of a return to heterosexual femininity.

In recent times, there has been a shift towards a very different sort of image of lesbianism – as young, glamorous and ultra-feminine. Lesbian-themed series, such as *Sugar Rush* and The *L-Word* have been of importance here, alongside lesbian characters, romances and encounters in a range of series, including *Brookside, Buffy the Vampire Slayer, Home and Away, Guiding Light* and *Grey's Anatomy*. Such representations have the potential to blur some of the boundaries of dominant femininity and perhaps even to raise questions about the automatic equation of feminine glamour with the male gaze.

As well as being the exception rather than the rule, however, lesbianism within mainstream soap operas or drama series often consists of a moment of temporary exploration or a one-off relationship. Such encounters tend to be followed by either a return to heterosexuality or being written out of the series – both of which function to restore the heterosexual equilibrium on which such shows are based. The narrative conventions of soap opera, in particular, make it difficult to accommodate homosexual characters for a significant period of time, simply because there are unlikely to be a sufficient number of potential partners in the predominantly heterosexual communities depicted to enable any more than a single relationship. Meanwhile, although it challenges some boundaries, the trend towards glamorous, traditionally feminine lesbian representations seems liable to reinforce dominant notions of female beauty and particularly the notion of femininity as sexualized display. Within the world of the narrative, the male gaze may be secondary to female-to-female sexual attraction, but the spectacle of the young, glamorous lesbian encounter onscreen may also be read, in some cases, as a sexualized female display orientated towards the male viewer.

Gay men have probably been more frequently represented in mass media than lesbians and other sexual minorities, with a range of male game show hosts, pop stars and actors openly identifying themselves as homosexual, but depictions of male gay intimacy remain rare. Stereotypes of feminine, camp eccentricity have dominated, often establishing the gay male as a freakish, theatrical figure of fun, positioned at a safe and visible distance from dominant constructions of masculinity. Male homosexuality is also frequently represented in its most middle-class, sanitized and unthreatening guise (Arthurs, 2004). The largely asexual 'gay best friend' has become a particularly familiar stereotype in female-orientated television series, including *Will and Grace* and *Sex and the City*, as well as in romantic comedy films, such as *My Best Friend's Wedding*.

Such representations could be argued to be 'positive', in that they tend to present gay men as likeable and friendly members of society, but, as well, as being guilty of a form of pigeonholing, their orientation tends to exclude some of the less socially accepted elements of homosexual identities. Notably, the same-sex encounters or romances of the gay best friend tend to be marginalized and, in particular, explicit male-to-male intimate and sexual contact remains unusual. A similar point could be made, perhaps, in relation to the numerous high-profile gay male artists in the popular music industry, many of whom have tended to avoid explicit or clear expressions of their sexuality in lyrics, imagery, interviews or public appearances in order to ensure that they remain sufficiently palatable to heterosexual audiences (Doty and Gove, 1997).

The example of the gay best friend character also exemplifies a tendency for gay, lesbian or bisexual characters to be secondary to predominantly heterosexual narratives. And according to Alexander Doty and Ben Gove, even if homosexuality *is* positioned more centrally, it tends to be focused on from a heterosexual point of view. 'Heterocentric narrative construction', they argue, 'will, finally, structure the plot to revolve around how straight characters and culture respond to lesbians, gays and queers', so that 'we see these characters primarily through straight gazes and narratives' (1997: 88). This connects to a further point, which is that the emphasis on attracting mainstream audiences causes non-heterosexual characters to be isolated within overwhelmingly straight environments or communities. As a consequence, we rarely see much evidence of broader gay peer groups or communities, let alone involvement in collective political activism (Arthurs, 2004).

This tendency for homosexual narratives to be marginal is not ubiquitous, of course. In addition to the lesbian-focused *Sugar Rush* and *The L Word*, the 1990s UK series, *Queer as Folk* focused in detail on the lives, relationships and encounters of homosexual men, enabling the exploration of a variety of different characters in the context of a gay scene. In contrast to the sanitized depictions elsewhere, the narratives of *Queer as Folk* centred on less socially accepted sides of the gay scene, with overtly sexual storylines, including a relationship between a 29-year-old and a 15-year-old and a number of explicit depictions of sexual encounters. More recently, the cartoon series *Rick and Steve* presented a satirical focus on the gay scene, complete with comic storylines about threesomes, lesbian motherhood and even HIV.

Another representation to break with desexualized or secondary representations was the Oscar-winning blockbuster *Brokeback Mountain*, which focused on a long-term secret love affair between two summer sheep herders in Wyoming. Significantly, *Brokeback Mountain*'s huge box office success enabled it to break out of the specialist gay content pigeonholes within which other productions, including *Queer as Folk* and *Rick and Steve*, have been located, reaching a huge, diverse audience around the world.

Encouraging though this may be, it remains the case that, outside of highbrow or specialist gay and lesbian media channels (see Chapter 12 for a discussion of the latter), non-heterosexuals are often either invisible or stereotyped as a fixed and familiar 'other', reinforcing the dominance of heterosexuality (Foucault, 1990).

It is important to recognize, however, that, while overt homosexual representations remain limited, there are many characters who are primarily coded as straight but offer the possibility of 'queer' readings among certain audiences (Doty and Gove, 1997). What were taken by some as occasional hints at an ongoing lesbian relationship between two of the main characters within the cult series *Xena: Warrior Princess*, for example, prompted many fans to understand and enjoy the characters as lesbian icons, even though they were not explicitly presented as homosexual. This was encouraged by the show's producers, who developed the lesbian subtext by means of further hints as the series continued. Meanwhile, as we saw earlier in this chapter, groups of straight, gay and bisexual fans engaged in online Slash fan fiction communities have regularly created storylines centred on queer interpretations of apparently straight characters in mainstream series.

The popularity among some audiences of 'queering' outwardly straight characters prompts Doty and Gove to note that 'almost every figure on television might be "representing" queerness in some way, to some degree, for some viewer' (1997: 89). Once again, we are reminded of the need to recognize the range of audience responses to textual representations and the ways in which such interpretations sometimes contribute to the subversion of dominant structures of meaning.

Conclusion: a balanced approach

While feminism has been largely responsible for the development of studies of gender and media, the growing body of research on masculinities has helped to establish the importance of understanding gender as a matter that concerns the construction and living out of both female and male forms of identity. Meanwhile, developing understandings of gay, lesbian and bisexual representations in media remind us, among other things, of the crucial link between the reinforcement of dominant understandings of sexuality and prevailing constructions of masculinity and femininity.

In order to develop a rounded understanding of the relationship between media and gender identities, it is equally important to balance emphasis on representations in the content of media texts with the ways in which audiences construct gendered and sexualized identities in their use of media. We should be cautious of both overly deterministic forms of textual criticism and of overly celebratory or uncritical audience studies. The role of the structure and motivation of media industries ought not to be forgotten either, particularly with respect to the relationship between particular constructions of gender and media profitability. After all, dominant representations of masculinity and femininity in media tend to be those that are most effective when it comes to the selling of advertising space or, indeed, the selling of consumer goods themselves.

QUESTIONS AND EXERCISES

1 a) Select an example of a recent blockbuster film and analyse the constructions of its male and female characters using Laura Mulvey's framework. To what extent does your film illustrate her conclusions?

   b) Do the representations of femininity in *Sex and the City* challenge or reinforce dominant understandings of gender?

   c) Should we celebrate the proliferation of glamorous female action heroes such as *Charlie's Angels*, *Lara Croft* and *Buffy the Vampire Slayer*?

2 a) What would a positive representation of femininity look like and why? How about masculinity? Try to think of examples of each.

(Continued)

(Continued)

    b) Why has feminist criticism of gendered media representations itself been subject to criticism?

3 a) Is there such a thing as a 'female genre'? What would you include in such a category?

    b) What contribution has been made by studies of female audiences? If audiences are active and creative, do we need to worry about what is depicted in media content?

4 Carry out an analysis of a recent edition of a lads' magazine, such as *FHM*, *Loaded* or *Nuts*. In what ways are masculinity and femininity constructed by the front cover and the different features, illustrations, commentaries and adverts in the magazine?

5 a) Does the increasing prevalence of glamorous young women involved in lesbian encounters or relationships in the media challenge or reinforce dominant understandings of gender and sexuality?

    b) In what ways have apparently straight characters or personalities been read or reinterpreted by some audience groups as gay? Think of as many examples as you can.

Suggested further reading

Doty, A. and Gove, B. (1997) 'Queer representation in the mass media', in A. Medhurst and S. Munt (eds), *The Lesbian and Gay Studies Reader*. London: Cassell.
Analysis of media representations of sexual minorities, including discussion of the 'queering' of characters and stories by audiences.

Gill, R. (2007) *Gender and the Media*. Cambridge: Polity Press.
Critical account of a broad range of debates and examples relating to media and gender.

Jackson, P., Stevenson, N. and Brooks, K. (2001) *Making Sense of Men's Magazines*. Cambridge: Polity Press.
Detailed study of men's magazines, from the point of view of industry, content and audience.

Mulvey, L. (1975) 'Visual pleasure and narrative cinema', *Screen*, 16 (3): 6–18.
Highly influential article that first established the notion of media depictions of women being orientated towards the male gaze.

Radway, J. (1987) *Reading the Romance: Women, patriarchy and popular literature*. London: Verso.
One of the first and most well-known feminist studies of the audiences of female-orientated media forms.

12

Media Communities: Subcultures, Fans and Identity Groups

Focal points
• Understandings of media as a force that dilutes distinct communities.
• Mass media moral panic as constructor of defiant minority forms of collective identity.
• Local and niche media as conscious facilitators and constructors of distinct communities.
• DIY media, online communication and debates about '*virtual community*'.
• Case studies, including youth subcultures, TV fan communities, consumer groupings and sexual minorities.

Introduction

A good deal of discussion about media, culture and society has focused on the relationship between large-scale or mass communications and the broad swathes of the population who form their audience or users. Many focus in general terms on the relationship between media and the opinion, intelligence, morality or identity of 'the public' or the nation, while the attention of others falls on the potential of mass media to facilitate a universal mass culture.

As we have seen in our discussions of ethnicity in Chapter 10, however, contemporary media can also be involved in the facilitation and development of smaller-scale, minority or specialist groupings. The representation of such marginal groups within broadly targeted mass media can play a role here, but of increasing significance are specialist and DIY forms of media that target particular groupings, whether they are based on locality, consumer taste, political persuasion, ethnic identity or sexual orientation.

Referring to a range of examples – including youth subcultures, television fan communities and sexual minorities – this chapter examines the nature of the relationship between media and small-scale forms of collective identity. We'll begin, however, by looking at approaches that regard community as something that exists outside and in opposition to media.

Media versus community

Homogenization and atomization

Media frequently are associated with a broad process of social change that is deemed to have brought about a decline in the significance of community. The nineteenth-century writings of German theorist Ferdinand Tönnies (1963) point to the gradual eclipsing of *gemeinschaft* (community) by *gesellschaft* (society) as the dominant mode of human association.

Tönnies understood gemeinschaft as a grass roots, intimate form of collective unity premised on the organic shared understanding, mutual dependence and self-sufficiency created by kinship, religion and the isolation of pre-industrial village life. Crucially, the collective entity itself is of greater importance than the individual self-interest of those who make it up. Although media are not the main focus of Tönnies' account, gemeinschaft is regarded as having declined in prominence as a result of forces of modernity and industrialization, including the movement of populations to large, anonymous cities, increased communication and trade between previously isolated localities and the growth of capitalist modes of production. Such developments are deemed to have led to the prominence of gesellschaft, which is larger-scale, more disparate and centred on mechanical, rational relationships of convenience between self-interested individuals (Delanty, 2003).

Tönnies' approach to gemeinschaft is adapted by Robert Redfield (1955), who specifies that, as well as being organic rather than chosen, community implies a homogenous group that is self-sufficient, distinctive and clearly bounded relative to the outside world, as well as being small enough to enable intense communication between all its members. It is not easy to find an example of so pure a community in modern societies, but the depiction of local collective identity in UK soap operas such as *Coronation Street* or *EastEnders* demonstrates at least some of the features. On the basis of the accident of their shared locality, the characters know each other, depend on each other, socialize in the same handful of local cafés, bars and shops and proudly defend their collective identity and values (Geraghty, 1991). Such representations strike a chord with audiences because, even if communities of this kind may be increasingly rare, the ideal of folk community as local, face-to-face and organic endures.

According to Zygmunt Bauman (2001), because it was dependent on isolation from the outside world, the traditional notion of community outlined by Tönnies and Redfield was bound to be undermined by the development of media. Ever-more intensive contact with people in other places would blur insider/outsider boundaries, he argues, and erode distinctiveness and mutual dependence, rendering community more a matter of choice than necessity. Others, too, have pointed to media as being key in the demise of communities. From the telegraph to the printing press, to television, satellite technology and the Internet, emphasis often is placed on the ways media increase the amount of contact and shared experiences between people based in different settlements, villages, towns and even countries (Anderson, 1991; Bauman, 2001; McLuhan, 2001; Meyrowitz, 1985). The implication is that the greater the penetration of media into people's lives, the more their communities would dissolve into larger, more anonymous social entities.

The argument is particularly stark in theories of mass culture. Such theories are well known for bemoaning the decline of elite high culture as a result of the growth of mass media that is orientated towards the satisfaction of ordinary tastes through superficial and standardized forms of culture. They tend to be equally vocal, however, on the part played by standardized mass media alongside broader processes of industrialization in the erosion of grass roots folk communities. For Dwight MacDonald, folk culture had reflected the organic face-to-face communication and cohesive community life of ordinary people, but it had been undermined and replaced by an artificial and undifferentiated mass culture imposed from above through mass media. This process is regarded as having led to 'a large quantity of people unable to express themselves as human beings because they are related to one another neither as individuals nor as members of communities' (1957: 59, cited in Strinati, 1995). Lamenting the decline of folk communities tied together by substantive belonging and distinctive traditions and values, he characterizes 'the mass man' as 'a solitary atom, uniform with and undifferentiated from thousands and millions of other atoms'.

From a different perspective, the early Frankfurt School's neo-Marxist approach to mass culture also portrays media as an homogenizing, atomizing force, of course (see Chapter 6). Emphasizing the financial incentive for the culture industries to market standardized products to the largest possible audience, Theodor Adorno castigates the 'abstractness and self-sameness to which the world has shrunk' (1990: 57).

Resisting mass culture (and media): youth subcultures

Some theorists challenged the pessimism of mass cultural theories, arguing that it remained possible in a media-dominated society for meaningful, creative and even oppositional forms of community to emerge.

Theorists at Birmingham University's Centre for Contemporary Cultural Studies (CCCS) carried out a series of studies in the 1960s and 1970s focused on the emergence of distinctive, stylistically marked groups of young people, including teddy boys, mods, skinheads and punks, each of which centred on a strong and defiant form of collective identity. The prevailing view among the CCCS theorists is that such subcultures represented a form of collective, grass roots youth resistance via style and, more specifically, a subversive reaction to the decline of traditional working-class forms of community and the rise of mass consumer culture (Clarke et al., 1976; Cohen, 1972).

Rather than being insulated from media and consumer culture, such groups were centred on music and fashion. Yet, in contrast to the mass consumer culture around them, subcultural participants are deemed to have formed communities centred on using culture industry products in subversive ways. Previously unconnected products were subject to a process of *bricolage*, whereby they were appropriated, placed alongside one another and given new, resistant meanings never envisaged by the companies that manufactured them. In the case of mods, for example, scooters, smart clothes and metal combs became associated with a brash, hedonistic subcultural identity that, according to Dick Hebdige (1979), parodied and defied mass culture. In contrast to the massification happening all around them, then, subcultural participants used media and commercial products as raw materials to generate defiant and distinctive grass roots communities.

In some respects, CCCS's accounts of subcultures challenged traditional notions of community by asserting that, rather than automatically destroying all forms of community, media and popular cultural products could, if consumed in active ways, form the basis for distinctive, resistant forms of collective identity. They may not have been isolated, long-term or self-sufficient, but these modern, consumer-based subcultures, based on an attachment to distinct sets of symbols (Cohen, 1985), exhibited clear distinctiveness, commitment and mutual identification. By establishing this principle, the CCCS paved the way for later studies of audience and fan communities – a subject to which we shall return to later in this chapter.

Yet, in other respects, the CCCS's approach reinforces the notion that community is, by definition, separate from and counterposed to media. The role of the culture industries in their account, after all, is limited to that of unwitting provider of the raw materials of style, while subcultures themselves are presented as organic, grass roots creations borne of a natural, creative response by young people to the social circumstances in which they found themselves. In contrast, the world outside such subcultures is implied to be thoroughly shaped by media and, as a consequence, homogenous (Thornton, 1995). That direct media involvement is regarded as being fundamentally incompatible with grass roots communities in this account is made particularly clear in Hebdige's description of the process of *incorporation*. Here, it argued that, after having emerged as subversive grass roots communities, subcultures eventually become the focus of exploitation by media and commerce, triggering the appearance of watered-down versions of the style in newspapers, television or high street shops (Hebdige, 1979). For Hebdige, subcultural communities lose their substance and significance as soon as this media co-optation takes place. Once again, media are presented, essentially, as a force of dilution and homogenization that erodes community.

Intriguingly, media are attributed a comparable role by some critics of subcultural theory, who doubt the possibility of distinctive, meaningful youth communities emerging, particularly in more recent times. Leaving aside the question of whether or not the CCCS's account was valid at the time, such critics argue that expansions and diversifications in the operation of media and commerce since the 1970s have created a situation in which it is no longer conceivable that young people can develop authentic style or music communities. Desperate to generate profit from every tiny fragment and passing fad of youth culture, the culture industry is deemed to have become highly adept at promoting new styles or crazes at the first available opportunity. 'Cool hunters' are employed to enable the industry to latch on to and exploit street styles before they are even fully conceived, while youth media constantly shape and promote new scenes (Osgerby, 2004).

What this suggests is that, rather than being incorporated by the culture industry after an initial period as creative, grass roots communities, contemporary youth styles – from emo to the latest incarnations of underground hip hop – are fully implicated in media and commerce from their very conception. With no chance of forming organic communities, young people are seen as having no option but to choose between the various stylistic options the culture industry has created from above (Polhemus, 1997).

Lacking the group commitment or mutual dependence of organically developed subcultures, these media-constructed consumer styles are ideally suited to being quickly tried on and cast off. Young people may loosely coalesce at times into discernable scenes, but, because there will always be a range of other styles to buy into, such groupings are regarded as being likely to be transitory and loosely bounded (Muggleton, 1997).

Sometimes referred to as *neo-tribes*, these loose, temporary groupings are understood to be more notable for the movement of individuals from one style to another than for their substance as communities (Bennett, 1999). In this formulation, then, a culture saturated by media and consumer choice is understood to mitigate against the development of substantive communities. Here too, then, media tends to be presented as a force for the dilution of community.

Although diverging in other respects, the approaches and examples focused on above all illustrate a tendency to characterize media as a significant part of processes whereby substantive communities are eroded. Sure enough, media probably can and do contribute to this sort of social de-differentiation in some or even many circumstances. Yet there remain situations in which media can also do the opposite. That is, they can play a key role in the facilitation and construction of small or marginal forms of community. Such communities seem unlikely to live up to the isolated, self-sufficient ideals of Tönnies or Redfield, but, nevertheless, can exhibit levels of collective identity worthy of our analytical attention. Specialist forms of mediated communication are of great importance to such groups, including local, niche and *DIY media*. Before we take a look at these, however, we'll examine the construction of marginal communities through negative forms of mass media coverage.

Moral panic and mass media stigmatization

As we saw in Chapters 9 and 10, ethnic, sexual and other minority groups have often found themselves stereotyped or stigmatized in mainstream newspapers, television programmes or films. Far from subsuming all differences into a unified or atomized mass, such representations can amplify collective difference by constructing marginalized groups as internally homogenous and essentially different. Theories of deviance, labelling and moral panic emphasize that, as well as contributing to broader prejudice and discrimination, this can actually strengthen the shared identity, distinctiveness and mutual commitment of those groups on the receiving end. From delinquent gang cultures (A. Cohen, 1955) to drug users (Becker, 1963; Young, 1971), studies have demonstrated that the experience of being collectively rejected and labelled can prompt those involved in marginal groups to become more tightly knit, more distinct in their values and more hostile to broader society – sometimes to the extent of developing ever more deviant or counter-hegemonic approaches to life. The media labelling of people as deviant or 'other', then, can become a *self-fulfilling prophesy*.

Stan Cohen's (1972) account of the media moral panic surrounding violence between groups of young mods and rockers in the 1960s provides a classic case study. For Cohen (1972), a stream of sensationalist headlines about actual or expected violence had the effect of stigmatizing mods and rockers as folk devils – that is, dangerous 'others' who posed a threat to ordinary society.

One of the functions of this, according to Cohen, was to reinforce the perceived normality of mainstream values against the caricatured figure of the outsider, but the coverage is also deemed to have triggered a classic labelling process with respect to mods and rockers themselves. The distinctive characteristics and meaning of each group, including their mutual animosity, became cemented in the minds of participants. Their coherence and distinctiveness as subcultures was strengthened and the notoriety and excitement with which they were associated attracted new recruits while concentrating the involvement of existing members.

Resentment about media stigmatization, meanwhile, is deemed to have prompted an amplification in the deviance of group participants, to the extent that aspects of their behaviour came to resemble the media representations. As Cohen puts it, 'the societal reaction not only increases the deviant's chance of acting at all, it also provides him with his lines and stage directions' (S. Cohen, 1972: 137).

Since that time, countless moral panics have taken place in response to a variety of events, with hysteria often targeted at particular groups of 'others', whether in the form of inner city youth, striking workers, new age travellers, 'binge drinkers', goths or immigrants. Sarah Thornton (1995) demonstrates that negative newspaper coverage of rave culture played an important role in the eventual strength and size of the movement. Panic-stricken headlines about drug-fuelled free parties, combined with the banning of records from radio, police clamp-downs and repressive legislation all strengthened the resolve, commitment and sense of unity of ravers, as well as attracting a wave of enthusiastic new participants. Arguing that 'negative newspaper and broadcast news baptise transgression' (1995: 129), Thornton suggests that, by publicizing and stigmatizing the movement, such coverage helped to turn rave from a transitory fad into a far more committed and long-lasting movement, centred on a strong and defiant sense of collective identity.

Labelling and moral panic theories, then, illustrate the ways in which mass media can inadvertently define, construct and strengthen distinctive communities. They raise questions about the notion that communities can only exist as spontaneous entities in the absence of media. In particular, Cohen and Thornton's work suggests that, rather than being entirely spontaneous communities, as in the CCCS's account, strongly held youth subcultural identities may have been partially constructed by negative mass media coverage. Nevertheless, we should acknowledge that the construction of community as a result of mass media stigmatization is probably limited to a small number of highly distinctive or visible minorities and that moral panics also play a role in reinforcing the dominance of the 'normal' culture of the majority, against which such abnormal groups are offset. It is when we begin to examine the role of more positive coverage in smaller-scale, more narrowly orientated outlets that the contribution of media to the development of greater numbers of communities across society becomes clearer.

Targeting community

Amidst all the attention afforded to broadly targeted mass media, it some-times is forgotten that many media outlets are more specifically orientated towards the concerns of smaller population groups. Such specialist media are of great interest here because, in the course of targeting subsections of society, they sometimes can contribute to the development or consolidation of community. This is increasingly important in a contemporary media environment that is becoming more and more fragmented as a result of pro-cesses of deregulation and digitalization. There are, however, some examples of specifically targeted media that are neither new nor particularly high-tech. Among the most obvious of these are local newspapers and radio.

Local media

Most early newspapers were orientated towards the populations of par-ticular localities and, despite the rise to prominence of state or national media, local press have continued to comprise an important element of the identity of cities, towns and sometimes villages ever since. Similarly, there are multitudes of radio stations orientated towards particular local popula-tions. Alongside the more recent addition of locally orientated Internet facilities, such media illustrate that, even in the case of local populations for whom regular face-to-face contact remains feasible, the use of media may sometimes contribute *towards* cohesion and shared identity rather than weakening them.

Widely consumed within particular areas and rarely encountered outside them, local media construct a sense of collective exclusivity among their audience. Residents who may otherwise have little to do with one another are brought into the same communicative space to share in an agenda of events, debates or forms of entertainment.

The result could perhaps be regarded as a small-scale localized version of the 'imagined community' discussed by Benedict Anderson (1991), except that, in this case, the prospect of meeting or knowing other members is greater. Local media content often explicitly emphasizes the significance of place as a focus for shared identity and outlets often adopt the specific role of champion of local opinion. People are continually reminded of their status as locals and the significance of this for their identity in a manner comparable to Michael Billig's (1995) explanation of the flagging of banal nationalism (see Chapter 9 for discussion of Anderson and Billig).

Local media also facilitate direct contact between residents, enabling communities to speak to themselves. Whether they cover local politics, crime, school fêtes or sport, articles are full of the opinions and voices of residents themselves, as well as their experiences and achievements. Letters pages and phone-ins, meanwhile, offer forums for the direct exchange of local views. Unlike their national cousins, meanwhile, local media also regularly facilitate and publicize face-to-face events within their locality, whether in the form of editorial coverage or by acting as a community noticeboard so that organizers can promote things for themselves.

This doesn't mean that local media always realize their potential, however. Writers such as Bob Franklin and David Murphy (1998) and Andrew Crisell (1998) express concern that the increasing commercialization of local media may be restricting their value. Most 'local' newspapers are owned by national or global media corporations and declining sales have forced publications to reduce or abandon their cover prices, leaving them increasingly dominated by advertising. According to Franklin and Murphy, as well as filling pages with commercials, this has resulted in a populist news agenda dominated by crime, entertainment, lifestyle features and consumer guides. Rather than providing an in-depth examination of matters of local importance and constructing a strong sense of mutual responsibility, then, it is argued that local newspapers offer a bland, commercialized agenda.

Sometimes local media are not even particularly local. Crisell points out, for example, that the need to maximize audiences often prompts local radio stations to fill most of their airtime not with local community issues but national and international pop music. It is also important to bear in mind that, even in the case of the most richly detailed, locally orientated media, their impact on overall levels of community cohesion within the area they serve may remain relatively low as a result of patchy levels of consumption among the population as a whole, as well as the fact that those who do avidly read or listen are also liable to consume a range of national and global media. Nevertheless, the case study shows how media can contribute to community facilitation, even if there are limits to their impact.

Niche magazines and consumer groupings

While local media target the diversity of people who happen to live within a given place, *niche media* are orientated towards geographically dispersed segments of the population united by particular characteristics or interests. Predated by long-running highbrow newspapers aimed at particular social elites, the proliferation of what is sometimes termed *narrowcasting* coincided with the late twentieth-century diversification of consumer culture.

The first half of the century was dominated by both broadly targeted mass media and *Fordist* approaches to commerce, whereby massive quantities of standardized, universally targeted goods would be produced in massive assembly line factories and sold to the largest number of people possible. As disposable income rose and commerce boomed in the post-war years, however, this standardized approach – which had inspired some of the complaints of mass culture theorists – morphed into *post-Fordism*, characterized, among other things, by a movement away from the 'one size fits all' approach and towards the development of a broader range of products, each of which carefully targeted at the needs or aspirations of distinct groups of people, or, *niche markets*. Sophisticated consumer research and marketing techniques enabled companies to cultivate such consumer segments and market goods in such a manner that they would became symbolically associated with the collective identities of such groupings (Osgerby, 2004).

This shift towards niche markets was mirrored in some sectors of media. The final decades of the twentieth century saw a proliferation of magazines and other specialist publications orientated towards a plethora of demographic and interest-based identity groups. The specialist content of such publications became highly profitable by drawing in precisely the kinds of niche consumer groups that advertisers were desperate to reach. Not only do such publications filter the population into clearly identifiable segments but they also often specifically tap into and cultivate a sense of collective identity among their members – something that advertisers can then latch their products on to. Magazines, then, can sometimes both reflect *and* construct community among their readers.

Sometimes the groups towards which magazines are orientated are fairly broad. General categories of women's or men's magazines target niche markets that are clearly defined but far from cohesive, while general consumer car or hi-fi magazines are specialist in content, but orientated towards interests which are widespread. Other publications, though, covet more committed and clearly defined identity groups. Magazines orientated towards minority activities such as rock climbing, surfing, snowboarding or motorbiking, for example, involve more tightly knit audience

FIGURE 12.1   Consumer magazines
©Torbjorn Lagerwall

groups, each with distinct community values, knowledges and identities. By providing an exclusive media space for such groups, magazines can contribute to the generation of shared agendas and experiences, to the exchange of ideas and to the communication of information about events and equipment.

Specialist publications orientated towards intense fans of cult mass media products such as *Star Trek* or *Doctor Who* are a further example. Providing a range of inside information and gossip relating to make-up, scripting, special effects and casting decisions, they feed the desire of such intensive fan communities to differentiate themselves from other members of the mass audience for their favourite shows (Jenkins, 1992). For Matthew Hills (2002) such fan-orientated publications, which include *Cult Times* and *Doctor Who Magazine,* commercially exploit the intense loyalty that characterizes fan groups. It is equally important to recognize, however, that such publications facilitate, construct and intensify such loyalty.

Specialist youth music magazines can play a similar role, with publications orientated towards all manner of different genres, each feeding a range of collective identities. In contrast to the CCCS's model of subcultural community as spontaneous and resistant, the decades that followed their work have seen niche media play a substantial role in the construction of youth style and music groupings from above.

For Sarah Thornton (1995), negative newspaper moral panics did not comprise the only role of media in the development of rave culture. Such negative stigmatization, she argues, operated in tandem with extensive positive coverage orientated towards insiders in the pages of youth-orientated lifestyle magazines such as *ID* and *The Face*. The tone of such 'subcultural consumer magazines' (1995: 155) aligned itself with participants, sharing and giving voice to their disdain for newspaper misunderstandings, while both reflecting and reinforcing subcultural rhetoric and values.

For Thornton, it wasn't just a question of reinforcing acid house culture once it had taken root – such magazines are deemed to have played a key role in the initial crystallization of a disorganized handful of sounds and events into a singular movement with a name and an identity. Thornton concludes the following about niche media: 'They categorize social groups, arrange sounds, itemize attire and label everything ... they baptize scenes and generate the self-consciousness required to maintain cultural distinctions' (1995: 151). Rather than watering down initially organic communities by a process of incorporation or creating styles so superficial that young people rapidly buy into and then out of them, niche media appear sometimes to contribute extensively to the construction of communities characterized by strong collective distinctiveness, identity and commitment.

A further example of the role of niche print media in the construction of community is provided by the gay and lesbian press. An ever-expanding range of lifestyle magazines, led by market leaders such as *Gay Times*, compete to offer a space for the expression of homosexual identities and to deliver the much vaunted 'pink pound' to their advertisers. Providing much needed specialist forms of information, discussion and entertainment for groups that often are excluded or stigmatized by mass media, such publications court and construct particular versions of gay identity, complete with appropriate styles, tastes, perspectives and insider knowledge. In so doing, they contribute to community commitment and cohesion and to the establishment of boundaries of inclusion and exclusion.

The market is somewhat dominated by publications orientated towards a particular white, affluent, youthful gay male identity, while separate lesbian-orientated magazines, such as *Diva* and *Curve*, also tend to be orientated towards middle-class consumers – something at least partly attributable to the greater value of this group to advertisers. With the partial exception of more inclusive, political and news-orientated publications, such as the UK's *The Pink Paper*, working-class and non-white homosexuals, alongside bisexuals and other minorities, tend to be somewhat under-represented. One of the consequences of this is that, at the same time as offering crucial forms of representation and inclusion, such publications may sometimes contribute to the continuing prominence of particular, limited versions of homosexual identity. As in the case of constructions of nation and ethnicity (see Chapters 9 and 10), the construction of this community can have both positive and negative implications.

Niche digital media

While niche print media remain a prominent facilitator of community for some identity groupings, the digitalization of television and radio, alongside the development of the Internet, has drastically increased the range of specialist media on offer to contemporary consumers.

Where previously they had to settle for occasional runs of their favourite series on broadly targeted mixed channels, the sci-fi fan communities who read magazines such as *Cult Times* have also found themselves explicitly targeted by television narrowcasters, including Sky One and Bravo (Hills, 2002), which, at different points in the past, placed emphasis on showing UK premieres or reruns of cult sci-fi series, and the Sci Fi channel, which continues to do so and in an even more concentrated fashion. Such channels offer fans the prospect of concentrated consumption of the shows closest to their identities. They were already able to do this via DVDs, of course (Jenkins, 1992), but without the sense of a simultaneous shared experience that can be created by television.

To take one of our other examples, there are also now dedicated television channels for sexual minorities, including OUTtv in Canada and Logo in the USA, which offer a specialist range of content for lesbian, gay, bisexual and transgender communities on a medium so often associated with their exclusion or stigmatization.

Turning to music, if, in the 1980s, fans could rarely expect to see or hear specialist artists on broadcast media, then by the 2000s an array of niche music television channels had emerged, catering for distinct genres, many of which associated with subcultural affinities of one kind or another. In the UK, for example, viewers can choose from R&B and urban (MTV Base, Flava, Channel AKA), rock (Q), metal (Kerrang!, Scuzz) dance music (MTV Dance), classic rock (VH1 Classic) and alternative rock (MTV2, NME, Rockworld TV), among others.

Meanwhile, an increasing range of digital and Internet radio stations and streaming facilities offer even more finely honed services. Some are more specialist than others but many of these television and Internet services orientate themselves towards the loyal markets provided by particular scenes and subcultures, reinforcing the cohesion of existing movements and constantly seeking to tap into and amplify new developments. The onset of the Internet has also prompted the development of commercial websites orientated towards music scenes, including official band sites and online versions of magazines.

DIY media and Internet communication

Recent developments in communications technology have also led to a proliferation of even smaller-scale and more narrowly orientated 'micro' or 'DIY' media. While such media are not always 'subcultural' (Atton, 2002), they often are produced by and for the members of distinct communities and play an integral part in the facilitation of such groups.

Fanzines

The most talked-about form of DIY media prior to the days of the Internet are fanzines or 'zines', defined by Marion Leonard as 'self-published, independent texts devoted to various topics including hobbies, music, film and politics [which are] usually non-profit making and produced on a small scale by an individual or small group of people'(1998: 103). Preceded by early science fiction fan magazines and also by the larger-scale 'underground press' associated with 1960s counter-culture, the growth of fanzines culminated in their extensive importance to punk subculture (Atton, 2002). In the years that followed, fanzines remained a significant component of youth style subcultures, sports fan cultures, marginal political groups and a variety of sci-fi, horror and other media fan communities. Typically distributed for free, sold at cost price or exchanged for the publications of fellow producers, fanzines have gradually become cheaper and easier to produce as a result of the increasing accessibility of printing technologies.

Narrower in audience than professional niche media, fanzines represent a decentralized form of communication close to the grass roots networks of communities (Leonard, 1998). Henry Jenkins (1992) places emphasis on the interactive and reciprocal nature of fanzine discourse in television fan communities. The content of such publications in his study included critical commentary and discussion, illustrations and artwork of various kinds and *fan fiction*, which refers to stories written by fans based on the characters or context of television shows.

Not only were the entry barriers to producing one's own 'zine low, but it was equally easy to contribute to fan discourse by sending material to other people's publications. The boundary between production and consumption, then, was thoroughly blurred in an ongoing network of fanzine conversations. In contrast to the operation of commercial niche media, fanzine culture is deemed to have centred on reciprocality and a mutual interest in the perpetuation of fan culture itself as a community (Jenkins, 1992).

Despite their decentralized operation, the potential contribution of fanzines to the cohesion and togetherness of distinctive communities has been extensive. Thornton (1995) emphasizes their importance as a trusted purveyor of subcultural values and a crucial means by which experiences were shared and reinforced within rave culture. My own studies of the late 1990s UK goth scene, meanwhile, illustrated that, at a time when this subculture was largely ignored by the commercial music press, fanzines acted as an important source for the exchange of discourse about bands, events, fashion or controversies, as well as a noticeboard for goth venues, events, retailers and record labels. Almost entirely unavailable outside of the subculture, such publications collectively facilitated everyday subcultural involvement by garnering the interest and enthusiasm of participants and providing them with information about where to be and what to buy. Their editors became low-level gatekeepers for what was or was not on the collective subcultural agenda, helping to shape the incorporation of new developments into the style, at the same time as reinforcing the bounded distinctiveness of the subculture (Hodkinson, 2002).

Online micro-communication

The Internet has transformed and expanded the role of DIY media as a part of the contemporary communications environment. Many of those who would in the past have contributed to fanzines are today editing or submitting content to websites, blogs and forums. And as the production of online content has become easier and more accessible over time, a broader range of individuals have begun to produce content, whether by contributing reviews, illustrations or stories to fan websites, participating in debates on discussion forums, posting original music, photographs or videos or keeping a blog, journal or social networking site profile. Far larger in scale than the previous DIY media landscape, this revolution in grass roots communication has prompted much debate about questions of power and influence (see Chapter 9), but has equally important implications for patterns of identity and community.

Offering the potential to connect interactively with anything or anyone we choose at the touch of a button, the Internet may at first seem like a final nail in the coffin of the cohesive, distinctive and highly committed community. 'Where do you want to go today?' asked Microsoft in 1995, implying that we could instantaneously 'go' anywhere, consume or create anything and interact with anyone – and that tomorrow we could make an entirely different set of choices. All this seems about as far removed as one could imagine from the geographically isolated communities of necessity discussed by Tönnies and Redfield. After all, if we can do different things with different people every day, then why would we remain rooted anywhere in particular? It is for this reason that some early commentators argued that the Internet was liable to prompt individuals to develop all sorts of different onscreen identities and even play out several at the same time (Turkle, 1995).

It has become clear, however, that, rather than frantically searching for new things to do, most people use the Internet as a means of extending their existing interests and relationships. In fact, the need to choose where to go and who to engage with is something most of us respond to by focusing on what's already familiar to us. Thus, most of the goths I interviewed during my research project on the subculture said their use of the Web was dominated by websites and forums relating to goth bands, clothes, events or people.

The efficiency of the Web in enabling people instantly to find sites on any subject and in enabling them to explore deeper into that subject by navigating the hyperlinks between sites has two important implications in this respect. First, the Internet maximizes the ease with which those already interested in a subculture, such as the goth scene, can find one another and access materials relevant to their identity. Second, because people generally find what they are looking for and surf further into existing topics rather than across topics, it seems unlikely that many users will *accidentally* stumble on specialist set of sites and materials, such as those orientated towards goths (Hodkinson, 2002). This suggests, according to Leah Lievrouw, that use of the Internet is liable to 'reinforce people's identification with narrow interests' and 'their sense of difference from other groups' (2001: 22). Counter-intuitively, perhaps, through use of a medium that offers us instant access to *anything*, groups might actually sometimes be strengthened rather than weakened.

Virtual community

As a consequence, many theorists have explored the possibility that use of the Internet might even bring about a *resurgence* of community.

Studies of so-called 'virtual' or 'cyber' communities originally focused on the growth of a range of specialist, all-to-all message forums orientated towards things like political groupings (Hill and Hughes, 1998), specialist rock fans (Watson, 1997) or avid soap opera viewers (Baym, 2000). Clearly labelled by their topic, such forums are argued to have drawn together those with a strong existing mutual interest, providing a shared space for the grass roots establishment or reinforcement of community. In the case of fan cultures, they have enabled the collective pooling of knowledge and helped to legitimate and reinforce the passions of individual fans by enabling instant, everyday contact with a group of like-minded others (Baym, 2000; Jenkins, 2002).

Researchers have often emphasized the extensive levels of belonging and commitment exhibited by the participants of such groups, as well as the frequency and intensity of their communication with one another (Watson, 1997). This sometimes has led to strong familiarity between core participants, as in an e-mail list for Kate Bush fans that was dominated by 'long-term contributors who all knew one another well and often shared personal information and long-running jokes' (Vroomen, 2004: 249).

Researchers also emphasize that such groups have tended to display clear and consistent values and norms that would be rigorously policed, both by group moderators and participants themselves. Transgressions often would result in the offender being ignored or, worse still, 'flamed' (verbally attacked) by other participants. For Nessim Watson, the collective delivery of such corrective measures illustrates an emphasis on group responsibility:

> The awareness of behavioural norms and the frequency of conduct-policing by other members ... strongly implies that sense of community in which individual actions are always executed within the known constraints of a forum (1997: 111).

As well as regulating insider behaviour, such maintenance of norms acts as a means by which groups 'vigorously and successfully defend their electronic boundaries' (Hill and Hughes, 1998: 69). In contrast to notions of the Internet as a boundless space, even enthusiastic 'newbies' often are expected to earn the respect of other members over a period of time before being treated as equals (Whelan, 2006). Despite not having access to all the physical cues that accompany face-to-face contact, then, many online groups develop their own ways of differentiating between insiders and outsiders.

Communities or individuals?

Studies of virtual communities are not without their problems, however. In some cases, individual discussion groups are focused on in a rather isolated manner and, as a consequence, insufficient attention is paid to the relationship between such groups and the broader fan communities or political groupings of which they often were a part. Similarly, discussion group engagement tends not to be contextualized within the everyday lives and identities of participants. Use of the term 'virtual community' reinforces a sense of separation between the Internet spaces focused on by studies and the 'real' lives of participants, when it might have been more useful to research online communication as an integral part of broader identities lived out in a range of physical and virtual spaces (Miller and Slater, 2000). We aren't told as much as we might have been, then, about what Baym's soap fans or Watson's rock fans were up to 'off-list'. Did they spend most of the rest of their time conversing with the same people about the same topics in their e-mail, instant messenger, phone and face-to-face interactions or were their communicative lives divided between a wide range of different interests and social networks?

Consideration of this final question has prompted some theorists to doubt the strength of people's ties within online communities. According to Barry Wellman and Milena Gulia (1999), such groups often play only a partial role in the identity of participants, competing for their attention with a range of other affiliations and networks, each related to different aspects of their everyday lives. The interactions on discussion groups may exhibit a certain distinctiveness, argue Wellman and Gulia, but, rather than encouraging the development of broadly based, *strong ties* between members, the requirement to stay on topic can cause relationships to be confined to specialist, pragmatic exchanges rather than deeper, lasting attachments.

Wellman and Gulia are confident that the Internet has the capacity to extend the quantity of such specialist *weak ties* that each of us may generate across different online spaces, but are less sure about whether discussion groups are likely to facilitate intense, broadly based attachments. Manuel Castells takes a similar approach, arguing that discussion groups are characterized by 'low entry barriers and low opportunity costs' and that this implies each one is liable to form just one component of complex individual 'portfolios of sociability' (2001: 132).

There remain some cases, however, where research has pointed to the facilitation of deep and strong attachments to tightly knit communities. In my study of goths, participants exhibited extensive levels of commitment to their subculture and to their networks of friendships within the group, which typically were lived out across a range of physical and virtual spaces, of which online discussion groups were just one. Use of the Internet enhanced the community by enabling participants to exchange information, take part in debates, generate enthusiasm and develop and strengthen their subcultural friendships (Hodkinson, 2003). Similarly, Henry Jenkins (1992; 2002) shows how different forms of Internet communication have enhanced committed forms of collective identity among intensive fans of television genres, while Maria Bakardjieva (2005) illustrates the importance of Internet communication to the development of cohesive transnational ethnic communities (see Chapter 10).

It should be acknowledged that such examples may not be typical ones. Many discussion groups and websites are not orientated towards such committed communities, but rather more widely dispersed subject matter – home repairs, sightings of celebrities, cheats for computer games or gardening advice, for example. Likewise, many Internet users are less committed than goths or some TV fan cultures are to a single group and, as a consequence, may utilize the Internet from a fairly eclectic, multi-affiliated starting point, rendering the pursuit of existing interests an exercise in negotiating a range of subjects and networks. It remains the case, however, that, in certain circumstances, grass roots use of specialist websites and discussion groups can facilitate community.

Importantly, though they remain centrally important for some, the all-to-all discussion groups on which much virtual communities research has been based have declined in their overall importance. Diary-style blogs and journals have become highly important for some groups of users (Bruns and Jacobs, 2006), but by far the biggest recent development has been the growth of social networking sites such as Bebo, Facebook, MySpace and Twitter. These often include community facilities, but their central focal point is the personal identity of the individual user, who develops a constantly updated display of selected elements of their everyday self and identity (boyd, 2008; Livingstone, 2008).

Rather than communicating in the shared, public space of a predefined community, this user interacts on their own terms with an individually hand-picked set of friends. This doesn't mean that social networking sites *cannot* facilitate community. The friends lists of goths who use such facilities, for example, are usually dominated by other goths, indicating that members of existing communities may utilize social networking sites to enhance their collective affiliations (Hodkinson, 2007). For others, however, social networking sites may facilitate more disparate networks of communication involving a wider range of subject matter and friends from a variety of different spheres of life. We'll discuss the significance of social networking sites further in Chapter 13.

Conclusion: all about definitions?

Having started the chapter by outlining arguments that placed media and small-scale community as mutually exclusive, we have identified a number of ways in which the former can contribute to the development or reinforcement of the latter.

This discussion has involved a recognition that, rather than being monolithic, media can be divided into different types, each of which may have different sets of implications for patterns of identity and community. Negative mass media coverage may prompt defiance and cohesion within marginal communities, while the positive, exclusive tone of local or niche media can contribute to the provision of a shared space for ideas, interaction and collective identity. Meanwhile, the increasing range of grass roots or DIY media, both off and online, offer extensive possibilities for the bottom-up construction and facilitation of community in some cases, even if they also can contribute to rather less cohesive networks in others.

Substantial arguments remain, however, about the levels of substance and meaning of the various media communities we have discussed. Many would probably recognize the strength of identity and cohesiveness of certain sexual minority groups who, as with the ethnic minority groups we examined in Chapter 10, tend to be excluded from or stigmatized by mainstream media and are reliant on niche and grass roots communication. Yet, the situation may be rather less clear when it comes to the make-up of groups centred on particular hobbies or consumer choices, for example. Do extreme sports fanatics, sci-fi fans or youth music scenes really constitute substantive communities or are such groupings really too loose-knit, diverse and transitory to warrant such a description? The answer may well depend on one's initial definition of community.

For some of those who take seriously traditional definitions, such as those of Tönnies and Redfield, community implies a long-term mutual togetherness and commitment that can only realistically exist in a situation of forced mutual dependence (Bauman, 2001). The organic strength of genuine tight-knit communities is deemed to have reflected *ascribed* factors that people were born into and had no choice about – most notably mutual geographical isolation, but also things such as shared social class, ethnicity or religious traditions.

From this point of view, by removing barriers of distance and offering people the possibility of a range of different connections across the social and cultural world, media have contributed to the introduction of *choice* in who or what to associate ourselves with. And the range of such choices has become progressively greater with the proliferation of media and consumer culture.

Partly as a consequence of this, it is argued that locality, social class, religion and a range of other stable sources of community, have declined in terms of the extent to which they shape our lives (Bauman, 2001). As a consequence, individuals are left without stable roots and expected to forge their own identities through the choices they make. For Zygmunt Bauman (2000; 2001), a burning desire for belonging prompts people to attach themselves to all sorts of apparent symbols and affiliations, many of which are associated with media and popular culture. Instead of being defined by the locality, class or religion into which we were born, then, we choose to identify ourselves as a horror film fans, golf supporters, gamers or celebrity watchers.

From the point of view of theories of *individualization*, because these media and consumer-related identities are chosen, they can be just as easily unchosen, so that our community attachments are always 'until further notice' (Beck and Beck-Gernsheim, 2001). People buy into and then out of a multitude of partial and temporary attachments, it is argued, rather than attaching themselves in a committed way to any in particular. Instead of demonstrating the unshakeable strength of mutual feeling and responsibility that characterize communities, then, such groups are themselves fleeting and superficial. Far from being more important than the individual self-interest of each of their members – as Tönnies had envisaged in his definition of gemeinschaft – such groups are subordinate to the fickle individuals who float between them. From this point of view, the more extensive and expansive they become and the greater the range of choices they provide us with, the more media contribute to an *individualized* society – that is, one centred on floating multi-affiliated individuals rather than stable, substantive communities (Bauman, 2000).

What is suggested by this perspective is that the apparent communities facilitated by local media, specialist magazines, niche television channels, DIY fanzines and narrowly orientated Internet facilities are liable to lack the levels of substance and commitment the term implies. Our ability to join and leave them at will renders them not communities but temporary amalgamations of personal convenience.

The adoption of such an absolutist initial view of community may not be necessary, however. If we insist the only groups that warrant being described as communities are those involving 100 per cent self-sufficiency and commitment as a result of enforced mutual dependence or isolation, then, as well as risking a romanticization of the past, we may fail to recognize the presence of clear and important communal features within some contemporary groupings and miss out on the opportunity to understand the role of media in their facilitation.

They may involve an element of choice and may not always be life-long or exclusive, but a considerable number of small-scale social groupings continue to display a strong sense of belonging and commitment, a distinctive set of values and practices and intense internal communication. Rather than dismissing the significance of such groups on the grounds that they fail to live up to an idealized set of standards from the past, we should continue to explore the extent and nature of their communal features and the role played by different forms of media in providing the spaces, representations and interactions that contribute to their development.

QUESTIONS AND EXERCISES

1　In what way do the following approaches tend to regard media as something that dilutes community?

  a)　Theories of mass culture.
  b)　CCCS's subcultural theory.
  c)　Theories of individualization.

2　Think of an example of a recent media moral panic targeted at a particular social group. In what ways might such coverage construct community?

3　Conduct a close analysis of the content of a local newspaper or radio station. In what ways does this media form construct or facilitate community? What sort of community is constructed here – who is included and excluded? To what extent does your example illustrate the criticisms of local media made by Franklin and Murphy and Crisell?

4　a)　What is it that makes the targeting of distinct identity groups by media a profitable exercise?
  b)　Are the kinds of groups targeted by consumer magazines and specialist television stations really close-knit enough to be regarded as communities? Does the availability of such media strengthen group attachments?

5　a)　In what ways have theories of virtual community been criticized? Are such criticisms justified?
  b)　Is the Internet likely to strengthen existing community attachments or encourage individuals to develop increasing numbers of transitory ties?

Suggested further reading

Atton, C. (2002) *Alternative Media*. London: Sage.
  Detailed discussion of the use of small-scale media by different individuals and groups across society.

Bauman, Z. (2001) Community: *Seeking safety in an insecure world*. Cambridge: Polity Press.
  Theoretical analysis of the ongoing quest for lost community in an individualistic society.

Baym, N. (2000) *Tune In, Log On: Soaps, fandom and online community*. London: Sage.
  Influential online study of an Internet discussion group orientated towards avid soap opera fans.

Osgerby, W. (2004) *Youth Media*. Abingdon: Routledge.
  Critical overview of the relationship between a range of different forms of media and contemporary youth culture.

Thornton, S. (1995) *Club Cultures: Music, media and subcultural capital*. Cambridge: Polity Press.
  Influential study of rave culture that places particular emphasis on the role of different forms of media in the construction of the subculture.

13

Saturation, Fluidity and Loss of Meaning

Focal points

- The increasing saturation of contemporary life by media and consumer culture.
- Postmodernist theories that suggest saturation is blurring boundaries between media representations and reality.
- The notion that identities are becoming fluid, fragmented and centred on media and popular culture.
- Understandings of the Internet as a postmodern culture of image and simulation.
- Criticisms of postmodern interpretations of media saturation.

Introduction

At various points during this book we have revisited questions about whether or not media should be regarded as reflective mirrors on society or as shapers of that society. In simple terms, it has been suggested that, rather than innocently mirroring the world, media construct very particular representations of it and that the selectiveness of these media versions of reality have the capacity to influence future social relations, cultural values and so on (see Chapter 1).

This circular way of thinking offers an improvement on the more partial and simplistic poles of reflection and *shaping theory*, providing a convenient framework for making sense of the different topics we have covered. The selective representations approach, however, may itself be vulnerable to the criticism that, despite regarding the media–society relationship as a complex, two-directional one, it continues to place emphasis on a fundamental distinction between media representations and the 'real world', which they are taken to refer to and to influence. This simplification may be valuable in making sense of how media work, but it is important to realize that, ultimately, media operate within and as part of this real world rather than outside it, forming an integral part of our broader social and cultural environment (Alexander, 2003).

Postmodern theorists argue that media representations have become so central to everything we see, think, say and do that it is impossible to conceive of any sort of reality separate from them. From this point of view, contemporary societies are so saturated by media that reality and media representation are one and the same – that is, representations are reality and reality consists of a myriad of representations. Everything – from understandings of contemporary events to the construction of individual identities – is inseparable from media.

This chapter is about some of the proclamations and predictions of theorists who argue that the saturation of society by media has reached such an extent that truth, stability, certainty and meaning are rapidly disappearing. The ideas we'll be looking at here are some of the most compelling, fascinating, important and controversial we examine in this book, but they are not always the easiest to grasp, so let's take it one step at a time.

Saturation as loss of meaning

Consumerism: expansion and speed-up

Driven by a combination of profitmaking and new technologies, the amount of media communication and consumer goods circulating within society and their importance throughout culture and everyday life has expanded rapidly in recent decades. Important here has been the transition outlined in Chapter 12 from a standardized *Fordist* economy to a *post-Fordist* one dominated by an ongoing and disorganized proliferation of different sorts of media and cultural products, each orientated towards distinct consumer segments.

The sharp growth of disposable income across developed societies, alongside intense competition within increasingly unregulated markets meant, according to postmodernist theorist Fredric Jameson, that the culture industries had become increasingly focused on a constant drive to develop as many new and different things for us to consume as possible. As well as developing as many variations as possible within existing genres or product categories, this search for 'ever more novel-seeming goods' entailed an ongoing search for new markets (Jameson, 1991: 4; see also Featherstone, 2007).

As well as cultivating more and more niche markets, media and commerce have penetrated into more areas of our everyday lives, routines and identities. Sure enough, it has become difficult to think of many cultural activities that are *not* centred on or shaped by profit-making interests in some way. Popular sports fandom, for example, has become a thoroughly media-driven pursuit, every element of which is focused on and shaped by making money – auctioned television rights, replica shirts, club sponsorship deals, commercials at grounds and on screen, as well as gambling, fan magazines, websites, calendars, computer games, mugs and so on. Participation in sport and outside activities is equally exploited, with constant efforts to develop new and novel-seeming forms of equipment, clothing and a range of other consumer and media items.

Another theme of this proliferation of goods is that consumers have been increasingly urged to part with their money because of the symbolic value of goods as a marker of identity and status, rather than just because of their practical use. If the primary role of our televisions, clothes, cars, mobile phones, computers and household decor is to make a symbolic statement about who we are, then there are fewer limitations to the number of such items we might buy or the regularity with which we might replace them. My television might work perfectly well, but I still feel the need to buy another one in order to look up to date or sophisticated. My existing clothes could keep me warm for years, but new ones might help to make me look more in touch with the appropriate fashion for my social group. The triumph of symbolic value drastically expands the intensity of consumerism and the rapidity with which we can be persuaded to replace existing consumables with new ones.

An intense speed-up in the turnover rates for new products and the cycles of fashion with which they are associated, then, is argued to be a further key feature of contemporary media and commerce (Harvey, 1989). The lifespan of any one product or set of products becomes shorter as companies compete to shift our attention and money elsewhere as soon as possible. A picture is painted of an increasingly frantic and chaotic proliferation of more and more different symbolic products and services into all aspects of our lives.

Information overload

Media, of course, have formed a key component in this expansion of post-Fordist consumerism and it is no coincidence that they too have proliferated and diversified in recent years. Aided by the decline of public service broadcasting and other forms of government regulation, as well as the development of satellite, cable, digital and Internet technologies, media have shifted from a small number of products distributed to huge audiences towards a complex and ever-expanding array of specialist services, many of which are available to consumers at the time of their own choosing.

The proliferation of media channels has been matched by an increase in their collective saturation of contemporary life. We watch television or listen to radio as we get up, we listen to music in our cars, we view bill-boards, posters and digital displays around the city and we surf the Web or read newspapers at work. We then spend our evenings watching DVDs, playing computer games or watching more television at home or, if we go out, we watch films in the cinema or consume television, newspapers or music in bars. The increasing capacity of portable media, meanwhile, means that many of us take the Internet, computer games, our entire music collections and various other forms of content with us everywhere we go. Wherever we are, it seems, multiple media messages from different sources are competing for our attention. Some of us even consume media to help us sleep.

For some, this everyday plethora of images and information is cause for celebration. Proponents of the deregulated free market regularly point to the amount of choice on offer to us, while enthusiasts of digital democracy point to the emancipatory possibilities of such unprecedented access to information. However, for Jean Baudrillard (1983) – who was perhaps the most well-known postmodernist theorist – rather than being *enhanced* by the proliferation of electronic media, meaning, understanding and sub-stance are being drowned out by noise. According to this view, the more the channels of communication multiply, the more we all suffer from infor-mation overload.

Nick Stevenson illustrates Baudrillard's point by asking his readers to 'imagine a man sitting in a bar surrounded by a bank of television sets, advertising posters, the global press and the constant chatter of the radio' (2002: 161). As the man constantly shifts his attention between these dif-ferent information sources, he is only able to engage with each at the most superficial level. The amount of simultaneous information 'exceeds the interpretive capacity of the subject' (2002: 162) and understanding is replaced by a range of superficial surfaces.

The content transmitted by each channel, meanwhile, is increasingly orientated, Baudrillard argues, to immediate stimulation and excitement, as it is only by doing so that it can hope to garner our attention amid the din. Across genres, the emphasis is on fast-moving, ever-changing images that almost immediately are abandoned and replaced by something different. Rather than developing a complex, in-depth or coherent understanding of anything in particular, then, the attention of the man in the bar – or, indeed, the person flicking between television channels in his or her living room while surfing the Internet on a laptop – constantly switches between a myriad of temporarily engaging images and representations. Context and history become less important and our responses to the images placed before us are dominated by emotional reactions, snap judgements and, ultimately, a thirst for the next bite-sized snippet of content.

Media = reality

For Baudrillard, the extent of the saturation of our lives by this barrage of media messages suggests that there is no longer any distinction between such representations and society itself. The centrality of media to our everyday experiences means that their cumulative impact throughout our lifetimes is overwhelming – they define and dominate our broader cultural relations, values, experiences and understandings of the world. Even in those rare moments when we are not 'tuned in', our thoughts and activities are defined in relation to the myriad of previous media experiences through which our lives are constructed. Similarly, each of our encounters with media in the present are defined by existing understandings that can be traced back to past media encounters.

For theorists such as Baudrillard, this multilayered media saturation makes it impossible to envisage any sort of real society, authentic cultural identity or truthful account of the world that lies beneath all the images and representations. Active audience theories emphasize that engagement with media consists of a two-way interaction between media and the existing social and cultural contexts of consumers, but if the latter are themselves inseparable from a myriad of previous media experiences then might the situation not be better described as an interaction of new media representations with the outcome of previous ones?

Our understanding of public issues such as those concerning politics, wars, famines or the environment, then, should be regarded as entirely dependent on layers of media representations, whether via news, documentaries, film, magazines, television series or websites. We understood the events of September 11th 2001 by means of a series of direct media representations in the form of television, Internet and newspaper coverage at the time and there was no way for any of us to access an 'objective' view of events to assess them against 'reality'. And each of our interpretations of the direct media coverage we encountered was shaped by a range of past media experiences – disaster films, previous news stories and all manner of narratives about goodies, baddies, victims, terrorists and war.

When current media representations can only be understood via past media representations, the notion of an unmediated truth or reality beneath it all, according to Baudrillard, is difficult to envisage. He famously illustrates this point by declaring that the 1991 Gulf War did not happen – that there was no discernable reality beneath the barrage of media images of the conflict (Baudrillard, 1995b).

Understandings of issues and experiences associated with the private sphere are no less media saturated. The ways in which we live out our relationships, family lives, interests, hobbies and everyday behaviour are developed in relation to past and present media representations of these aspects of life – not least in the form of novels, soap opera, films, magazines, news stories, chat shows and advertising, to say nothing of the ever-expanding range of 'reality TV' programmes. We could perhaps add to this that our own use of DIY media such as digital cameras and social networking sites increasingly shapes and structures our lives rather than merely representing them, so that the boundaries between private and public become blurred.

As well as forming a key part of our everyday routines, media dominate our frames of reference in terms of the values we live by and the ways in which we understand our place in the world. Our understandings of ourselves and our everyday lives, then, are as intertwined with media images as are our perspectives on the broader world.

From truth, to ideology, to simulacra

Baudrillard (1995a: 6) locates media saturation as part of a four-phase transformation in the cultural role of images and representations – or, more precisely, signs. In the first two phases, signs are counterposed with 'a profound reality'. In the second two, the signs have proliferated to such an extent that they replace reality.

In the first phase, images perform the traditional symbolic role of the sign, acting as a means to faithfully represent real facets of the world. To use the language of semiology, we could say that signifiers have a clear referent – an object they refer to that is located in reality. In Baudrillard's second phase, instead of faithfully representing the real world, the predominant role for signs and images is to obscure or distort that reality. This phase equates with Marxist-derived notions of media as a form of ideology that blinds the population to the true nature of the circumstances in which they live (see Chapter 6). Crucially, although it is hidden by inaccurate representations, reality is still present beneath the images at this stage.

The transition to the third phase is the crucial one in Baudrillard's schema. Here, the proliferation of images has proceeded to such an extent that there is no longer any unmediated reality underneath them all. Rather than either representing or misrepresenting reality, the image 'plays at being an appearance' (1995a: 6) – in other words, it misleads us into thinking that it is a representation of something real. Even in the act of obliterating reality through their very proliferation, then, images still present themselves to us as signifiers of the real. In so doing, they hide from us the fact that nothing is real any more.

For Baudrillard, television is particularly effective at masking the absence of reality. Its fast-moving blend of sound sequences and moving images invite us to experience it as a set of representations of an external world when, in fact, the world amounts to no more or less than a myriad of television images. Theme parks such as Disney World provide another example of this masking of unreality. Disney World, Baudrillard argues, presents itself to us as a miniature, fantasy representation of something real – America. Some might understand it, then, as a first phase symbol of reality, while others may suggest it is a second phase ideological distortion that blinds people to the failures and exploitations of US capitalism. For Baudrillard, however, the function of Disney is not to either represent or misrepresent the reality of America, but, rather, to conceal the absence of any such reality. Disney 'plays at being an appearance', then, when, in fact, there is no reality to represent because America consists of no more than the same kinds of images and signs from which Disneyland is constructed.

This brings us on to a fourth and final phase, in which images no longer even play at being appearances or representations, referring only to one another. They are not signs or symbols at all, only empty *simulacra* – images without a referent, style without substance, surface without depth.

In this world, it is impossible for us to talk about the relationship between media and reality, about whether media are sufficiently real, truthful or accurate or about whether they might be biased. Media do not reflect or shape society – they *are* society. This is the world of the *hyperreal*, in which there is no distinction between truth and falsehood, only a myriad of different stories, discourses, ideas and images. After all, how can I discern whether an image, statement or story is 'true' or not if there is no longer any media-free reality to measure it against?

There are all manner of examples we might use to illustrate the sort of depthless, self-referential images described by Baudrillard, covering a wide range of genres, both 'factual' and fictional'. One of the most obvious and illustrative case studies is provided by the phenomenon of celebrity culture.

Celebrity culture as hyperreal

In many respects, celebrities are the ultimate media creation and, as such, embody the notion of simulacra.

Since the early cultivation of 'stars' as a mark of familiarity with which to market films and popular music many years ago, a huge industry has emerged, the primary role of which is the careful construction and publicizing of the personality, brand and image of celebrities (Turner, 2004). This industry intersects with a range of different media that utilize, reference and contribute to the manufacture of celebrities. So, celebrities not only appear 'in character' in film and television but also 'as themselves' in chat shows, magazines, adverts, reality television programmes and news media. More visibly than any other area, the celebrity industry revolves around media referring to other media, forming an interchangeable array of empty simulations that rarely, if ever, refer to any reality outside themselves.

How else could we interpret the domination of news headlines or documentaries, for example, by the antics of Britney Spears, Angelina Jolie, Tom Cruise or Paris Hilton? All are, if we follow Baudrillard's way of thinking, media simulacra. The 'real' personalities emphasized so much in celebrity coverage are every bit as constructed as the 'fictional' roles they play, and yet the soap opera inhabited by such personalities increasingly dominates even those 'factual' genres of media that claim the closest relationship with reality. At times, celebrities have even formed the centre of enormous media events characterized by the outpouring of public emotion – most notably in the case of the untimely deaths of Princess Diana, Michael Jackson and, in the context of the UK at least, of *Big Brother* star Jade Goody. For Baudrillard, the sight of such huge popular grieving in response to the deaths of those who, for everyone except their friends and relatives, are little more than media characters, would surely have represented a near-perfect example of *hyperreality*.

The role of celebrity in contemporary societies can also be used to illustrate Baudrillard's third phase, in which the image 'plays at being appearance', masking the absence of reality. The façade of a distinction between the 'real' personalities of film stars and the 'fictional' characters they play provides one example. We could also note that the branding of 'reality television' programmes such as *Big Brother* implies that the personalities to emerge from them are more authentic than other celebrities. The irony, of course, is that this association with 'reality' is merely a part of the artificial branding of the likes of Jade Goody, whose adult life and death were largely defined by a plethora of media discourse. Indeed, the notion of 'reality television' itself is a media inversion, in the sense that it presents itself to us as a media representation of the real when what it more plausibly demonstrates is the colonization of real life by media.

Yet, there is still another more fundamental layer of phase three concealment in the case of the celebrity industry. In presenting itself to us as a separate world of media spectacle and fantasy, the celebrity industry may serve to obscure the extent to which the 'real' society we inhabit every day is saturated by empty media symbols and images. The penetration of celebrity discourse itself within everyday lives, aspirations, understandings and identities across society represents one example of such saturation.

Identity: fragmentation and fluidity

Among the many implications of media saturation and hyperreality for Baudrillard is that the identities of individuals have become increasingly defined by and attached to the floating signifiers circulating around us. That is, we define ourselves and differentiate ourselves from others on the basis of not the place we live or the nature of the work we do but the symbolic value associated with things such as clothes, cosmetics, music, household decor, cars and other consumables.

This focus on identities centred on media images and consumer goods has been of importance for other theorists, too. Some are postmodernists while others avoid this particular label, but what unites them is a suggestion that, as a result of their symbolic relationship with the world of media and consumption, identities have become increasingly fragmented and unstable.

Recycling and pastiche

Outlining what he describes as the 'postmodern condition', Fredric Jameson (1991) suggests that the increasingly fast proliferation and turnover of consumer goods makes it harder and harder to associate any of them with fixed meanings. From this point of view, 'use value' has been almost entirely replaced by 'symbolic value' and, furthermore, symbolic value itself has become increasingly malleable and hard to pin down. One of the impacts of pressure to develop 'novel-seeming' consumables, for Jameson, is a constant reformulation and recirculation of styles and fashions from the past. It isn't hard to think of examples of this in the worlds of music and fashion, from individual items such as flares or tight jeans, to broader categories such as rock 'n' roll, glam, goth or new romantic. Crucially, the connection between such styles and their original contexts and symbolic meanings is argued to loosen more with each reuse.

Sometimes reuses might form a conscious revival, whereby selective caricatures of the style's original associations are either embraced wholeheartedly or subjected to knowing kitsch or *parody*. Here there remains a clear reference to an original symbolic meaning, even if it is a loose or simplified one. For Jameson, however, parody has become less significant as a mode of reuse than another approach – *pastiche*. Here, instead of referring back to an original set of meanings, objects or styles are extracted from previous associations in the process of being fused together with one another to create new products for new consumers in new contexts. Iain Chambers (1985), for example, draws attention to the tendency of emerging genres of popular music to mix together selected elements of previous genres, with the effect that the boundaries between such genres – along with the lifestyles, values or groupings with which they were associated – become blurred. Similarly, Dick Hebdige argues that music had, by the 1980s, become dominated by the 'raiding and pasting together of rhythms, images and sounds from multiple sources' (1988: 212). A particular focus for such claims was the emphasis on sampling, reusing and arranging sequences from a variety of sources in dance music (Connor, 1997).

The broader implication of all this is that the more the ongoing process of recycling and pastiche continues, the more empty and meaningless the newly manufactured hybrids become. They no longer have substantive meanings and, instead, represent only 'their own transitory practice' (Chambers, 1985: 199). All the while, boundaries between styles and genres are blurred and even broader divisions, such as the partition between high art and popular culture, are challenged as elements from each are fused and merged.

The implication, then, is that, while, previously, the symbolic meanings of objects were restricted, we now inhabit something of a free-for-all, where an endless stream of hybrid consumables can be selected and combined at will and can mean what we want them to mean. This is argued to have significant implications for identify formation. As our identities become more and more attached to floating, transitory, polysemic simulacra, it is argued that we, ourselves, become increasingly hybrid and fluid, our understanding of self consisting of an ever-changing multiplicity of temporary styles and objects. We can adopt selected elements of punk style, it is argued, without attending a punk gig and we can listen to versions of hip hop with no knowledge of its inner city roots. Such fragments can mean what we want them to mean and we can discard them in favour of new ones tomorrow.

For Ted Polhemus, in the postmodern 'supermarket of style' we might even come to regard authenticity and meaning as unimportant, revelling instead in the artificiality of it all: 'While fashion celebrated change and subcultural style celebrated group identity, the inhabitants of Styleworld celebrate the truth of falsehood, the authenticity of simulation, the meaningfulness of gibberish' (1997: 149–50).

Not everyone accepts that contemporary consumer goods and media images are quite this flexible in terms of their meaning or that consumers are no longer even interested in constructing and conveying meaning and authenticity. Nevertheless, the emphasis placed by postmodernists on the fragmentation and fluidity brought about by media and consumption coheres with the theories of individualization emphasized at the end of Chapter 12. Without going as far as Baudrillard and Jameson regarding the issue of meaninglessness, theorists such as Bauman (2000) and Beck and Beck-Gernsheim (2001) emphasize that identities are increasingly connected to consumer and media habits and that, because of the vast choice of objects and symbolic meanings on offer to individuals, the extent of our attachment to any one affiliation is liable to be both partial and temporary. The individual here is still regarded as intact, but, as with postmodern approaches, identity is fluid and highly complex.

The Internet as virtual playground

Simulated identity?

Not surprisingly perhaps, for some of its earliest theorists, the Internet represented a particularly concentrated manifestation of the hyperreal culture of simulacra and meaninglessness described by Baudrillard, among others. Describing the Internet as 'a culture of simulation', Sherry Turkle suggests that, in their onscreen lives, people consist of no more than a set of arbitrary words and images – symbols, in other words, interacting with other symbols (1995: 10). And, for Turkle, the lack of physical presence renders the extent of any connection between these virtual symbols and any substantive or 'real' person ambiguous. Given that limitations of physical presence and distance are removed, users are rendered free to develop their virtual identities in whatever way they so desire. We can play at the construction of personalities according to this view, adapting and adjusting our virtual gender, sexuality, ethnicity, nationality and all manner of other characteristics. Online freedom from physical constraints is argued to enable identities to become particularly malleable and fluid. Not only can the images and text that represent us onscreen change as often as we like, but the technology also enables us to sustain multiple virtual identities at any one moment in time. Referring to the connection between Microsoft's market-leading operating system and the Internet, Turkle claims that 'the life practice of Windows is that of a decentred self that exists in many worlds and plays many roles at the same time' (1995: 14).

Rather than being a unified individual consisting of a stable inner core and physically located body, then, online selves are understood as incoherent, multiply located and always shifting. Further, as greater and greater amounts of time, energy and emotions are exhausted on parallel virtual personas, it becomes increasingly unclear which identity is 'real' and which artificial. There may even be ambiguities as to whether or not the life of the person sitting at the screen is any more authentic than the actions and affiliations of their virtual onscreen personalities. Cyborg identities on the Internet, then, are argued to be blurring the boundary between human and technology, authentic and artificial, real and representation: 'Are we living life on the screen or in the screen?' Turkle asks (1995: 21), going on to suggest that 'people are increasingly comfortable with substituting representations of reality for the real' (23).

FIGURE 13.1   Screenshot from *Second Life*
© Linden Labs. Second Life is a trademark of Linden Research, Inc. Certain materials have been reproduced with permission of Linden Research, Inc.

Although Turkle's work was focused on multi-user dungeons (MUDs) in the early days of the Internet, we can illustrate her point in relation to contemporary virtual environments such as *Second Life* (see Figure 13.1). Here, users are encouraged to develop 'fictional' characters and explore, work, play, buy, sell and develop relationships with other characters in an entire world of virtual spaces and places (Boellstorff, 2008; Geser, 2007a; 2007b). The question of interest to many sociologists in relation to such environments is that, as users put more and more time and energy into these 'virtual' characters and their 'fictional' relationships, at what point, if any, do the latter become more important or more real than their identity off the screen? In 2008, a British couple – Amy Taylor and David Pollard – got divorced in the 'real' world as a result of a virtual 'affair' between the husband's character on *Second Life* and the character of another user.

Another theorist who focuses on the specific role of the Internet as part of the development of a postmodern culture of simulation is Mark Poster (1995; 2001). Poster regards the Internet as part of a final stage in the decline of Enlightenment notions of a coherent, autonomous individual subject who is able to observe, understand and act on an external reality. In a manner somewhat reminiscent of Marshall McLuhan's *medium theory*, each of the stages set out by Poster corresponds to developments in media technology.

In the first stage – the age of print media – the informed, critical, rational individual subject is deemed to have been shaped and moulded by the contextual depth and individualistic orientation of books and newspapers.

In stage two – the age of broadcast media – the subject is partly extended by still being addressed and constituted as such by a small number of media producers, but increasingly undermined in other respects. In a clear echo of Baudrillard, Poster argues that a proliferation in the number of depthless media images on television led to a situation in which they increasingly referred to one another rather than to an external world. The individual subject may have been intact, but it was becoming increasingly fragmented and its ability to observe or act on external reality was becoming ambiguous:

> Printed discourses and newspapers ... appeared as representations of an outside world ... To some extent broadcast media perform the same operation but to a greater degree they undermine the relation of representation to an outside and foreground a relation of representation to themselves (Poster. 2001: 15).

In the final stage – the age of the Internet – the notion of an observable external world implodes altogether, while the subject itself fragments. The Internet precipitates a massive further expansion in the range and volume of media content, while the interactivity of the medium diversifies the range of sources for such content. The division between consumers and producers is blurred and the greater the proliferation of content, the more self-referential it becomes.

Consistent with Turkle's account, Poster argues that, on the Internet, there is little distinction between reality and representations of reality and everything is of the order of depthless image or simulacra. In other words, on the Internet, everything is an image on a screen referring to another image on a screen and another and so on. The range of media simulacra on offer, meanwhile, brings about a fragmentation of the collective audience so important to the broadcast age and, ultimately, the break-up of the individual subject, which at this point exists only as a set of different virtual roles being played out within the virtual world. There is no external 'real' world for the subject to observe or understand, then. Instead, the subject finds itself operating within a virtual world of images: 'the self is no longer a subject since it no longer subtends the world as if from outside but operates within a machine apparatus as a point on a circuit' (Poster, 2001: 16).

Internet as extension of everyday life

Though they make a number of salient observations, postmodernist approaches to the Internet such as those of Turkle and Poster tend to exaggerate the social impacts on which they focus. Such accounts are guilty of *technological determinism*, in that they present the technologies of the Internet as primary instigators of social change, with insufficient weight afforded to the role of individuals, organizations and broader social contexts in the development and use of such technologies. They turn selective readings of the possibilities of the Internet into confident and generalized predictions. It is assumed by Turkle, for example, that, because Internet technology creates the potential for people, under certain circumstances, to experiment with or expand their identities, we can expect that, as a direct result, identities across society will become fluid and fragmented and that virtual identities will be essentially separate from and as important as offline ones. But why should we assume that people will want to take up the opportunity to develop entirely new virtual identities, especially when the internet offers equally strong possibilities to consolidate one's existing position in the world?

A further problem is that Turkle's emphasis on the distinctiveness of the virtual sphere as the perfect embodiment of the meaninglessness and fragmentation emphasized in postmodern theory is confusing because it seems implicitly to admit that offline society fails to live up to such postmodern proclamations. The implication is that, in contrast to the postmodern virtual world lived out on the Internet, life in the physical world retains fixity, boundaries and meaning. This sort of analysis would surely have troubled Baudrillard. It seems likely that he would have regarded Turkle's singling out of the Internet as a move that only serves to hide the media saturation and hyperreality which, as he saw it, characterizes *all* social life.

Leaving aside the level of 'reality' or 'unreality' there is in the world as a whole, the presentation of the Internet as distinct from something else that counts as the 'real' or physical world is now widely regarded as mistaken. Such an interpretation probably fitted with the experience of some early 1990s multi-user dungeon users and it may retain some currency as a means of understanding contemporary 'parallel' online environments such as *Second Life* and *World of Warcraft*, in which participants are explicitly encouraged to develop identities, personalities and friendships that are different from those they live out elsewhere. For most contemporary users, however, the Internet does *not* comprise an alternative virtual world, but, rather, constitutes a set of communication tools that they put to use in the enhancement of their existing life and identities. For all the excitement about it, most of us use the Internet to do mundane, everyday things that are intimately connected with our offline lives – checking railway timetables, researching essays, shopping, checking the weather, searching for jobs, reading the news and, of course, communicating with friends, relations and communities (Wellman and Haythornthwaite, 2002).

That the Internet is thoroughly embedded in our everyday lives does not mean we should dismiss the suggestions of Turkle, Poster and others out of hand, however. Poster's work, for example, is valuable in drawing attention to the role of the Internet as a catalyst for the increasingly disorganized proliferation of images and messages that are saturating culture and society, whether or not we accept all his conclusions about the death of the subject and loss of the real.

Neither should we necessarily abandon the suggestion that Internet use might facilitate looser, more complex or changeable identities. In Chapter 12 we saw that, for writers such as Wellman and Gulia (1999) and Manuel Castells (2001), the existing complexity of people's identities, together with the ease with which they can access online images, information or fellow conversants on any subject, makes it likely they will end up negotiating between a range of different sites, interests and affiliations.

Connecting the Internet with the broader theoretical approaches of the likes of Zygmunt Bauman (2001), Barry Wellman and Caroline Haythornthwaite explicitly suggest that the Internet encourages what they term 'networked individualization', through enabling each of us to act as a social switchboard at the centre of our own set of personal networks (2002: 32). Here, the argument isn't that the subject is dead or that the self is no longer meaningful but that the floating multi-affiliated individual, rather than fixed entities such as nation, the local community or the social class grouping, is now the primary organizing unit in society.

Case study: social networking sites

The use by millions of people of social networking sites such as Facebook, Bebo, MySpace and Twitter provides a useful case study for exploring the connections between Internet use and people's everyday worlds and identities.

Unlike older discussion forums and chat rooms, which provided the basis for earlier writings about the Internet and were dominated by high-intensity early Internet adopters, social networking sites are now used by millions of ordinary people as a regular part of their everyday lives. In January 2009, for example, Facebook was accessed by over 68 million unique users, while the fastest-growing social networking site at that time was Twitter, which achieved almost six million unique users during the same month (Kazeniac, 2009).

The first observation to make about the use of social networking sites is that, consistent with the discussion above, they tend to be intimately connected to the broader everyday lives of users. Early media panics about young people coming into contact with anonymous strangers have receded a little as academic research has repeatedly demonstrated that most people use software such as MySpace, Facebook, Bebo and Twitter to communicate with people they already know offline (boyd, 2008; Livingstone, 2008). Indeed, many use the privacy features on such sites to establish boundaries around their online space, enabling only hand-picked existing friends to view their profiles or converse with them.

The content of people's communication on such platforms, meanwhile, tends to consist of short statements or images related to mundane aspects of everyday life off the screen, from reflections on the weekend, to comments about work and complaints about the weather. There also tends to be a clear connection between people's overall presentation of self on social networking sites and the identities they display and live out elsewhere. People may well exaggerate certain features and play down other ones, but few construct entirely fictitious or parallel identities. A certain amount of trying on and experimenting with different facets of identity is inevitable, but the construction of identity on social networking sites tends to be a means of consolidating, mapping and making sense of one's place in the world.

As with the decoration of the walls of the teenage bedroom, social networking sites enable people to map, construct and perform a coherent and unified identity from the range of contexts, interests and relationships that make up their lives (Hodkinson and Lincoln, 2008). Far from accelerating the postmodern decline of the self, then, the use of such sites is often a means of 'writing oneself into being' (boyd, 2008). And, consistent perhaps with the notion of networked individualism, social networking sites enable each user to act as a social switchboard, conversing from their single personal online space with a variety of individuals and groups connected to different aspects of their past or present.

Despite their intimate connection with everyday life, the fact that social networking sites centre on the floating individual rather than any particular community may enable them to facilitate and perhaps even encourage a degree of identity fluidity. In comparison to community sites and forums, there may be less need to conform to predetermined topics or demonstrate the extent of one's group commitment. Rather, users are encouraged to illustrate their uniqueness as individuals by displaying an ever-changing collage of different interests, affiliations and everyday reflections. The unification of one's overall identity remains of central importance in this construction, but, rather than being rooted in anything in particular, this identity may for many people consist of multiple, shifting locations and focal points. By making it easier for people to manage and develop such shifting identities, then, social networking sites could be said to contribute in some way towards identity fluidity, even if, as we saw in Chapter 12, they also offer some possibilities for the furtherance of existing group attachments.

The widespread use of social networking sites could also be interpreted as a further example of the saturation of the world with superficial images and messages. The users of sites such as Twitter and Facebook contribute to and consume an ongoing barrage of one-line status updates, or 'tweets', most of which concern ordinary activities, feelings, emotions and opinions – from 'Paul is eating his breakfast' to 'Paul is trying to write about media saturation' to 'Paul wishes it was the weekend'. Often of little real consequence and nearly always devoid of detail and context, the stream of friend updates on most users' news feeds is so extensive that each message can only retain our attention momentarily before being replaced by a torrent of new ones from other friends.

Everyday lives, then, are being populated with a multiplicity of superficial, momentary snippets of information via social networking sites. If we connect this with the vast range of other bite-sized and momentary snippets of information we encounter throughout our daily existence, then the use of such sites could be regarded as a further extension of the information overload and hyperreality discussed by Baudrillard, Poster and others. Among all of the superficial chatter, how are we to identify, focus on and develop any understanding of messages of consequence?

Conclusion: saturated but real?

Postmodern theories of media have offered insights that are of value in any attempt to understand the relationships between media, culture and society. Their primary contribution in relation to the concerns of this book may be the observation that, rather than being a separate, external mirror or shaper of social and cultural life, media lie right at the heart of society, saturating our understandings, values, lifestyles and identities. It is truly hard to envisage an activity, an event, a set of values or a group of people within the developed world that could be said to lie substantially outside of the world of image and communication.

Meanwhile, emphasis on the sheer number of channels and messages surrounding us, and on the increasingly superficial and momentary character of such images, has drawn crucial attention to the danger of assuming, when it comes to 'information', that more is always better. Similarly, postmodern theorists have provided useful insights into the massive speed-up and saturation of culture by a disorganized proliferation of commercial objects and images – and of the drift towards layer upon layer of symbolic value to the extent that we purchase images and messages which have little relation to anything outside of themselves. As a consequence of all this, it also makes sense to conclude that a range of boundaries have become somewhat less clear than they used to be, not least distinctions between 'factual' and 'fictional' media, between different cultural genres and styles, between different places, between different sorts of identity and community and, finally, between authenticity and artifice.

The problem is that postmodernists such as Baudrillard and Jameson tended to overgeneralize the implications of what they observed into sweeping claims about the wholesale loss of meaning, reality and subjectivity – claims backed up only in relation to carefully selected examples. For example, the valid observation of an intensification of the operation of symbolic value in society becomes exaggerated, as Dominic Strinati (1995) has pointed out, into an implication that use value has all but disappeared. If we consider a range of examples of everyday consumables – from cars to glasses to vacuum cleaners to computers – it becomes apparent that things are far from being this clear-cut. To be sure, all of these items have a substantial symbolic role as images about our identities. Dell's 2009 advertisement for its latest range of laptop computers, for example, focused primarily on their colour and style. Yet, to suggest that Dell's laptops, or any of the other goods mentioned above, have no practical use or that their practical features are of no importance seems an unnecessary exaggeration.

Likewise, it is one thing to suggest that developed societies are increasingly saturated by media images – or even to recognize an increasing tendency for media representations to refer to one another – but quite another to claim that reality has entirely disappeared, that identities, lifestyles and understandings consist of nothing but simulacra and that self and subject are obliterated. The claim that reality and truth are entirely indistinguishable from artifice and the relativist implication therein that all representations and images should be regarded as equally valid is particularly important. Such a claim has huge significance for the way in which we should understand and assess media, not least those claiming to be informational, such as news, documentaries, books, 'factual' websites and even academic papers and research reports.

It may be that we *are* largely reliant on layers of media representations and that all such representations are manufactured, making it difficult to gauge accuracy or reliability, but this does not mean that the representations on which we rely have no relationship whatsoever to real events or that we have no possibility of judging between comparatively more or less faithful and honest accounts. Castigating Baudrillard for his infamous claim that the 1991 Gulf War consisted of nothing more than a media spectacle, Frank Webster argues that 'it is demonstrably the case that all news worthy of the term retains a representational character' (2002: 256). In other words, for Webster, the words and images in 'factual' media often *do* relate to very real events and situations and it is imperative that we do all we can to understand and assess the nature of this relationship.

Ultimately, as well as being an exaggeration, the argument that there is no reality or truth and only a myriad of equally valid symbols and representations is a contradictory and self-defeating one. The statement that there is no truth is, itself, a truth claim – about as big a truth claim as one could make, in fact. If there is no possibility of discerning truth from fiction, then on what basis can Baudrillard ask us to accept *his* particular claims about the world over those of other theorists? Like many other postmodernist theorists, he denies the validity of all truth claims except for his own. Indeed, he so confident in the latter that he is able to identify 'false' understandings of the world, such as those relating to Disneyland, which mask the truth, as he asks us to see it (Larrain, 1994).

The biggest problem with the more exaggerated postmodernist claims we have addressed in this chapter, however, is that, even in those cases where they are critical of the media-saturated, meaningless situation we face, they undermine attempts to learn about and improve the situation. As a consequence, they let the media industry off the hook, all but exempting them from criticism. After all, if one cannot judge between truth and fiction, honesty and dishonesty, quality and superficiality or valuable and harmful, then there seems little point in further analysis – we might as well all just make what we can of our fragmented, incoherent media-driven identities and enjoy the show.

Readers will not be surprised to hear, however, that that is not the conclusion of this chapter or this book. On the contrary, the increasing saturation of the social and cultural world by media renders it more important than ever that we understand, as definitively as possible, how processes of communication work. It is equally important that such understandings be used to hold media organizations to account and ensure the operation of communications within society is such that, as far as possible, its potential to enhance lives, identities and democracies is realized more than its potential to undermine or damage them.

QUESTIONS AND EXERCISES

1   Is it really accurate to suggest that the whole of contemporary culture and society is saturated by media and consumerism? Try to identify some elements of private or public life that are not defined or dominated by media.

2   a) Why does Baudrillard connect the media saturation of society with a loss of meaning and a gradual erosion of the relationship between media images and reality?

    b) What are the implications of Baudrillard's argument for the way in which we assess the value of news media?

3   In what ways does celebrity culture help to illustrate Baudrillard's concept of hyperreality? Try to identify some other examples.

4   a) To what extent does participation in virtual environments such as *Second Life* and *World of Warcraft* suggest a postmodern fragmentation of the self and a blurring of boundaries between fiction and reality?

    b) How typical is the behaviour of users in such environments compared to that of Internet users as a whole?

5   Does the use of social networking sites such as Twitter and Facebook offer an illustration of postmodern theories of media or does it draw attention to the limitations of such theories?

Suggested further reading

Baudrillard, J. (1995a) *Simulacra and Simulation*. Ann Arbor, MI: University of Michigan Press.
Frequently cited discussion of the saturation of culture and society by simulacra and the loss of meaning.

boyd, d. (2008) 'Taken out of context: American teen sociality in networked publics'. PhD thesis, University of California. Available online at: www.danah.org/papers/TakenOutOfContext.pdf.
Ethnographic study of the role of social networking sites in the development of young people's identities.

Featherstone, M. (2007) *Consumer Culture and Postmodernism* (2nd edn). London: Sage.
Influential analysis of the expansion of consumerism through the lens of postmodern theory.

Polhemus, T. (1997), 'In the supermarket of style', in S. Redhead (ed.), *The Club Cultures Reader*. Oxford: Blackwell.
Postmodern perspective on the proliferation of styles and identities on offer to young consumers.

Turkle, S. (1995) *Life on the Screen: Identity in the age of the Internet*. London: Phoenix.
Early study of Internet culture, focused on the blurring of boundaries and multiplicity of identities.

Glossary

Agency
The ability of individuals to be self-determining. Often discussed in relation to the ways in which agency is constrained by social *structures*.

Agenda setting
The notion that, as a result of their decisions about which issues and events to focus on, news and other 'informational' media can shape the priorities of the public.

Alienation
Used by Marx to refer to the estrangement of workers from the objects that their labour produces within capitalist societies. For Marx, alienation from the object of one's labour effectively amounted to alienation from oneself.

Assimilation
The process whereby members of ethnic minority or other marginal groups are encouraged or required to adopt the way of life, cultural values and identity of the majority.

Asynchronous communication
Communication that does not take place in real time. Newspapers are asynchronous, as are books, letters and e-mails.

Audience ethnography
An approach to media research geared towards the development of a rich understanding of the role of media in the lives of users, usually by means of in-depth observation and/or interviews.

Bias
Partiality or lack of objectivity in a person, an organization, a statement, a news report and so on.

Bourgeoisie
Used by Marx to refer to the capitalist ruling class, who own and control the means of production.

Bricolage
Used in subcultural theory to refer to the forming of new styles by bringing together a disparate set of previously unconnected objects, each of which acquires subversive meanings in its new context.

Burden of representation
The constraining expectation on ethnic minority artists, directors, actors, presenters and other public figures that they or their work will be taken to represent their entire ethnic group. Also applicable to members of sexual or other minority groups.

Censorship
A form of regulation concerned with restricting or banning particular kinds of content on the basis that they are offensive or socially harmful.

Centrifugal
Used in the study of media and society to refer to the process whereby a fragmented, plural media system contributes to the movement of different groups and individuals away from a common centre.

Centripetal
Used in the study of media and society to refer to the process whereby common media usage has the effect of drawing disparate individuals and groups together.

Citizen journalism
The active participation of ordinary members of the public in amateur journalistic practices, from taking and distributing newsworthy photographs to conducting interviews, posting reports or comment pieces on the Internet and so on.

Commodity fetishism
The separation of commercial objects from the social conditions in which they were produced. A social relationship becomes reified into a relationship between objects and money.

Community
A group of people who share a set of values, interests and experiences and feel a sense of affiliation and commitment to one another. Sometimes restricted to the most tightly knit or isolated local communities, but often used to refer to a variety of different sorts of group.

Connotation
Used by Roland Barthes to refer to the 'second order', associative or inferred meaning of a signifier or set of signifiers. See also *denotation*.

Consumer culture
A culture saturated by the buying and selling of material goods, to the extent that consumerism dominates cultural life and consumption habits become markers of identity, status and happiness.

Content
The messages, discourse or cultural forms communicated via media technologies.

Content analysis
A systematic, quantitative approach to the study of content, focused on the frequency with which designated types of content occur across statistically generalizable samples of texts.

Convergence
The process whereby the boundaries between previously distinct types of communication begin to blur.

Cool media
Used by Marshall McLuhan to refer to low-intensity, high-participation media forms, such as, in his view, television.

Critical discourse analysis
See *discourse analysis*.

Cultivation theory
George Gerbner's contention that, over a period of time, the versions of the world presented by television begin to dominate the symbolic realities of audiences, cultivating particular attitudes, opinions and understandings.

Cultural/culturalist perspective
Connected with the broader discipline of cultural studies, the term 'cultural' or 'culturalist' is sometimes used to refer to an approach to the study of media that is deemed to focus particularly on questions of discourse and meaning, often through the detailed study of media texts or their interpretation by audiences. Often contrasted with *political economy*.

Cultural capital
Used by Pierre Bourdieu to refer to forms of cultural knowledge, taste and experience that confer status and socio-economic advantages on those who have them. Transmitted via one's milieu or habitus, cultural capital is deemed to contribute to the maintenance of class boundaries.

Cultural imperialism theory
A critical interpretation of processes of globalization that emphasizes the cultural domination of small countries by multinational companies distributing Western media and cultural products.

Culture
A complex term, the use of which here implies the ways of life associated with a particular society or group and/or the forms and practices of creative and artistic expression associated with a particular society or group.

Culture industry
Used by Theodor Adorno and Max Horkheimer to refer to the apparatus responsible for the commercial mass production and distribution of standardized cultural products.

Denotation
Used by Barthes to refer to the 'first order' or most immediate and explicit meaning of a signifier or set of signifiers. See also *connotation*.

Deregulation
The process whereby government-driven regulation of an industry is relaxed, enabling a greater role for market forces.

Diaspora
A group of people who share a common point of origin and identity and have become dispersed around the globe as a result of patterns of migration.

Diaspora film
A film that depicts the life and experiences of one or more diaspora populations.

Digitalization
The process whereby analogue forms of media are replaced by digital communications.

Discourse analysis
An approach to the study of content that focuses on the construction of meaning via verbal or written forms of language use. Critical discourse analysis concentrates on the role of discourse in the reinforcement of dominant ways of seeing the world.

DIY media
Amateur and usually small-scale forms of media. Also sometimes referred to as micro-media.

Economic determinism
The belief that economic or material relations drive the course of history and determine the non-material facets of society, including cultural norms, ideas, beliefs and forms of expression. Closely related to the notion of material determinism or materialism.

Effects research
An empirical approach to the study of audiences that focuses on measuring the extent to which, and ways in which, media consumption influences attitudes or behaviour.

Ephemeral
Temporary or subject to constant change.

False consciousness
The adoption by members of the proletariat (or other subordinate groups) of distorted sets of ideas and beliefs that reinforce the system that oppresses them.

False needs
Used by Herbert Marcuse to describe distorted sets of priorities whose internalization by individuals – to the point that they are experienced and strived for as necessities – serves to reinforce oppression and subservience. Often used as a critique of consumerism.

Fan
An intensely, committed follower of a particular cultural form or set of cultural forms whose enthusiasm may form a significant part of his or her identity and/or involve participation in a fan community.

Fanzine
A small-scale amateur pamphlet or magazine associated with a particular topic or interest community.

Fluidity
Social or cultural instability, changeability or ephemerality.

Fordism
An approach to the organization of capitalist enterprise characterized, among other things, by the large-scale assembly line production of standardized, universally targeted goods and the mass marketing of such goods to broad groups of consumers.

Fragmentation
Social fragmentation implies a breaking up of once cohesive societies into a plurality of comparatively disconnected individuals and groupings.

Fraternity
Refers to a 'brotherhood' and sometimes is used by public sphere theorists to refer to the role of shared identity as part of the broader citizenship.

Functionalism
A perspective that seeks to explain different elements of the social world by reference to the role they play in contributing to the smooth functioning of society as a whole.

Gatekeeping
The process by which media organizations select which elements of the social world to include in their content. Often used to conceptualize news filtering processes.

Gemeinschaft
German term for community, used by Ferdinand Tönnies to refer specifically to the most intimate, affective and all-encompassing forms of collective unity and mutual dependence.

Genre analysis
An approach to the study of content that examines the relationship between individual texts and broader genres – or categories – that each have distinct sets of conventions and audience expectations.

Gesellschaft
German term for society, used by Tönnies to refer to a social entity that, in contrast to *gemeinschaft*, consists of a plurality of complex, pragmatic and self-interested relationships within a broad, disparate group of people.

Globalization
The process, in which media form a key component, whereby different parts of the world become intensively interconnected, in terms of trade, finance, politics, social life and culture.

Global village
Term coined by Marshall McLuhan to refer to the effective shrinking of the globe as a result of increased international communication brought about by media technologies.

Hegemony
Hegemony, or sometimes cultural hegemony, is associated with the work of Antonio Gramsci and refers to domination over the realm of culture and ideas by the ruling class. Rather than being predetermined by economic relations, cultural hegemony is constantly subject to ideological challenge and struggle.

Horizontal integration
The expansion of media corporations across different media sectors (such as television, newspapers, books, gaming, music and so on) via takeovers and mergers. See also *vertical integration*.

Hot media
Used by McLuhan to refer to high-intensity, low-participation media forms. Including most forms of print media, hot media were deemed isolating and undemocratic.

Hyperreality

Used by Jean Baudrillard to refer to a situation in which society is so saturated by layer upon layer of simulacra that it becomes impossible to discern any sort of external reality or truth beneath all the empty images.

Icon

A semiological term meaning a signifier that bears a resemblance to its *signified*, for example through appearance or sound.

Ideological state apparatus

Used by Louis Althusser to describe a set of institutions, including the family, education system, religious organizations and media, that, although relatively autonomous, are determined by the economic base of society 'in the last instance' and function to reinforce dominant ideology.

Ideology

A set of ideas, beliefs and assumptions about the world. Often used (for example, in Marxist theories) to refer specifically to dominant and/or misleading sets of ideas that reflect and reinforce prevailing power relations.

Imagined community

Used by Benedict Anderson to refer to the symbolic sense of shared identity experienced by those who share the same nationality, despite never meeting or knowing one another.

Index

A semiological term meaning a *signifier* that does not resemble but is causally or sensorially connected with its *signified* and, therefore, not arbitrary.

Individualization

The notion that individuals are increasingly detached from traditional sources of stability, security and direction and, as a consequence, float freely between a range of temporary and partial foci for identity.

Industry

Media industry refers to the body of organizations that dominate the development, operation and distribution of media.

Instrumental reason

Development and use of the human capacity for imagination, judgement, reasoning and rationality as a means to an end (for example, to increase productivity, efficiency or profit) rather than as an end in itself.

Interpersonal media

Media that enable interactive communication between small numbers of people.

Labelling theory
The argument that the negative labelling of 'outsider' groups or individuals by society (such as via media coverage) can amplify their sense of difference and cause them to identify more strongly with the values or people associated with the label.

Male gaze
The objectifying look of the heterosexual male voyeur to whom many representations of femininity are argued to be directed. Associated with Laura Mulvey's work on gender and cinema and widely adopted in other contexts.

Marxism
A perspective based on the ideas of Karl Marx that focuses on the exploitative and alienative relations deemed to define capitalist societies and the determination of non-economic spheres of society (culture and ideas, for example) by economic relations. Marxist perspectives on media tend to focus on the way in which mass communications reflect and/or reinforce capitalist material relations.

Mass culture theory
Theories that lament the replacement of elite high culture and/or grass roots folk culture with a superficial and standardized mass culture attributable to mass media and consumer culture. Connected to notions of mass society, which emphasize the replacement of distinct participatory communities with an atomized mass.

Mass media
Usually used to refer to the one-directional distribution of media by powerful corporate institutions to large and demographically broad audiences.

Media
Plural of *medium*. Also sometimes used to refer to the collective make-up, activities or impact of large-scale media organizations.

Medium
The technological means by which content is communicated between an origin and a destination, such as a telegraph, telephone, television, book and so on.

Medium theory
A theory that focuses on the ways in which communications technologies act as a force for social and cultural change.

Monopoly
A situation in which all or most of the products and services for a particular market are supplied by a single provider.

Moral conservativism
A political perspective focused on protecting traditional moral values.

Moral panic
An intense societal reaction – usually fuelled by sensationalist media coverage – against a perceived threat to prevailing social values or ways of life. Those associated with the threat are invariably stigmatized, according to Stan Cohen, as 'folk devils'.

Myth
Used by Barthes to refer to broad sets of dominant or 'common sense' understandings that are tapped into and reinforced by the connotations of individual texts.

Narcissism
The gaining of pleasure by gazing at and/or admiring one's own image. Associated with Jacques Lacan's 'mirror stage' of child development and adapted to discussions of the representation of gender in media.

Narrative analysis
An approach to the study of content that focuses on the role of structures and conventions of storytelling in media texts.

Narrowcasting
The distribution of media to clearly defined, specialist audiences.

Neo-liberalism
A political doctrine that revived some of the free market ideas of eighteenth- and nineteenth-century liberal economics, including the work of Adam Smith. Neo-liberal perspectives on media endorse the relaxation of state intervention, from controls on content to the funding of public service broadcasters.

Neo-Marxism
A perspective that adapts or amends the ideas of Karl Marx (see also *Marxism*) in some way, as in the case of theorists such as Antonio Gramsci and Louis Althusser.

Neo-tribe
Used by Michel Maffesoli to refer to loose-knit affinity groupings with porous boundaries and adopted by some youth cultural theorists as a replacement for the notion of subculture.

New ethnicities
Used by Stuart Hall to refer to the complex and fluid nature of ethnic identities. Particularly associated with research on multifaceted ethnic identities of second- and third-generation ethnic minority youth.

News values
The set of priorities that form the basis of decisions made by news organizations about the selection, positioning and construction of stories.

Niche media
Forms of media that are targeted narrowly towards particular groups or types of consumers.

Oligopoly
A situation in which a particular market is overwhelmingly dominated by a small number of powerful companies.

Panopticon
A prison in which every cell is visible from a single watchtower. Often used as a metaphor for the capacity of electronic media technologies, such as the Internet, to subject individuals to surveillance throughout their everyday lives.

Paradigmatic analysis
An approach to semiological analysis concerned with comparing each element of a text with a paradigm of alternatives that might have been used in its place. See also *syntagmatic analysis*.

Parody/pastiche
A distinction used by Frederick Jameson between ironic reuses of images that refer to the context of the original use (parody), and reuses which remove all reference to the previous context by combining the image with a range of others (pastiche).

Patriarchy
Used here to refer to a social system centred on male authority and female subordination.

Pluralism
A perspective or state of affairs whereby the coexistence of a range of voices and viewpoints is valued.

Political economy
A political economic perspective on media is one that focuses particularly on the workings of the media industry and the broader economic and political context in which it operates.

Polysemic
A semiological term referring to the capacity of a sign to have multiple meanings.

Population
The overall group of people or body of content that a *sample* in a research study is intended to represent.

Post-Fordism
A flexible approach to capitalist enterprise, characterized, among other things, by the precise targeting of niche markets and the capacity to rapidly develop and promote new and different kinds of products in response to market changes.

Preferred meaning
The meaning that the encoding of a media text is deemed to encourage.

Proletariat
Used by Marx to refer to the working class, by which he meant the non-wealth-owning majority, who sell their labour to make a living.

Pseudo-individualization
Used by Theodor Adorno to refer to the guise of difference and originality with which standardized cultural products present themselves to us.

Public service broadcasting (PSB)
A form of broadcasting whose objective is to benefit society – an orientation usually achieved via government-driven funding and/or regulation.

Public sphere
A space for the collective exchange and development of ideas located between the realm of government and the domestic and commercial spheres of society. Often discussed in relation to the role of media in the facilitation of public debate and/or shared culture.

Reflection theory
An approach that suggests media reflect or 'mirror' existing social values or relations.

Regulation
Controls imposed by government or government-appointed bodies on the activities of media organizations.

Reification
The transformation of what is human, subjective or social into an object or thing. For example, the dehumanization of workers into being mere cogs in the capitalist machine or the theoretical decontextualization of technologies from their human context by technological determinist theorists.

Relative autonomy
Used by Althusser to describe the partial independence of non-economic spheres of society – including the realm of culture and ideas – from their economic base.

Representation
Refers to the way media content symbolizes or stands in for social or cultural phenomena. Often used to refer to the selective portrayal of events, people, groups, cultural trends, social relations and so on.

Sample
A selection of people or examples of content that is designed to represent the broader *population* in which a research study is interested.

Saturation
Media saturation refers to the domination of all or most facets of society, culture and everyday life by layer upon layer of mediated communication, information and imagery.

Scopophilia
The gaining of pleasure by subjecting others to a voyeuristic, objectifying gaze. Adapted from psychoanalytic understandings of childhood in Laura Mulvey's discussion of the significance of the *male gaze* in cinema.

Self-fulfilling prophesy
A prediction or representation whose own influence causes it to be fulfilled. For example, high-profile media discussion of the likelihood of violence at a protest march may render violence more likely to occur there by affecting the mood of participants.

Semiology
An approach to the study of media content which focuses on the generation of meaning through arrangements of signs.

Shaping theory
An approach that suggests media have a direct influence on society.

Signified
A semiological term meaning the concept represented by a *signifier*.

Signifier
A semiological term meaning the means by which a concept, or *signified*, is represented.

Simulacra
Used by Baudrillard to refer to the meaningless images that, in his view, had saturated social and cultural life. Rather than referring to any sort of external reality or truth, simulacra refer only to one another.

Social democratic
A political perspective which embraces democracy and elements of market capitalism while endorsing substantial state intervention in the interests of equality, social justice and the public good.

Society
A network of institutions, relationships, interactions and culture within which individual lives take place.

Stereotype
A familiar and often-repeated characterization of the members of a particular social group or category (ethnic, gender, age or sexual categories, for example) the prevalence of which has the effect of reducing, simplifying and generalizing the features of the group as a whole.

Strong ties
Broad, substantive and sustained relationships that involve extensive individual familiarity and commitment and are sustained across numerous sites of interaction.

Structure(s)
The set of established social institutions, groupings, hierarchies, norms and ways of living into which people are born. Often regarded as constrainers or shapers of individual lives and identities. See also *agency*.

Subculture
Contested term associated with youth cultural theory that usually refers to a group of people characterized by a strong sense of identity and centred on a set of styles, values or tastes that differentiate them from the broader culture of which they are a part.

Symbol
A semiological term meaning a *signifier* that has no a priori relationship to its *signified* and is therefore arbitrary. Also sometimes used in a more general sense to refer to any sort of signifier.

Symbolic value
The value that derives from the symbolic meanings associated with a commodity. For example, an object may have significance as a marker of identity or status.

Synchronous communication
Communication that takes place in real time. A telephone call is synchronous, as is radio listening and TV watching.

Syntagmatic analysis
An approach to semiological analysis centred on developing an understanding of the relationship between different elements of a text in the construction of meaning.

Technological determinism
The belief that technologies act as independent shapers of the social and cultural world and are the most important instigators of social change. Often used as a term with which to draw attention to the perceived shortcomings of *medium theory*.

Technology
For media technology, see *medium*. In its broader sense, the term refers to the practical application of scientific knowledge for a particular purpose and/or the outcomes of such an endeavour.

Tokenism
The inclusion of one or a small number of people from a minority or marginalized group in an organization, event or a cultural text in order to appear inclusive.

Two-step flow
A model of communication that suggests media influence on people is channelled and filtered by influential members of their community.

Users
The range of ordinary people who utilize media, whether as audiences, interpersonal interactants or non-professional producers and distributors of content.

Uses and gratifications
A research approach focused on the active selection and use of media by individuals in order to fulfil needs and achieve gratifications.

Use value
The value that is derived from the practical function of a commodity.

Vertical integration
The expansion of media corporations – via mergers or takeovers – up and down the different stages of production and distribution. See also *horizontal integration*.

Virtual community
A contested term used to refer to a community that is primarily generated or sustained via Internet communication.

Volunteer audience
An audience that is deemed wilfully to have chosen to consume a particular type of content (rather than accidentally stumbling on it by channel hopping, for example).

Weak ties
Narrow and limited relationships that lack intensity or commitment and are often confined to a particular sphere of interest/commonality and/or a single site of interaction.

References

Adorno, T. (1990; 1941) 'On popular music', in S. Frith and A. Goodwin (eds), *On Record: Rock, pop and the written word*. London: Routledge.

Adorno, T. (1991; 1944) 'The schema of mass culture', in J. Bernstein (ed.), *The Culture Industry: Selected essays on mass culture*. London: Routledge.

Adorno, T. and Horkheimer, M. (1997; 1944) *Dialectic of Enlightenment*. London: Verso.

Allan, S. and Thorsen, E. (eds) (2009) *Citizen Journalism: Global perspectives*. New York: Peter Lang.

Alexander, C. (2000) *The Asian Gang: Ethnicity, identity, masculinity*. Oxford: Berg.

Alexander, V. (2003) *Sociology of the Arts: Exploring fine and popular forms*. Oxford: Blackwell.

Allen, A. and Zelizer, B. (2004) *Reporting War: Journalism in wartime*. Abingdon: Routledge.

Althusser, L. (1971) *Lenin and Philosophy and Other Essays*. London: New Left Books.

Anderson, B. (1991) *Imagined Communities*. London: Verso.

Ang, I. (1985) *Watching Dallas: Soap opera and the melodramatic imagination*. London: Methuen.

Ang, I. (1996) *Living Room Wars: Rethinking media audiences for a postmodern age*. London: Routledge.

Antony, R. (2009) 'Second-generation Tamil Youth in London'. Ongoing PhD Project, University of Surrey.

Appadurai, A. (1996) *Modernity at Large: Cultural dimensions of globalization*. Minneapolis, MN: University of Minneapolis Press.

Arthurs, J. (2004) *Television and Sexuality: Regulation and the politics of taste*. Maidenhead: Open University Press.

Atton, C. (2002) *Alternative Media*. London: Sage.

Back, L. (1996) *New Ethnicities and Urban Culture: Racisms and multiculture in young lives*. London: Routledge.

Bagdikian, B. (2004) *The New Media Monopoly*. Boston, MA: Beacon Press.

Bakardjieva, M. (2005) *Internet Society: The Internet in everyday life*. London: Sage.

Baker, W. and Dessart, G. (1998) *Down the Tube: An inside account of the failure of US television*. New York: Basic Books.

Baker, J., Houston A., Diawara, M. and Lindeborg, R. (eds) (1996) *Black British Cultural Studies: A reader*. Chicago, IL: University of Chicago Press.

Bandura, A., Ross, D. and Ross, S. A. (1961) 'Transmission of aggression through imitation of aggressive models', *Journal of Abnormal and Social Psychology*, 63: 575–82.

Bandura, A., Ross, D. and Ross, S. A. (1963) 'Imitation of film-mediated aggressive models', *Journal of Abnormal and Social Psychology*, 66: 31–41.

Barker, M. (1981) *The New Racism: Conservatives and the ideology of the tribe*. London: Junction Books.

Barnett, S. (1998) 'Dumbing down or reaching out: is it tabloidisation wot done it?', in J. Seaton (ed.), *Politics and the Media: Harlots and prerogatives at the turn of the millennium*. Abingdon: Blackwell.

Barthes, R. (1968; 1964) *Elements of Semiology*. London: Cape.

Barthes, R. (1972; 1957) *Mythologies*. New York: Hill & Wang.

Baudrillard, J. (1983) 'The ecstasy of communication', in H. Forster (ed.), *Postmodern Culture*. London: Pluto Press.

Baudrillard, J. (1988) *The Ecstasy of Communication*. Cambridge, MA: MIT Press.

Baudrillard, J. (1995a) *Simulacra and Simulation*. Ann Arbor, MI: University of Michigan Press.

Baudrillard, J. (1995b) *The Gulf War Did Not Take Place*. Bloomington, IN: Indiana University Press.

Bauman, Z. (2000) *The Individualized Society*. Cambridge: Polity Press.

Bauman, Z. (2001) *Community: Seeking safety in an insecure world*. Cambridge: Polity Press.

Baym, N. (2000) *Tune In, Log On: Soaps, fandom and online community*. London: Sage.

Beck, U. and Beck-Gernsheim, E. (2001) *Individualization*. London: Sage.

Becker, H. (1963) *Outsiders: Studies in the sociology of deviance*. New York: Free Press.

Bell, A. (1991) *The Language of News Media*. Oxford: Blackwell.

Bennett, A. (1999) 'Subcultures or neo-tribes? Rethinking the relationship between youth, style and musical taste', *Sociology*, 33(3): 599–617.

Berelson, B. (1952) *Content Analysis in Communication Research*. New York: Free Press.

Berelson, B., Lazarsfeld, R. and McPhee, N. (1954) *Voting: A study of opinion formation in a presidential campaign*. Chicago: University of Chicago Press.

Berkowitz, L. (1984) 'Some effects of thoughts on anti- and pro-social influence of media events', *Psychological Bulletin*, 95 (3): 410–27.

Billig, M. (1995) *Banal Nationalism*. London: Sage.

Boellstorff, T. (2008) *Coming of Age in Second Life: An anthropologist explores the virtually human*. Princeton, NJ: Princeton University Press.

Bourdieu, P. (1984) *Distinction: A social critique of the judgement of taste*. London: Routledge.

boyd, d. (2008) 'Taken out of context: American teen sociality in networked publics'. PhD thesis, University of California. Available online at: www.danah.org/papers/TakenOutOfContext.pdf

Boyd-Barrett, O. (1977) 'Media imperialism: towards an international framework for the analysis of media systems', in J. Curran, M. Gurevitch and J. Woollacott (eds), *Mass Communication and Society*. London: Arnold.

Briggs, A. (1961) *The History of Broadcasting in the United Kingdom: Birth of broadcasting, Volume 1*. Oxford: Oxford University Press.

Bruns, A. and Jacobs, J. (eds) (2006) *Uses of Blogs*. New York: Peter Lang.

Brunsden, C. and Morley, D. (1978) *Everyday Television: Nationwide*. London: British Film Institute.

Bull, M. (2007) *Sound Moves: iPod culture and urban experience*. Abingdon: Routledge.

Butler, J. (1990) *Gender Trouble: Feminism and the subversion of identity*. New York: Routledge.

Butler, J. (1993) *Bodies That Matter: On the discursive limits of 'sex'*. London: Rouledge.

Butsch, R. (ed.) (2007) *Media and Public Spheres*. Houndmills, Basingstoke: Palgrave Macmillan.

Carlyle, T. (1849) 'Occasional discourse on the negro question', *Fraser's Magazine*, February.

Castells, M. (2001) *The Internet Galaxy*. Oxford: Oxford University Press.

Castells, M., Fernandez-Ardevol, M., Linchuan Qui, J. and Sey, A. (2006) *Mobile Communication and Society: A global perspective*. Cambridge, MA: MIT Press.

Chambers, I. (1985), *Urban Rhythms: Pop music and popular culture*. London: Macmillan.

Chandler, D. (1994a) 'The transmission model of communication'. Available online at: www.aber.ac.uk/media/Documents/short/trans.html

Chandler, D. (1994b) 'Semiotics for beginners'. Available online at: www.aber.ac.uk/media/Documents/S4B/semiotic.html

Chandler, D. (1995) 'Technological or media determinism'. Available online at: www.aber.ac.uk/media/Documents/tecdet/tecdet.html

Clarke, J., Hall, S., Jefferson, T. and Roberts, B. (1976) 'Subcultures, cultures and class: a theoretical overview', in S. Hall and T. Jefferson (eds), *Resistance Through Rituals: Youth cultures in post-war Britain*. London: Hutchinson.

Cohen, Albert (1955) *Delinquent Boys: The culture of the gang*. London: Collier-Macmillan.

Cohen, Anthony (1985) *The Symbolic Construction of Community*. Chichester: Ellis Horwood.

Cohen, P. (1972) 'Subcultural conflict and working class community', *Working Papers in Cultural Studies*, 2: 5–70.

Cohen, S. (1972) *Folk Devils and Moral Panics: The creation of the mods and rockers*. London: MacGibbon & Lee.

Cohen, S. and Young, J. (eds) (1973) *The Manufacture of News: Social problems, deviance and the mass media*. London: Constable.

Collins, R. (1990) *Culture, Communications and Political Economy*. Toronto: University of Toronto Press.

Collins, E. and Murroni, C. (eds) (1996) *New Media, New Policies: Media and communications strategies for the future*. Cambridge: Polity Press.

Connell, R. W. (2000) *The Men and the Boys*. Cambridge: Polity Press.

Connor, S. (1997) *Postmodernist Culture: An introduction to theories of the contemporary* (2nd edn). Oxford: Blackwell.

Corea, A. (1995) 'Racism and the American way of media', in J. Downing, A. Mohammadi and A. Sreberny-Mohammadi (eds), *Questioning the Media: A critical introduction*. London: Sage.

Crisell, A. (1998) 'Local radio: attuned to the times or filling time with tunes?', in B. Franklin and D. Murphy (eds), *Making the Local News: Local journalism in context*. London: Routledge.

Croteau, D. and Hoynes, W. (2000) *Media/Society: Industries, images and audiences* (2nd edn). Thousand Oaks, CA: Pine Forge Press.

Curran, J. and Seaton, J. (2003) *Power Without Responsibility: The press, broadcasting and new media in Britain* (6th edn). New York: Routledge.

Dahlgren, P. (1995) *Television and the Public Sphere: Citizenship, democracy and the media*. London: Sage.

Dayan, D. (1998) 'Particularistic media and diasporic communications', in J. Curran and T. Liebes (eds), *Media, Ritual and Identity*. London: Routledge, 103–13.

de Certeau, M. (1984) *The Practice of Everyday Life*. Berkeley, CA: University of California Press.

Delanty, G. (2003) *Community*. London: Routledge.

de Saussure, F. (1974; 1915) *Course in General Linguistics*. London: Fontana.

Devlin, P. (1965) *The Enforcement of Morals*. London: Oxford University Press.

Dobson, A. (2008) 'The "grotesque body" in young women's self-presentation on MySpace', Conference Paper, TASA Conference, University of Melbourne. Available

online at: www.tasa.org.au/conferences/conferencepapers08/Social%20Networks/
Dobson,%20Amy,%20Session%2010%20PDF.pdf

Dorfman, A. and Mattelart, A. (1971) *How to Read Donald Duck: Imperialist ideology in the Disney comic*. New York: International General.

Doty, A. and Gove, B. (1997) 'Queer representation in the mass media', in A. Medhurst and S. Munt (eds), *The Lesbian and Gay Studies Reader*. London: Cassell.

Downing, J. and Husband, C. (2005) *Representing Race: Racisms, ethnicity and the media*. London: Sage.

Drabman, R. and Thomas, R. (1974) 'Does media violence increase children's toleration of real-life aggression?', *Developmental Psychology*, 10: 418–21.

Du Gay, P., Hall, S., Janes, L., Mackay, J. and Negus, K. (1997) *Doing Cultural Studies: The story of the Sony Walkman*. London: Sage.

Dworkin, A. (1981) *Pornography: Men possessing women*. London: Women's Press.

Dworkin, A. (1995) 'Pornography and male supremacy', in G. Dines and J. Humez (eds), *Gender, Race and Class in Media: A reader*. London: Sage: 237–43.

Dyson, M. (1993) *Reflecting Black African-American Cultural Criticism*. Minneapolis, MN: University of Minnesota Press.

Edwardson, R. (2008) *Canadian Content: Culture and the quest for nationhood*. Toronto: University of Toronto Press.

Eldridge, J., Kitzinger, J. and Williams, K. (1997) *The Mass Media and Power in Modern Britain*. New York: Oxford University Press.

Elstein, D. (1986) 'An end to protection', in C. MacCabe and O. Stewart (eds), *The BBC and Public Service Broadcasting*. Manchester: Manchester University Press: 81–91.

Fairclough, N. (1995) *Critical Discourse Analysis: The critical study of language*. Harlow: Longman.

Featherstone, M. (2007) *Consumer Culture and Postmodernism* (2nd edn). London: Sage.

Federal Communications Commission (FCC) (2008) 'Obscure, indecent and profane broadcasts', *FCC Consumer Facts*. Available online at: www.fcc.gov/cgb/consume-facts/obscene.html

Feshbach, S. (1961) 'The stimulating versus cathartic effects of a vicarious aggressive activity', *Journal of Abnormal and Social Psychology*, 63: 381–5.

Fiske, J. (1987) *Television Culture*. London: Methuen.

Fiske, J. (1990) *Introduction to Communication Studies* (2nd edn). London: Routledge.

Fiske, J. (1991a) *Understanding Popular Culture*. London: Routledge.

Fiske, J. (1991b) *Reading the Popular*. London: Routledge.

Fiske, J. and Hartley, J. (1988; 1978) *Reading Television*. London: Routledge.

Flew, T. (2003) *New Media: An introduction*. Oxford: Oxford University Press.

Foucault, M. (1990; 1976) *The History of Sexuality: Volume 1*. Harmondsworth: Penguin.

Franklin, B. (1997) *Newszak and News Media*. London: Arnold.

Franklin, B. and Murphy, D. (1998) 'Changing times: local newspapers, technology and markets', in B. Franklin and D. Murphy (eds), *Making the Local News: Local journalism in context*. London: Routledge.

Fulton, H., Huisman, R., Morphet, J. and Dunn, A. (eds) (2005) *Narrative and Media*. Cambridge: Cambridge University Press.

Galtung, J. and Ruge, M. (1973) 'Structuring and selecting news', in S. Cohen and J. Young (eds), *The Manufacture of News: Social problems, deviance and the mass media*. London: Constable.

Garnham, N. (1978) *Television Monograph 1: Structures of television*. London: British Film Institute.

Garnham, N. (1992) 'The media and the public sphere', in C. Calhoun (ed.), *Habermas and the Public Sphere*. Cambridge, MA: MIT Press.

Garnham, N. (1995; 1979) 'Contribution to a political economy of mass communication', in O. Boyd-Barrett and C. Newbold (eds), *Approaches to Media: A reader*. London: Arnold.

Gauntlett, D. (1998) 'Ten Things Wrong With the Effects Model', in R. Dickenson, R. Harindranath, and O. Linné, (eds) (1998), *Approaches to Audiences: A reader*, London: Arnold.

Gauntlett, D. (2008) *Media, Gender and Identity: An introduction* (2nd edn). Abingdon: Routledge.

Gellner, E. (1983) *Nations and Nationalism*. Oxford: Blackwell.

Georgiou, M. (2001) 'Crossing the boundaries of the ethnic home: media consumption and ethnic identity construction in the public space: the case of the Cypriot Community Centre in North London', *International Communication Gazette*, 63(4): 311–29.

Georgiou, M. (2002) 'Diasporic communities on-line: a bottom up experience of transnationalism', *Hommes & Migrations*, 1240: 10–18. Also available online at: www.lse. ac.uk/collections/EMTEL/Minorities/papers/hommesmigrations.doc

Georgiou, M. (2006) *Diaspora, Identity and the Media*. Cresskill, NJ: Hampton Press.

Geraghty, C. (1991) *Women and Soap Opera: A study of prime-time soaps*. Cambridge: Polity Press.

Gerbner, G. (1956) 'Toward a general model of communication', *Audio Visual Communication Review IV*, (3): 171–99.

Gerbner, G. (1994) 'Reclaiming our cultural mythology', *In Context*, 38.

Gerbner, G. (2002) 'Global media mayhem', *Global Media Journal*, 1 (1). Also available online at: http://lass.calumet.purdue.edu/cca/gmj/fa02/gmj-fa02-gerbner.htm

Gerbner, G. and Gross, L. (1976) 'Living with television: the violence profile', *Journal of Communication*, 26: 173–99.

Gerbner, G., Gross, L., Jackson-Beeck, M. Jeffries-Fox, S. and Signorielli, N. (1977) 'TV violence profile No. 8: the highlights', *Journal of Communication*, 27 (2): 171–80.

Geser, H. (2007a) 'Me, my self and my avatar: some microsociological reflections on "Second Life"', in online publication *Sociology in Switzerland: Towards cybersociety and vireal social relations*. Available online at: http://socio.ch/intcom/t_hgeser17.pdf

Geser H. (2007b) 'A very real virtual society: some macrosociological reflections on "Second Life"', in online publication *Sociology in Switzerland: Towards cybersociety and vireal social relations*. Available online at: http://socio.ch/intcom/t_hgeser18.pdf

Gidley, B. (2007) 'Youth culture and ethnicity: emerging youth multiculture in South London', in P. Hodkinson and W. Deicke (eds), *Youth Cultures: Scenes, subcultures and tribes*. New York: Routledge.

Gilder, G. (1992) *Life after Television: The coming transformation of media and American life*. New York: Norton.

Gill, R. (2007) *Gender and the Media*. Cambridge: Polity Press.

Gillespie, M. (1995) *Television, Ethnicity and Cultural Change*. London: Routledge.

Gillespie, M. (2006) 'Narrative analysis', in M. Gillespie and J. Toynbee (eds), *Analysing Media Texts*. Maidenhead: Open University Press.

Gillmor, D. (2006) *We the Media: Grass roots journalism by the people for the people*. Sebastopol: O'Reilly Media.

Gilroy, P. (1987) *There Ain't No Black in the Union Jack: The politics of race and nation*. London: Hutchison.

Gilroy, P. (1993) *The Black Atlantic: Modernity and double-consciousness*. London: Verso.

Gitlin, T. (1998) 'Public sphere or public sphericules', in T. Liebes and J. Curran (eds), *Media, Ritual and Identity*. London: Routledge.

Gitlin, T. (2000) *Inside Prime-Time* (revised edn). Abingdon: Routledge.

Glasgow University Media Group (1976a) *Bad News*. London: Routledge & Kegan Paul.

Glasgow University Media Group (1976b) *More Bad News*. London: Routledge & Kegan Paul.

Glasgow University Media Group (1982) *Really Bad News*. London: Writers' and Readers' Publishing Cooperative.

Global Media Monitoring Project (2005) 'Who makes the news?: Global Report 2005'. Also available online at: www.whomakesthenews.orgreports/2005-global-report.html

Golding, P. and Murdock, G. (1991) 'Culture, communications and political economy', in J. Curran and M. Gurevitch (eds), *Mass Media and Society* (3rd edn). London: Arnold: 70–92.

Goffman, E. (1979) *Gender Advertisements*. London: Macmillan.

Gore, A. (2007) *The Assault on Reason*. London: Bloomsbury Publishing.

Gramsci, A. (1971) *Selections From the Prison Notebooks*. London: Lawrence & Wishart.

Gray, A. (1992) *Video Playtime: The gendering of a leisure technology*. Abingdon: Routledge.

Gray, J., Sandvoss, C. and Harrington, C. (eds) (2005) *Fandom: Identities and Communities in a Mediated World*. New York: New York University Press.

Greenslade, R. (2003) 'Their master's voice', The *Guardian*, 17 February. Also available online at: www.guardian.co.uk/media/2003/feb/17/mondaymediasection.iraq

Gross, L. (1995) 'Out of the mainstream: sexual minorities and the mass media', in G. Dines and J. Humez (eds), *Gender, Race and Class in Media*. London: Sage: 61–70.

Gunter, B. (2000) *Media Research Methods*. London: Sage.

Habermas, J. (1987; 1981) *The Theory of Communicative Action, Volume 2: Lifeworld and system – a critique of functionalist reason*. Cambridge: Polity Press.

Habermas, J. (1992; 1964) *The Structural Transformation of the Public Sphere*. Cambridge: Polity Press.

Habermas, J. (1996) *Between Facts and Norms: Contributions to a discourse theory of law and democracy*. Cambridge: Polity Press.

Habermas, J. (2001) *The Postnational Constellation: Political essays*. Cambridge: Polity Press.

Hall, S. (1973) 'The determination of news photographs', in S. Cohen and J. Young (eds), *The Manufacture of News*. London: Constable.

Hall, S. (1982) 'The rediscovery of "ideology": return of the repressed in media studies', in M. Gurevitch, T. Bennett, J. Curran and J. Woollacott (eds), *Culture, Society and the Media*. London: Routledge.

Hall, S. (1992) 'New ethnicities', in A. Rattansi and J. Donald (eds), *Race, Culture and Difference*. London: Sage.

Hall, S. (1993; 1980) 'Encoding, decoding', in S. During (ed.), *The Cultural Studies Reader*. London: Routledge: 90–103.

Hall, S. (1997) 'The spectacle of the other', in S. Hall (ed.), *Representation: Cultural representations and signifying practices*. London: Sage.

Hall, S., Critcher, C., Jefferson, T., Clarke J., and Roberts, B. (1978) *Policing the Crisis: Mugging, the state and law and order*. London: Macmillan.

Halloran, J. (1970) *The Effects of Television*. London: Panther.

Hannerz, U. (1996) *Transnational Connections: Culture, people, places*. London: Routledge.

Harrison, M. (1985) *Television News: Whose bias?* London: King's Fund.

Hartley, J. (1982) *Understanding News*. London: Methuen.

Hartley, J. (2009) 'Less popular but more democratic?: *Corrie*, Clarkson and the Dancing *Cru*', in G. Turner and J. Tay (eds), *Television Studies After TV: Understanding television in the post-broadcast era*. Abingdon: Routledge.

Harvey, D. (1989) *The Condition of Postmodernity: An enquiry into the logics of social change*. Oxford: Basil Blackwell.

Hayes, I. (1971) *Theme From Shaft*. Enterprise (music recording).

Hebdige, D. (1979) *Subculture: The meaning of style*. London: Methuen.

Hebdige, D. (1988) *Hiding in the Light: On images and things*. London: Routledge.

Herman, E. and Chomsky, N. (1998; 1988) *Manufacturing Consent: The political economy of the mass media*. London: Vintage.

Hermes, J. (1995) *Reading Women's Magazines*. Cambridge: Polity Press.

Hesmondhalgh, D. (2002) *The Cultural Industries*. London: Sage.

Hesmondhalgh, D. (2006) 'Discourse analysis and content analysis' in M. Gillespie and J. Toynbee (eds), *Analysing Media Texts*. Maidenhead: Open University Press.

Hill, K. and Hughes, J. (1998) *Cyberpolitics: Citizen activism in the age of the Internet*. Oxford: Roman & Littlefield.

Hills, M. (2002) *Fan Cultures*. Abingdon: Routledge.

Huq, R. (2006) *Beyond Subculture: Pop, youth and identity in a postcolonial world*. Abingdon: Routledge.

Hodkinson, P. (2002) *Goth: Identity, style and subculture*. Oxford: Berg.

Hodkinson, P. (2003) 'Net.Goth: Internet communication and (sub) cultural boundaries', in D. Muggleton and R. Weinzeirl (eds), *The Post-Subcultures Reader*. Oxford: Berg: 285–97.

Hodkinson, P. (2007) 'Interactive online journals and individualisation', *New Media and Society*, 9 (4): 625–50.

Hodkinson, P. and Lincoln, S. (2008) 'Online journals as virtual bedrooms: young people, identity and personal space', *YOUNG*, 16 (1).

Hussain, Y. (2005) *Writing Diaspora: South Asian women, culture and identity*. London: Ashgate.

Innes, H. A. (1951) *The Bias of Communication*. Toronto: University of Toronto Press.

Jackson, P., Stevenson, N. and Brooks, K. (2001) *Making Sense of Men's Magazines*. Cambridge: Polity Press.

Jameson, F. (1991) *Postmodernism or the Cultural Logic of Late Capitalism*. London: Verso.

Jenkins, H. (1992) *Textual Poachers: Television fans and participatory culture*. London: Routledge.

Jenkins, H. (2002) 'Interactive audiences?', in V. Nightingale and K. Ross (eds), *Critical Readings: Media and audiences*. Maidenhead: Open University Press.

Katz, E. (1959) 'Mass communications research and popular culture', *Studies in Public Communication*, 2: 10–19.

Katz, E., Blumler, J. and Gurevich, M. (2003; 1974) 'Utilization of mass communication by the individual', in K. Nightingale and A. Ross (eds), *Critical Readings: Media and audiences*. Maidenhead: Open University Press.

Katz, E., Gurevitch, M. and Haas, H. (1973) 'On the use of mass media for important things', *American Sociological Review*, 38: 164–81.

Katz, E. and Lazarsfeld, P. (1955) *Personal Influence*. New York: Free Press.

Katz, E. and Liebes, T. (1985) 'Mutual aid in the decoding of *Dallas*: preliminary notes from a cross-cultural study', in P. Drummond and R. Patterson (eds), *Television in Transition*. London: British Film Institute: 187–98.

Kazeniac, A. (2009) 'Social networks: Facebook takes over top-spot, Twitter climbs', *Compete*, 9 February. Available online at: http://blog.compete.com/2009/02/09/face book-myspace-twitter-social-network

Kellner, D. (1995) 'Advertising and consumer culture', in J. Downing, A. Mohammadi and A. Sreberny-Mohammadi (eds), *Questioning the Media: A critical introduction* (2nd edn). London: Sage: 329–44.

Kerlinger, F. N. (1986) *Foundations of Behavioural Research*. New York: Holt, Rinehart & Winston.

Kipling, R. (1899) 'The white man's burden', *McLure's Magazine*, 12 February.

Klein, N. (2000) *No Logo*. London: Flamingo.

Kress, G. and Hodge, R. (1979) *Language as Ideology*. London: Routledge & Kegan Paul.

Lacan, J. (2001; 1977) *Écrits: A selection*. Abingdon: Routledge.

Langer, J. (1998) *Tabloid Television: Popular television and the 'other news'*. London: Routledge.

Larrain, J. (1994) *Ideology and Cultural Identity*. Cambridge: Polity Press.

Lasswell, H. (1948) 'The structure and function of communication in society', in L. Bryson (ed.), *The Communication of Ideas*. New York: Institute for Religious and Social Studies.

Lazarsfeld, P., Berelson, B. and Gaudet, H. (1944) *The People's Choice*. New York: Columbia University Press.

Leonard, M. (1998) 'Paper planes: travelling the New Grrrl geographies', in T. Skelton and G. Valentine (eds), *Cool Places: Geographies of youth cultures*. London: Routledge.

Liebes, T. (1998) 'Television's disaster marathons: a danger for democratic processes?', in T. Liebes and J. Curran (eds), *Media, Ritual and Identity*. London: Routledge.

Lievrouw, L. (2001) 'New media and the "pluralization of live-worlds": a role for information in social differentiation', *New Media and Society*, 3 (1): 7–28.

Livingstone, S. (2008) 'Taking risky opportunities in youthful content creation: teenagers' use of social networking sites for intimacy, privacy and self-expression', *New Media and Society*, 10 (3): 393–411.

Livingstone, S. and Lunt, P. (1994) *Talk on Television*. London: Routledge.

Lyon, D. (1998) 'The world wide web of surveillance: the internet and off-world power flows', *Information, Communication & Society*, 1 (1): 91–105.

MacDonald, D. (1957) 'A theory of mass culture', in B. Rosenburg and D. White (eds), *Mass Culture*. Glencoe, IL: Free Press.

MacKinnon, C. (1988) *Feminism Unmodified: Discourses on life and law*. Cambridge, MA: Harvard University Press.

Malik, S. (2002) *Representing Black Britain: Black and Asian images on television*. London: Sage.

Malm, K. and Wallis, R. (1993) *Media Policy and Music Activity*. London: Routledge.

Mander, J. (1978) *Four Arguments for the Elimination of Television*. New York: William Morrow.

Marcuse, H. (1964) *One Dimensional Man: Studies in the ideology of advanced industrial society*. London: Routledge & Kegan Paul.

Marshall, P. D. (1997) *Celebrity and Power: Fame in Contemporary Culture*. Minneapolis, MN: University of Minnesota Press.

Marx, K. (1844) 'A contribution to the critique of Hegel's philosophy of right', *Deutsch-Französische Jahrbücher*, February.

Marx, K. (2000) 'Preface to a contribution to a critique of political economy', in D. McLellan (ed.), *Karl Marx: Selected Writings*. Oxford: Oxford University Press.

McChesney, R. (1999) *Rich Media, Poor Democracy: Communication politics in dubious times*. New York: New Press.

McCombs, M. and Shaw, D. (1972) 'The agenda-setting function of the press', *Public Opinion Quarterly*, 36 (2): 176–87.

McCracken, E. (1992) *Decoding Women's Magazines: From 'Mademoiselle' to 'Ms'*. London: Macmillan.

McDonnell, J. (1991) *Public Service Broadcasting: A reader*. London: Routledge.

McLuhan, M. (1962) *The Gutenberg Galaxy: The making of typographic man*. Toronto: University of Toronto Press.

McLuhan, M. (2001; 1964) *Understanding Media*. Abingdon: Routledge.

McQuail, D., Blumler, J. and Brown, J. (1972) 'The television audience: a revised perspective', in D. McQuail (ed.), *Sociology of Mass Communications*. Harmondsworth: Penguin.

McRobbie, A. (2000) *Feminism and Youth Culture* (2nd edn). London: Macmillan.

McRobbie, A. (2008) *The Aftermath of Feminism: Gender, culture and social change*. London: Sage.

mediawatch-UK (2005) 'Towards a decent society', News Release 2005. Also available online at: www.mediawatchuk.org.uk/index.php?option=com_content&task=view&id=155&Itemid=124

Mepham, J. (1990) 'The ethics of quality in television', in G. Mulgan (ed.), *The Question of Quality*. London: British Film Institute.

Mercer, K. (1990) 'Black art and the burden of representation', *Third Text*, 10.

Meyrowitz, J. (1985) *No Sense of Place: The impact of electronic media on social behaviour*. New York: Oxford University Press.

Mill, J. S. (1975; 1859) 'On liberty', in J. S. Mill and R. Wollheim, *Three Essays: 'On liberty', 'Representative government', 'The subjection of women'*. Oxford: Oxford University Press.

Miller, D. and Slater, D. (2000) *The Internet: An ethnographic approach*. Oxford: Berg.

Miller, M. C. (1988) 'Cosby knows best', in M. C. Miller (ed.), *Boxed-In: The culture of TV*. Evanston, IL: Northwestern University Press: 69–78.

Modleski, T. (1982) *Loving with a Vengeance: Mass produced fantasies for women*. New York: Routledge.

Moran, A. (1998) *Copycat TV: Globalisation, programme formats and cultural identity*. Luton: University of Luton Press.

Morgan, R. (1980) 'Theory and practice: pornography and rape', in L. Lederer (ed.), *Take Back the Night*. New York: William Morrow: 134–40.

Moritz, M. (2004) 'Old strategies for new texts: how American television is creating and treating lesbian characters', in C. Carter and L. Steiner (eds), *Critical Readings: Media and gender*. Maidenhead: Open University Press.

Morley, D. (1980) *The Nationwide Audience: Structure and decoding*. London: British Film Institute.

Morley, D. (1988) *Family Television: Cultural power and domestic leisure*. London: Routledge.

Morley, D. (1992) *Television, Audiences and Cultural Studies*. London: Routledge.

Morley, D. (2000) *Home Territories: Media, mobility and identity*. Abingdon: Routledge.

Muggleton, D. (1997) 'The post-subculturalist', in S. Redhead (ed.), *The Club Cultures Reader: Readings in popular cultural studies*. Oxford: Blackwell.

Mulvey, L. (1975) 'Visual pleasure and narrative cinema', *Screen* 16 (3): 6–18.

Murdock, G. (1992) 'Citizens, consumers and public culture', in M. Skovmand and K. Schroder (eds), *Media Cultures: Reappraising transnational media*. London: Routledge.

Murdock, G. and Golding, P. (1995; 1973) 'For a political economy of mass communications', in O. Boyd-Barrett and C. Newbold (eds), *Approaches to Media: A reader*. London: Arnold.

Murdoch, J. (2009) 'The absence of trust', *MacTaggart Lecture, 2009 Edinburgh International Television Festival*. Available online at: http://image.guardian.co.uk/sys-files/Media/documents/2009/08/28/JamesMurdochMacTaggartLecture.pdf

Murdoch, R. (2001) 'Freedom in broadcasting versus the public service tradition', in B. Franklin (ed.), *British Television Policy: A reader*. Abingdon: Routledge: 38–40 (extract from 1989 lecture).

Negroponte, N. (1996) *Being Digital*. New York: Vintage Books.

Nightingale, V. and Ross, K. (2003) 'Introduction', in V. Nightingale and K. Ross (eds), *Critical Readings: Media and audiences*. Maidenhead: Open University Press.

Norman, E. (1988) *The Psychology of Everyday Things*. New York: Basic Books.

Ofcom (2004) *Ofcom review of public service television broadcasting*. London: Ofcom. Also available online at: www.ofcom.org.uk/consult/condocs/psb/psb.pdf

Ofcom (2005) *Ofcom review of public service television broadcasting: Phase 3 – Competition for quality*. London: Ofcom. Also available online at: www.ofcom.org.uk/consult/condocs/psb3

Ofcom (2007a) *The promotion of equal opportunities in broadcasting: Report for 2007*. London: Ofcom. Also available online at: www.ofcom.org.uk/tv/ifi/report07/equal_ops.pdf

Ofcom (2007b) *Ethnic minority groups and communications services*. London: Ofcom. Also available online at: www.ofcom.org.uk/research/cm/ethnic_minority

Ofcom (2009) *The Ofcom Broadcasting Code*. London: Ofcom. Also available online at: www.ofcom.org.uk/tv/ifi/codes/bcode/undue

Ong, W. J. (1977) *Interfaces of the Word*. Ithaca, NY: Cornell University Press.

Osgerby, W. (2004) *Youth Media*. Abingdon: Routledge.

Peet, R. (1989) 'The destruction of regional cultures', in R. Johnston and P. Taylor (eds), *A World in Crisis?: Geographical Perspectives*. Oxford: Basil Blackwell.

Peirce, C. (1931–1948) *Collected Papers*. Cambridge, MA: Harvard University Press.

Penley, C. (1991) 'Brownian motion: women, tactics and technology', in C. Penley and A. Ross (eds), *Technoculture*. Minneapolis, MN: University of Minnesota Press.

Perry, I. (2003) 'Who(se) am I? The identity and image of women in hip hop', in G. Dines and J. M. Humez (eds), *Gender, Race and Class in Media* (2nd edn). London: Sage: 136–48.

Pickering, M. (2001) *Stereotyping: The politics of representation*. Houndmills, Basingstoke: Palgrave Macmillan.

Pieterse, J. P. (1992) *White on Black: Images of Africa and Blacks in Western popular culture*. Newhaven, CT: Yale University Press.

Polhemus, T. (1997) 'In the supermarket of style', in S. Redhead (ed.), *The Club Cultures Reader*. Oxford: Blackwell.

Poster, M. (1995) *The Second Media Age*. Cambridge: Polity Press.

Poster, M. (2001) *What's the Matter with the Internet?* Minneapolis, MN: University of Minnesota Press.

Postman, N. (1987) *Amusing Ourselves to Death: Public discourse in the age of show business*. London: Methuen.

Postman, N. and Powers, S. (1992) *How to Watch TV News*. London: Penguin.

Propp, V. (1968) *Morphology of the Folktale*. Austin, TX: University of Texas Press.

Radway, J. (1987) *Reading the Romance: Women, patriarchy and popular literature*. London: Verso.

Redden, G. (2007) 'Makeover morality and consumer culture', in D. Hellar (ed.), *Makeover Television*. London: I. B. Tauris.

Redfield, R. (1955) *The Little Community*. Chicago, IL: University of Chicago Press.

Rettie, R. (2009) 'SMS: exploiting the interactional characteristics of near-synchrony', *Information, Communication and Society*, 12 (8).

Rheingold, H. (2000) *The Virtual Community: Homesteading on the electronic frontier* (revised edn). Cambridge, MA: MIT Press.

Riesman, D. (1953) *The Lonely Crowd: A study of the changing American character*. Garden City, NY: Doubleday.

Rock, P. (1973) 'News as eternal recurrence', in S. Cohen and J. Young (eds), *The Manufacture of News: Deviance, social problems and the mass media*. London: Constable: 73–80.

Rojek, C. (2005) 'P2P leisure exchange: net banditry and the policing of intellectual property', *Leisure Studies*, 24 (4): 357–69.

Rose, T. (2008) *The Hip Hop Wars: What we talk about when we talk about hip hop – and why it matters*. New York: Basic Books.

Rosengren, K. E. and Windahl, S. (1972) 'Mass media consumption as a functional alternative', in D. McQuail (ed.), *Sociology of Mass Communications*. Harmondsworth: Penguin.

Ruggiero, T. (2000) 'Uses and gratifications theory in the 21st century', *Mass Communication & Society*, 3 (1): 3–37.

Sandvoss, C. (2005) *Fans: The mirror of consumption*. Cambridge: Polity Press.

Said, E. (1978) *Orientalism*. London: Routledge & Kegan Paul.

Scannell, P. (1989) 'Public service broadcasting and modern life', *Media, Culture and Society*, 11 (2): 135–66.

Scannell, P. (1990) 'Public service broadcasting: the history of a concept', in A. Goodwin and G. Whannel (eds), *Understanding Television*. London: Routledge.

Schiller, H. (1976) *Communication and Cultural Domination*. White Plains, NY: International Arts and Sciences Press.

Schiller, H. (1992) *Mass Communication and American Empire*. Boulder, CO: Westview Press.

Schilt, K. and Zobl, E. (2008) 'Connecting the dots: riot grrrls, ladyfests and the international Grrrl Zine network', in A. Harris (ed.), *Next Wave Cultures: Feminism, subcultures, activism*. Abingdon: Routledge.

Segal, L. (1992) 'Introduction', in L. Segal and M. McIntosh (eds), *Sex Exposed: Sexuality and the pornography debate*. London: Virago Press.

Shannon, C. and Weaver, W. (1949) *The Mathematical Theory of Communication*. Champaign, IL: University of Illinois Press.

Smith, A. (1904; 1776) *An Inquiry into the Nature and Causes of the Wealth of Nations* (5th edn). London: Methuen.

Solomon, S. (1976) *Beyond Formula: American film genres*. New York: Harcourt Brace Jovanovich.

Solomos, J. (1993) *Race and Racism in Britain*. Houndmills, Basingstoke: Palgrave Macmillan.

Sreberny, A. (1999) *Include Me In: Rethinking ethnicity on television*. London: Broadcasting Standards Council.

Sreberny-Mohammadi, A. and Ross, K. (1995) *Black Minority Viewers and Television: Neglected audiences speak up and out*. Leicester: Centre for Mass Communications Research.

Stevenson, N. (2002) *Understanding Media Cultures* (2nd edn). London: Sage.

Strinati, D. (1995) *An Introduction to Theories of Popular Culture*. London: Routledge.

Talbot, M. (2007) *Media Discourse: Representation and interaction*. Edinburgh: Edinburgh University Press.

Temple, M. (2006) 'Dumbing down is good for you', *British Politics*, 1 (2): 257–73. Also available online at: www.palgrave-journals.com/bp/journal/v1/n2/pdf/4200018a.pdf

Thompson, J. (1990) *Ideology and Modern Culture: Critical social theory in the era of mass communication*. Cambridge: Polity Press.

Thornton, S. (1995) *Club Cultures: Music, media and subcultural capital*. Cambridge: Polity Press.

Todorov, T. (1978) *The Poetics of Prose*. Ithaca, NY: Cornell University Press.

Tomlinson, J. (1991) *Cultural Imperialism: A critical introduction*. London: Pinter.

Tönnies, F. (1963) *Community and Society*. New York: Harper & Row.

Tracey, M. (1998) *The Decline and Fall of Public Service Broadcasting*. Oxford: Oxford University Press.

Tuchman, G. (1978) 'Introduction: the symbolic annihilation of women by the mass media', in G. Tuchman, A. Kaplan Daniels and J. Benet (eds), *Hearth and Home: Images of women in the mass media*. New York: Oxford University Press.

Turkle, S. (1995) *Life on the Screen: Identity in the age of the Internet*. London: Phoenix.

Turner, G. (2004) *Understanding Celebrity*. London: Sage.

Vroomen, L. (2004) 'Kate Bush: teen pop and older female fans', in A. Bennett and R. Peterson (eds), *Music Scenes: Local, translocal and virtual*. Nashville, IN: Vanderbilt University Press.

Watson, N. (1997) 'Why we argue about virtual community: a case study of the phish. net fan community', in S. Jones (ed.), *Virtual Culture: Internet and communication in cybersociety*. London: Sage.

Webster, F. (2002) *Theories of the Information Society* (2nd edn). Abingdon: Routledge.

Wellman, B. and Gulia, M. (1999) 'Virtual communities as communities: net surfers don't ride alone', in M. Smith and P. Kollock (eds), *Communities in Cyberspace*. Abingdon: Routledge: 163–90.

Wellman, B. and Haythornthwaite, C. (2002) 'The Internet in everyday life: an introduction', in B. Wellman and C. Haythornthwaite (eds), *The Internet in Everyday Life*, Oxford: Blackwell: 3–44.

Westley, B. and MacLean, M. (1957) 'A conceptual model for communication research', *Journalism Quarterly*, 34: 31–8.

Whelan, A. (2006) 'Do u produce?: subcultural capital and amateur musicianship in peer-to-peer networks', in M. Ayers (ed.), *Cybersounds: Essays on virtual music culture*. New York: Peter Lang.

Williams, R. (1974) *Television: Technology and cultural form*. London: Fontana.

Williams, R. (1988) *Keywords: A vocabulary of culture and society*. London: Fontana.

Williams, R. (1989) *Resources of Hope: Culture, democracy, socialism*. London: Verso.

Williamson, J. (1995; 1978) *Decoding Advertisements: Ideology and meaning in advertising*. London: Marian Boyars.

Willis, P. (1990) *Common Culture: Symbolic work at play in the everyday cultures of the young*. Milton Keynes: Open University Press.

Wimmer, R. and Dominick, J. (2006) *Mass Media Research: An introduction* (8th edn). Belmont, CA: Thomson Wadsworth.

Woodward, K. (1997) *Identity and Difference*. London: Sage.

Young, J. (1971) *The Drug Takers: The social meaning of drug use*. London: Paladin.

Index

Page numbers in *italics* refer to figures.

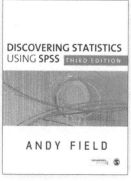
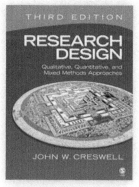

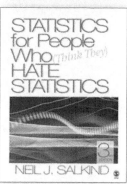

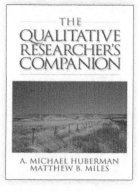

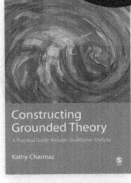

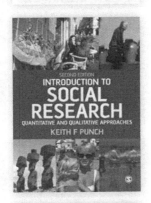
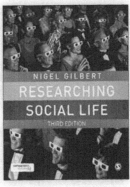

The Qualitative Research Kit

Edited by Uwe Flick

Read sample chapters online now!